REPUBLICANS

POLITICAL PARTY OR
THREAT TO OUR DEMOCRACY?

THOMAS GRAHAM JR.

Cover design by Susan Bard
Page design by Eric Butler

ISBN 978-1-0879-5271-0
Published by Indy Pub

To learn more about the author, visit his professional website:
www.thomasgraham.info

CONTENTS

Wisdom calls aloud in the streets.
She raises her voice in the public squares.
She calls out at the street corners.
She delivers her message at the city gates,
"You ignorant people.
How much longer will you cling to your ignorance?
How much longer will mockers revel in their mocking
and fools hold knowledge contemptible?"
Pay attention to my warning.

PROVERBS 1: 20—23

INTRODUCTION

ON THE EVENING OF JANUARY 30, 2022—about a year after he left office, having lost his bid for reelection against Democratic candidate Joe Biden—former president Donald Trump once again falsely asserted that the presidency had been stolen from him through voter fraud and that, as vice president, Mike Pence "had the ability to change the outcome of the election. . . . Unfortunately, he didn't exercise that power, he could have overturned the election!"[1] John McCormack of the *National Review* pointed out that "the former president's statement is a reminder that he didn't merely want an investigation into baseless claims of widespread voter fraud."[2] In other words, Trump had said explicitly what many Americans had already deduced: that his talk about voter fraud was only a smokescreen to hide the fact that he had done his utmost to simply steal a second presidential term.

Laurence Tribe, America's foremost constitutional lawyer, concurred with this assessment of the speech, saying on MSNBC that Trump had:

---

1   Philip Klein, "Trump's Continuing Disgrace," *National Review*, January 31, 2022, https://www.nationalreview.com/corner/trumps-continuing-disgrace/.
2   John McCormack, "Trump Admits He Wanted Pence to Overturn the Election," *National Review*, January 31, 2022, https://www.nationalreview.com/2022/01/trump-admits-he-wanted-pence-to-overturn-the-election/.

essentially confessed publicly and openly, without any coercion, without any pressure, to having committed the crime of conspiracy to engage in sedition. Seditious conspiracy [is] punishable by 20 years in prison. . . . He quite specifically said that he thought he had a right to overturn the election. . . . He also confessed publicly to inciting and fomenting, and more importantly, giving aid and comfort to an insurrection . . . which is punishable by ten years in prison and importantly, by permanent disqualification from ever holding office under the United States. . . . He basically is daring the United States government, and the attorney general, and the Justice Department, to enforce the rule of law. He is saying make my day, if you come after me, I am going to stir up an angry mob and you will suffer.[3]

Throughout the 2020 campaign Trump had made clear that he would only accept an election result that showed him the winner. Biden was declared winner by the Electoral College, and this result was ratified by Congress. After Trump's claims of victory had been rejected by all federal courts, by the Electoral College, and by Congress, he tried to overthrow the government by force in an attempted coup d'état on January 6, 2021.

He was not alone in that attempt. On May 2, 2021, the *Washington Post* published an editorial entitled "Democracy Can't Work If the GOP Is Devoted to Restricting Voters and Rejecting Their Decisions." The paper opined that "GOP leaders outside Washington are still acting on [Trump's] campaign of lies about the 2020 election, breaking norms and finding falsehoods in ways that further endanger the US system of government."[4] As Michael Gerson noted in his column

---

3   Cathy Blank, "Laurence Tribe: Trump Confessed to Seditious Conspiracy and Could Face 20 Years in Prison," *World News Era*, February 1, 2022, http://worldnewsera.com/news/politics/laurence-tribe-trump-confessed-to-seditious-conspiracy-and-could-face-20-years-in-prison/.

4   "Democracy Can't Work If the GOP Is Devoted to Restricting Voters and

the next day, "For the activist base of the Republican Party, affirming that Donald Trump won the 2020 presidential contest has become a qualification for membership in good standing . . . the lie of a stolen election is the foundational falsehood of a political worldview."[5]

Indeed, the Big Lie is currently the central principle of the Republican Party, however repugnant the notion of a party—with policies made whole-cloth of a falsehood—offering leadership *in a democracy*. Democracies cannot work this way. The effort to do so is what one expects of a personality cult—for example, those underlying such dictatorial governments as those of Nazi Germany, Mussolini's Italy, Franco's Spain, and Castro's Cuba. Or, alternatively, the Branch Davidians in Waco, Texas. Such a cult of personality is, of course, a hallmark of fascist regimes. An America governed by a national, fascist party masquerading as a Republican one—that appears to be the objective of those who follow Donald Trump. The Republican Party has become a cult devoted to benefiting one person and no one else.

Clearly there is not a shred of truth in the Trump Big Lie. All 50 election commissions around the country certified their votes, and multiple state recounts upheld the result in some 50 or so courts, many led by Trump-appointed judges. The Supreme Court rejected Trump's suits twice by votes of nine to zero. Trump's attorney general said he found no significant fraud, and Chris Krebs, the official designated to provide security for the election, publicly stated that it was the most secure election in our nation's history. And the election was not close; Biden won by more than seven million in the popular vote and by 74 electoral votes.

Rejecting Their Decisions," editorial, *Washington Post*, May 2, 2021, https://www.washingtonpost.com/opinions/republicans-are-still-waging-their-war-on-democracy-in-state-after-state/2021/05/01/3f2fa7f4-a9ef-11eb-8c1a-56f0cb4ff3b5_story.html.

5   Michael Gerson, "Elected Republicans Are Lying with Open Eyes. Their Excuses Are Disgraceful," *Washington Post*, May 3, 2021, https://www.washingtonpost.com/opinions/2021/05/03/trump-republicans-big-lie/.

Trump is continuing to advance his baseless claims of victory and is trying to persuade state legislatures to skew election law in their states so that no Democrat can win. Clearly, Donald Trump and the Republican Party represent an existential threat to American democracy and to the existence of this nation as a free society.

Only once before in our history has this country experienced such an existential threat—the passage of the Kansas-Nebraska Act in 1854, which terminated the Missouri Compromise and opened the door for Southern slaveholders to seize the power in the entire country and end America's constitutional attempt at government. In this book, that history will be presented. It will be explained how that history informs our current moment and what lessons we can learn from our nation's turbulent past. Also, readers will be guided through the history of the Republican Party, including the deeply American principles for which it once stood—a far cry from what it has become in recent years.

Hopefully, this time it won't take a civil war, as it did in the 1860s, to quell a direct assault on our liberties. Let us hope to avoid war, but let us also be prepared to do what it takes to ensure that our "government by the people, for the people, and of the people, shall not perish from the earth."

CHAPTER I

ORIGIN

THE ISSUE OF SLAVERY and its aftermath has been a threat to the moral compass and the cohesiveness of the United States since the Constitution was signed in 1787. The Constitution did not ban slavery, despite the desires of some that it do so. Rather, it made provision for slavery in that, for the purposes of determining congressional districts based on population, an enslaved person counted for three-fifths of a person in determining a state's total population. In subsequent discussions as the Constitution was gradually ratified by the states, Adams and Hamilton (among others) argued that slavery should be abolished by law. George Washington wanted its abolition as well, but gradually and carefully. In principle Jefferson and Madison supported a future without slavery but believed that slaveholding plantation states had to be permitted to keep an enslaved labor force for now. Without this proviso there could be no union. Adams, Hamilton, and Washington relented, recognizing that contending independent states based on different social and economic systems could create a highly unstable situation leading to war. If a strong union based on the principles of the Bill of Rights could be established, some Founders hoped that slavery would gradually wither away. Their comments reflected such sanguine hopes:

"Slavery in this country I have seen hanging over it like a black cloud for half a century."   —John Adams, 1821

"Negro Slavery is an evil of Colossal Magnitude."
                                                —John Adams, 1819

"I wish most sincerely that there was not a slave in this province."
                                                —Abigail Adams, 1774

"Were not the disadvantages of slavery too obvious to stand in need of it, I might enumerate and describe the tedious terrain of calamities inseparable from it."   —Alexander Hamilton, 1774

". . . it being among my first wishes to see some plan adopted, by the legislature by which slavery in this Country may be abolished by slow, sure & imperceptible degrees."   —George Washington, 1786

"This abomination must have an end, and there is a superior bench reserved in heaven for those who hasten it."
                                                —Thomas Jefferson, 1787

"American Citizens are instrumental in carrying on a traffic of enslaved Africans, equally in violation of the laws of humanity, and in defiance of those of their own country. The same just and benevolent motives which produced interdiction in force against the criminal conduct, will, doubtless, be felt by Congress, in devising further means of suppressing the evil."   —James Madison, 1810

"We intend this Constitution to be the great charter of human liberty to the unborn millions who may enjoy its protection, and who shall never see that such an institution as slavery was ever known in their midst."
                    —James Madison, regarding adding the word
                                    "slave" into the Constitution, 1787

In addition, there were strong dissenters to the eventual compromise that established the Union.

"As much as I value a union of all the states, I would not admit the Southern States into the Union, unless they agree to the discontinuance of this disgraceful trade, because it would bring weakness, and not strength, to the Union."

—George Mason, in a debate in the Virginia
Ratifying Convention, 1788

Over such scruples relating to slavery, the Constitution entered into force in 1788, and the first presidential election took place that fall. George Washington won, receiving 100 percent of the electoral votes. The Union was successful in many ways, but serious political conflict between the Hamiltonian and Jeffersonian wings soon appeared and became intense. The Hamiltonian wing became the Federalist Party and the Jeffersonian wing the Republican Party. Eventually the Federalist Party disappeared, to be replaced by the Whig Party (taking the English party name), and the Republicans became the Democrats. Several presidential administrations came and went—Washington, Adams, Jefferson, and Madison. With the election of James Monroe in 1816, some of the other original Founders were also still active, but the second generation was very much involved by that time. John Quincy Adams, who adamantly opposed slavery and who served as secretary of state under Monroe, would be elected president in 1824.

During Monroe's presidency, a serious attempt to limit slavery was made. In 1818, the Union was equally divided between free states and slave states. Missouri had first attempted to become a state in 1817, amidst passionate congressional debates over whether slavery would be permitted there. In 1819, John Adams weighed in with the pronouncement, "I am . . . utterly averse to admission of Slavery into the Missouri Territory, and heartily wish that every Constitutional measure may be adopted for the prevention of it."[1] The prominent statesman Henry Clay

---

1   "From John Adams to William Tudor Jr., 20 November 1819," Founders Online, National Archives, https://founders.archives.gov/documents/Adams/99-02-02-7261.

was then a member of the House of Representatives. He, along with others, fashioned what became known as the Missouri Compromise. Henry Clay skillfully influenced the votes in both houses of Congress and secured legislation admitting Maine as a free state and Missouri as a slave state, with the proviso that no infringements be made on the rights of Blacks living in Missouri who were already free and that no slavery be permitted in the future above the latitude of 36°30' (the westward end of the southern border of Missouri) to the Rocky Mountains in the Louisiana Purchase.

The Missouri Compromise kept the peace for 30 years—until the Mexican-American War created a new crisis between North and South that threatened the integrity of the Union. Vast territories had been ceded to the United States by Mexico as a result of the war. When California indicated that it wanted to enter the Union as a free state in 1849, the balance between free and slave states was threatened. Texas, itself newly admitted, claimed vast areas to its west. Henry Clay, for the second time, fashioned a compromise and introduced it to the Congress. It included admitting California as a free state; Texas giving up most of its claims to western lands; the territories of New Mexico and Utah being formed; and a stronger fugitive slave law being adopted. The Compromise of 1850 served to postpone the Civil War another ten years.

However, in 1854, one of Clay's supporters in the passing of the Compromise of 1850 sought to build a transcontinental railroad through Nebraska, which, along with its neighbor to the south, Kansas, was north of the Missouri Compromise line. Southerners, having always objected to the legislated line, now rebelled at the idea that they couldn't take their slave-based economic system everywhere it might prosper. Sen. Stephen Douglas and other Senate and House leaders passed the Kansas-Nebraska Act of 1854, which counter-manded the terms of the Missouri Compromise. The act made legal a policy of "popular sovereignty," which meant that whatever the people wanted in a particular state would determine its status—slave or free.

This, in effect, opened Kansas, Nebraska, and the entire undeveloped West to slavery.

Northerners were concerned that the Slave Power—the perceived dominant political power in the US federal government held by slaveholders—would not remain in Southern states but would take over the entire Union. Slavery, as an economic and political system, had essentially been an oligarchy within a free republic. One percent of each slave state's citizens controlled virtually all the wealth and political power in that state. The system was supported by a vast workforce of enslaved Blacks on plantations and poorer Whites who were able to buy a few enslaved Blacks to do most of the work on their small farms. Northerners saw the Kansas-Nebraska Act as a direct attack on the principles of the Declaration of Independence. It saw the South—the strongest and richest part of the country—exercising its considerable economic and political power to force its oligarchical system on the entire United States.

Many in the North regarded the act as the final blow to Northern liberties and were determined to resist. Northern leaders including *Chicago Tribune* editor Horace Greeley, Sen. Salmon Chase of Ohio, and Sen. Charles Sumner of Massachusetts were not prepared to sit back and watch an avalanche of pro-slavery settlers sweep across Kansas and Nebraska. Former representative Abraham Lincoln later recalled that the act "took us by surprise. . . . We were thunderstruck and stunned . . ."[2]

The Kansas-Nebraska Act convinced many Northerners that slavery threatened their society. Many expected their young people to go west to develop happy, free lives for themselves. They considered the Missouri Compromise practically one of the founding US documents. According to Heather Cox Richardson's account, on the morning after the Kansas-Nebraska Act passed on May 9, 1854,

---

2   Heather Cox Richardson, *To Make Men Free: A History of the Republican Party* (New York: Basic Books, 2014), 7.

Maine representative Israel Washburn invited some 30 antislavery representatives to a meeting in the rooms of two Massachusetts representatives, Thomas Eliot and Edward Dickinson, at Mrs. Crutchett's select boardinghouse at South and D Streets in Washington.[3] Rep. Edward Dickinson of Massachusetts was well known for his leadership at this time, but his place in history was perhaps more firmly to be secured by his daughter Emily, who wrote poetry.

The three men who called this meeting were all Northern Whigs, but others in attendance were from a variety of political parties. All left the elegant rooms in Mrs. Crutchett's boardinghouse determined to support a new organization that would stand firmly against the expansion of slavery into the West. Soon they referred to themselves as Republicans, initially because that was the name Thomas Jefferson had given to his party at its inception. An editorial by Horace Greeley in the *Chicago Tribune* in June of 1854 further fixed the name. He wrote:

> We should not care much whether those thus united (*against slavery*) were designated 'Whig,' 'Free Democrat' or something else; though we think some simple name like 'Republican' would more fitly designate those who had united to restore the Union to its true mission of champion and promulgator of liberty rather than propagandist of slavery.[4]

The nickname of the party, the Grand Old Party or GOP, did not come along until 1888, when the Republican Party was so designated by the *Chicago Tribune*. The *Tribune*, celebrating the first time that the Republican Party (as opposed to the Northern Democrats, Free Democrats, and Southern Democrats—the Democratic Party) had won both the presidency and the Congress since the Grant administration, wrote, "Let us be thankful that under the rule of the Grand

---

3   Richardson, 8.
4   "The Origins of the Republican Party," ushistory.org, https://www.ushistory.org/gop/origins.htm.

Old Party . . . these United States will resume the onward and upward march which the election of Grover Cleveland in 1884 partially arrested."[5] But the party was a very different organization in 1888 than it was at its beginnings.

After the party was founded in 1854, momentum built for voters to join the new antislavery organization. Political conventions throughout the Northern states appealed to free men to fight together "for the first principles of Republican government and against the schemes of the aristocracy, the most revolting and oppressive with which the earth was ever cursed or man debased."[6] Early in 1854 in Ripon, Wisconsin, there had been an exploratory meeting concerning a new party. In July 1854, a large mass meeting took place in Michigan—one that ultimately led to the first Republican official meeting in Pittsburgh, in 1856. Meanwhile, in the fall of 1854, as Richardson reports in her history, Northerners—many styling themselves Republicans—swept the board of "pro-Nebraska" politicians, who, being representatives, were up for reelection. There were 142 Northern seats in the House of Representatives, and new "anti-Nebraska" representatives were elected to 120 of those seats. The anti-Nebraska forces—on their way to becoming officially the Republican Party—also elected 11 senators and replaced Democrats in many state legislatures that the anti-Nebraska forces also took over.[7]

The Whig Party was falling apart, though Abraham Lincoln was still a member. According to the web archives maintained by the House of Representatives, Lincoln told a Springfield, Illinois, audience that the Northwest Ordinance, drafted by Thomas Jefferson and adopted by the Founding Fathers in 1784 under the Articles of Confederation, had prohibited slavery in the West. The Confederation Congress had approved a revision of Jefferson's ordinance in 1787, and the First

---

5   "The Origins," ushistory.org.
6   Richardson, *To Make Men Free*, 8.
7   Richardson, 9.

Federal Congress had renewed that revision in 1789.[8] Hence, Lincoln asserted, opposition to the extension of slavery beyond the South was a central American principle. Lincoln returned to his law practice, but like many, would not ignore the events of 1854. As Richardson writes, "It seemed that the Slave Power was bent on taking over the nation and only a new political organization could stop it."[9]

The next act in the drama saw civil war break out in Kansas in late 1855. Free-soil settlers were attacked by Confederate thugs, who aimed to determine the future of the majority-antislavery settlers by having a pro-slavery force seize power through violence and then fraudulently establish an authoritarian government. President Pierce sided with the pro-slavery marauders and called the antislavery settlers "outlaws" despite their having settled north of the Missouri Compromise line.

In May 1856, Sen. Charles Sumner gave a speech in the Senate entitled "The Crime Against Kansas," in which he compared the events in Kansas to the rape of an enslaved girl and—not stopping there—singled out certain senior Southern politicians infatuated with "the harlot, slavery." Sumner accused the Southern oligarchy of forcing slavery on the settlers of Kansas, thereby depriving American citizens of their rights. He mentioned by name a South Carolina senator, Andrew Pickens Butler, as the principal villain. Two days later Rep. Preston Brooks, Senator Butler's cousin and fellow South Carolinian, came up behind Senator Sumner on the Senate floor. Assisted by Rep. Laurence Keitt, another Democrat from South Carolina, he beat Sumner to within an inch of his life with a heavy cane, ultimately breaking the cane over Sumner's head. Several Southern senators nearby looked on without lifting a finger. Sumner was left by Brooks lying on the floor in a pool of blood. Brooks and Keitt were expelled

---

8   "The Northwest Ordinance of 1787," History, Art & Archives, US House of Representatives, https://history.house.gov/Historical-Highlights/1700s/Northwest-Ordinance-1787/.

9   Richardson, *To Make Men Free*, 9.

from Congress, but they were restored by voters the following year. It would be four years before Sumner could return to the Senate.

Initially, Republicans and others had backed away from Sumner because of the extreme nature of his speech. But now, after the attack, he looked very much in the right. Brooks was heard saying as he left the Senate floor after the attack, "I will have to kill him next time."[10] Sumner received widespread support in the North both personally and politically, and the attack was roundly condemned in mass meetings. One supporter wrote that the attack was "not only . . . a cowardly assault on a defenseless man, but a crime against the right of free speech and the dignity of a free state."[11]

The day of the attack on Sumner also brought news of more violence from Kansas. An armed guerrilla group had sacked the town of Lawrence and put the leaders of the free state under arrest. Those opposed to slavery had made it clear that "settler sovereignty" was contrary to the Missouri Compromise, which lived on in spirit. The armed group were labeled only "ruffians" by Southern politicians. Horace Greeley, however, was quick to comment in the *Chicago Tribune*, denouncing both actions as plots of the South. He wrote that "failing to silence the North by threats . . . the South now resorts to actual violence."[12]

The Dred Scott Supreme Court decision of 1857, holding that the Constitution did not include American citizenship for people of African descent (regardless of whether they were enslaved or free) and that the rights and privileges that the Constitution confers upon American citizens did not apply to them, felt to Northerners as though the South had struck the final blow. The decision convinced a strong majority of Northerners that the Slave Power intended to take over the entire country and dominate it. There was also a strong sense in

10 "The Origins," ushistory.org.
11 Richardson, *To Make Men Free*, 12.
12 "The Origins," ushistory.org.

the North that the Slave Power would succeed in its nefarious intent unless the North did something to halt it.

But the North was not quite ready to do this. The first Republican National Convention took place in Philadelphia after the earlier 1856 preparatory meeting in Pittsburgh. In Philadelphia the Republicans nominated John C. Frémont, a famous Western explorer, one of California's first two senators, and later a general officer in the Civil War. Another new party, the Know-Nothings, which opposed most immigration (particularly Irish Catholic), nominated Whig politician Millard Fillmore, former vice president under President Zachary Taylor and Taylor's successor upon his unexpected death. The Democrats nominated James Buchanan, whose milder disposition, it was hoped, might calm passions. The dominant issue was slavery.

Buchanan won the election, with Frémont quite close behind him. Buchanan announced in his inaugural that the Supreme Court would soon hand down a decision that might calm sectarian passions. He said that he expected to cheerfully submit "to this decision when the court ruled." Only days later the Supreme Court—at the time stacked in favor of slavery, with five of the nine justices coming from Southern states and another justice firmly pro-slavery, though not a Southerner—handed down the Dred Scott decision. Giving the lie to Buchanan's comments, it proved dreadfully divisive. Northerners saw a setup in that Buchanan seemed to know the contents of the decision in advance but delayed the announcement until after the election. Among other things, the decision also declared that the Missouri Compromise, sacred writ for Northerners, was unconstitutional and that Congress had no power to stop the spread of slavery into any part of the Western territory.

A combination of events—the revocation of the Missouri Compromise, civil war in Kansas, the attack on a sitting senator on the floor of the Senate, and the Dred Scott decision—brought the North across the Rubicon. This was made clear by Abraham Lincoln in his famous "House Divided" speech to the Illinois legislature on the occasion of his nomination for the Senate to replace Stephen Douglas, an avid supporter of slavery. Lincoln said that Douglas (author of the Kansas-Nebraska Act), Franklin Pierce (pro-slavery president of the US), Roger Taney (chief justice of the Supreme Court and author of the Dred Scott decision), and James Buchanan (the new president who overtly supported the Taney court):

> were all building a house that Lincoln used to symbolize the nation. When they were through, Lincoln warned, Americans would find that these carpenters had fitted slavery into every beam and nail in the framing. Slavery would be integral to every part of the nation: the South, the West and eventually the North.[13]

After Stephen Douglas returned to Illinois in July 1858, he (the incumbent senator) and Lincoln (the nominee) traveled around Illinois for the next three months debating the issues—principally slavery—in what came to be known as the Lincoln-Douglas debates. Douglas took a strong pro-slavery position, denying that Blacks had any inherent rights. According to Douglas, "This government of ours . . . was made by the white man, for the benefit of the white man, to be administered by white men."[14] Lincoln argued entirely in terms of the principles of the Declaration of Independence:

> We hold these truths to be self-evident, that all men are created equal, that they are endowed by their Creator with certain unalienable Rights, that among these are Life, Liberty and the pursuit of Happiness.—That to secure these Rights, Governments are instituted among Men, deriving their just powers from the consent of the governed.[15]

---

13 Richardson, *To Make Men Free*, 13–14.
14 Richardson, 14.
15 "The Declaration of Independence," National Archives, https://www.archives.gov/founding-docs/declaration.

There could be no compromise with equality, Lincoln argued. He suggested that Douglas and the Democrats were under the control of rich Southern slaveholders working to destroy America. The Republicans, having far less financial support than pro-slavery interests, had no choice but to fight it out on principle alone.

What principles were Republicans contesting? In March of 1858, South Carolina Democrat James H. Hammond gave a Senate speech outlining Southern principles of government, which Northern Democrats like Douglas had largely embraced. According to Richardson's account, Hammond described a strong society as having a bottom layer made up of drudges: stupid, unskilled workers who were strong, docile, and loyal to their superiors. He referred to them as "mudsills" after the timbers, in the building of a house or other structure, driven into the ground to support the structure above. Members of this class, Hammond said, were meant to stay where they were—indeed, were happier there. On the mudsill class rested higher civilization—men who brought progress and refinement.[16]

Hammond claimed that the Southern system of using non-voting enslaved Blacks as its mudsill class was the only safe one. He asserted that members of the mudsill class must have no say in government; otherwise they might demand a redistribution of wealth. The North courted danger when it used White men as mudsills. Poor Whites were a threat because they could vote and, as a result, had a potential to demand wealth-sharing and thereby destroy society. Poorer Whites in the South had small farms with a few enslaved people, who were content. All worked well. The largest Southern slaveholders were the wealthiest men in the country, proving that they alone had figured out a true system of political economy. Theirs was the best system and it should be spread throughout the nation.[17] Hammond described a true authoritarian oligarchy deeply antithetical to everything that the

16 Richardson, *To Make Men Free*, 15.
17 Richardson, 15.

United States of America stood for: a society in which only the top 1 percent had the right to life, liberty, and the pursuit of happiness. The rest had no control of their lives, no equality, and no liberty—or, in the case of poor Whites, compromised liberty, since the widespread practice of sharecropping made it structurally difficult or impossible to get ahead.

Hammond and his class apparently didn't worry about the discrepancy between American democracy and Southern notions of upper-class rule. In his view, self-government was never intended to be more than a slogan. The leaders would make all the decisions. Indeed, Congress would have no role—regular people should not be "annoyed with cares of the government." [18] This political philosophy was, of course, dramatically opposed to the views of Abraham Lincoln and the new Republican Party.

As repellent as it was, Hammond's theory of the ideal society, shared by South Carolinian John C. Calhoun, has been echoed by the political ideas of some leaders of the 20th and 21st centuries. Calhoun was a dominant figure in the Old South in the first half of the 19th century. Because of Calhoun's extensive writings supporting slavery and the Southern economic system built on slavery, historian Richard Hofstadter has referred to him as "the Karl Marx of the Master Class." [19] In more recent times, Calhoun's concepts have been seized upon by a relatively small number of billionaires on the radical right in the 21st century Republican Party, notably Charles Koch, in an effort to make America into an oligarchy like the one championed by Hammond and Calhoun.

Koch's America would be led by a master class of the very rich and served by drudges doing the necessary work to keep the economy going. According to historian Nancy MacLean, "The dream of this

---

18 Richardson, 15.
19 Nancy MacLean, *Democracy in Chains: The Deep History of the Radical Right's Stealth Plan for America* (New York: Penguin Books, 2017), 1.

movement, its leaders will tell you, is liberty."[20] But, in truth, it is only liberty from taxes and regulation for this small group of corrupt billionaires who pour hundreds of millions of dollars into American elections. This group has established many foundations with high-sounding names and "educational" programs, employing thousands to help them pursue their objectives. According to MacLean:

> What this cause really seeks is a return to oligarchy, to a world in which both economic and effective political power are to be concentrated in the hands of a few. . . . Its spokes-persons would like you to believe they are disciples of James Madison . . . [but] it is not true. Their intellectual lodestar is John C. Calhoun. He developed his radical critique of democracy a generation after the nation's founding, as the brutal economy of chattel slavery became entrenched in the South—and his vision horrified Madison.[21]

As in the resistance to school desegregation in the 1960s and the Tea Party anti-tax movement in the early 21st century, leaders today are seeking the political power needed to reduce taxes on the very rich in order to free more money to support their goals.

Koch's ilk ally themselves with the continuing effort by the Republican Party to reduce taxes on billionaires—for instance, the Trump administration's tax cut—putting more and more property in fewer and fewer hands. The chaos and destructiveness of the Trump administration only partially diverted this effort; Trump apparently didn't disagree with the objectives of the movement. He viewed its support as support for his administration, providing power and money primarily for himself. Trump's alliance with the movement will be discussed later in the book. Today, the movement continues with Charles Koch holding the banner as titular head. Now, as then,

---

20 MacLean, xxxii.
21 MacLean, xxxii.

the leaders seek Calhoun-style liberty for the few—the liberty to concentrate vast wealth so as to deny elementary fairness and freedom to the many.[22]

Today's Republican Party is no longer the party of Abraham Lincoln. His party held views antithetical to those of James Hammond, Stephen Douglas, John C. Calhoun, Charles Koch, Donald Trump, and all others who would snatch our republic from the hands of the American people and create in its place an oligarchical system based on chattel slavery (or the modern equivalent thereof) or, for that matter, the equivalent of the 18th-century monarchial systems of Great Britain and France. History shows the greatest glory for the Republican Party to have been during the days of Lincoln. Abraham Lincoln, after the founding generation, was the principal supporter and advocate for equality and liberty in America's history. He represented and still does represent America at its very best.

In September of 1859, Lincoln spoke at the Wisconsin Agricultural Fair. There he presented an alternative idea of political economy—one at odds with the ideas espoused by various supporters of the master class concept then and later, including those mentioned above. Lincoln asserted that the source of value is not capital but labor. It is labor that creates something out of nothing. When it receives political support— quality education, equitable economic opportunity, free access to the market—labor creates value and wealth. It is ridiculous to argue that laborers cannot move out of the situations into which they are born. Laborers, as they work, discover assets that society finds valuable. Those assets aren't created by men sitting in chairs smoking pipes. Viewed rightly, there is no conflict between capital and labor. Lincoln called capital simply "pre-exerted labor."[23] The value created by people working together on new ideas, on construction, on mining, and so forth, causes society to progress. Most unlike the master class theory,

---

22 Richardson, *To Make Men Free*, 234.
23 Richardson, 17.

this theory of political economy is wholly consistent with the principles of the Declaration of Independence, the Constitution, and the
Bill of Rights.

By 1859 Lincoln had shaped his central ideas into a worldview that
would become that of the new Republican Party. Congress should not
privilege an economic elite. Congress should ensure a level economic
playing field so that hardworking individuals can rise. The idea of
equality should mean more than government just staying out of the
way; government should support citizens as they improve themselves
and thereby better contribute to the nation. In terms of education,
for example, Congress should improve its quality and its availability.
In Heather Cox Richardson's words, "Republicans like Lincoln were
ready to adopt the idea that the government should actively promote
individual economic achievement."[24]

The country received an object lesson in the difference between
Republicans and Democrats during a recession in the spring of 1860.
The Buchanan administration saw government revenues falling dras-
tically and people being thrown out of work. Republicans in the House
proposed a tariff to cover the shortfall. The tariff would essentially be
levied on all manufactured goods coming from Europe. In addition,
the tariff would protect agriculture, mining, and fishing products in
America. Rep. Justin Morrill of Vermont introduced the bill, saying
it rested on the belief that all citizens shared a harmony of interest. Supporters declared that it was the duty of the government to
promote policies that advanced "the prosperity and happiness of the
whole people."[25] Rejecting Hammond's mudsill theory, Morrill said
that the government should treat all Americans "as members of one
family, all entitled to equal favor, and no one to be made the beast of
burden to carry the packs of others."[26] The legislation was intended
not only as a source of funds to ameliorate recession conditions but as

24 Richardson, 20.
25 Richardson, 21.
26 Richardson, 21.

a means to encourage hardworking Americans—free labor—to create their own manufacturing entities and thereby enrich the nation.

Republicans passed the tariff in the House in May, but Southern Democrats blocked it in the Senate. Clearly, Republicans' plans for governance—including a vision of supporting entrepreneurial labor—contrasted with those of Democrats.

At this time Republicans were split between a radical wing often referred to as the Radical Republicans, which wanted major national action against slavery everywhere, and a more moderate wing that simply wanted to return to the status quo before the Kansas-Nebraska Act. There were many candidates in the contest for the Republican nomination. The 1860 convention would take place in May in Chicago, giving Lincoln a home field advantage. William H. Seward, a Radical senator from New York, was seen as the favorite. Lincoln, more moderate, lent his efforts to bringing the two wings of the party together.

In February of 1860 the New York Republican Party, eager to undercut Seward, invited Lincoln to speak at the Cooper Union auditorium. Lincoln agreed to speak on the evening of February 27. The auditorium was filled to its capacity of 1,500. According to Richardson's account, Lincoln started slowly but warmed to his subject using a careful analytical approach. He effectively made the case that it was not the Republicans who were the radicals, but the Democrats, who were dangerously attempting to spread slavery beyond the South. The Republicans, he said, reflected the national vision of the Founding Fathers. When Lincoln stopped after an hour and a half, the audience stood and cheered. The newspapers printed 170,000 copies of the speech the next day. The speech made Lincoln a national figure in the Republican Party.[27]

A few months later Lincoln won the Republican nomination on the third ballot at the convention in Chicago. The Republicans were now united and the Democrats split—between Northern Democrats and

---

27 Richardson, 22.

Southern Democrats, with a small fourth Constitutional Union party that simply wanted the slavery problem to go away. Lincoln won the election with a little under 40 percent of the vote, and the Republicans won majorities in both houses of Congress. In just six years from its founding, the Republican Party had won control of Congress and elected Abraham Lincoln, perhaps the greatest president in American history. No political party in America has ever won an election as glorious as this one.

CHAPTER 2

WAR AND RECONSTRUCTION

SOME SIX YEARS PRIOR to the election of 1860 and the subsequent onset of the Civil War, former Whig Party member Abraham Lincoln had already identified in his own mind the argument that would block the Slave Power from seizing the entire Union via the ill-starred Kansas-Nebraska Act of 1854. Sen. Stephen Douglas of Illinois had led the effort to put the act on the books. In a speech in Peoria on October 18, 1854, Lincoln spoke out against this new pro-slavery legislative effort. He said that he objected to the new law "because it assumes that there *can* be *moral right* in the enslaving of one man by another." [1] In his opinion, Senator Douglas had acted to vitiate the promise made to all men and women in the Declaration of Independence—a promise referenced in the Constitution, the Bill of Rights, and the Missouri Compromise. Douglas's law attacked the declaration and destroyed the compromise. This must be rectified.

With the election of Lincoln, however, all compromise broke down.

---

1 Lewis L. Gould, *Grand Old Party: A History of the Republicans* (New York: Oxford University Press, 2014), 15. Accessed on ProQuest Ebook Central, https://ebook-central.proquest.com/lib/multco/detail.action?docID=1019505.

Eleven Southern states supporting the Slave Power seceded from the Union, calling themselves the Confederate States of America. South Carolina forces fired on the federal fort in Charleston Harbor, Fort Sumter, in April of 1861, and Lincoln decided to contest the secession. Thus Southern forces—the Confederate army—became rebels or traitors and were considered as such by the Union government.

The crisis of the Civil War shaped views of both the Democratic and the Republican parties.

> At some instinctive level, Republicans were convinced that their political opposition was less patriotic, even less American, than Republicans were in the nation's greatest crisis. As a result, while they did not question in principle the right of the Democrats to hold power, over the years, in the minds of Republicans, a Democratic president lacked legitimacy, especially if the chief executive had come to office with less than a majority of the popular vote. These attitudes originated during the Civil War when, as one writer noted in 1864, the Democratic Party gained "the taint of disloyalty, which whether true or false will cling to it, like the poisoned shirt of Nessus, for a century."[2]

That taint did cling, strengthening the resolve of the Republicans to effectively steal the election from the majority vote winner and probable Electoral College vote winner, the Democrat Sam Tilden, in 1876. But the writer was too conservative in his judgment; this attitude is with us still, some 161 years later.

The Civil War entirely transformed the Republican Party. Under their war leadership, the Republicans expanded the power and strength of the federal government, bringing it into the modern era. During the four years from 1861 to 1865, the nation:

---

2   Gould, 25.

achieved the destruction of slavery and the preservation of the Union in which the power of the South was much reduced. The war and Reconstruction that followed also created real political rights for African Americans in the United States for the first time. In 1865 the antislavery agenda of the Republicans had been realized in full.[3]

But the Republicans did much more. They took several steps in the economic sphere to strengthen the Union war machine. For instance, they created a national banking system, a national currency, and an income tax, and they built a transcontinental railroad. The federal government gained a powerful role in the development of the economy. Thus "a party that began as an attack on the existing political order became an organization that believed in an identity of interests of capitalists, labor, and farmers."[4]

Over time the capitalist part became more important. The Republican Party became the party of big business, which it remains today. It supports business, big business, and the contemporary equivalents of such robber barons as Rockefeller and Vanderbilt. Many of today's robber barons, however, are far more interested in their own political agendas, as seen in the Koch family's involvement with the libertarians. The robber barons of the late 19th century evolved into some of the greatest philanthropists in history, but with exceptions such as the Gates Foundation, with its efforts to support public health around the world, many today do not create great institutions for the country like Vanderbilt University, the Carnegie libraries, and the Rockefeller Foundation—institutions dedicated to the best interests of all humanity. Instead, they establish political institutions.

During the formative debates of the early 1860s, the Republicans— or National Unionists, as they called themselves for a time—were

---

3   Gould, 24.
4   Gould, 24.

divided into three parts. The "radicals," also known as the Radical Republicans, took a tough stance against the South, wishing to significantly expand the rights of Black Americans. By the later years of the decade, they counted among their numbers Senate president pro tempore Ben Wade and two of the most influential members of Congress, Sen. Charles Sumner—who had been badly beaten by two Southern representatives on the floor of the Senate as recounted above—and Thaddeus Stevens, a dominant figure in the House. Those styled "moderates" took a middle position. President Lincoln certainly fell into this category. The third faction—the "conservatives"—simply counted on winning the war; afterward, they hoped to return to the status quo, reverting to the terms of the Missouri Compromise before it was upset by the Kansas-Nebraska Act.

These factions of the party debated such issues as the future destiny of Black Americans and what to do about the South after the war was won. Lincoln acted as a conciliator among these divergent parts of the party. As historian Lewis Gould writes, "The size and strength of these factions shifted with specific issues and problems as Republican policy toward slavery and then Reconstruction emerged."[5] Lincoln's assassination in April 1865 left forever unsolved the mystery of what he would have done with the defeated South.

On the issue of slavery itself, Lincoln lived to work his will. Initially, as the war proceeded, he worried about the continued loyalty of the border states and held back on the Emancipation Proclamation until after the outcome of the Battle of Antietam in 1862. The outcome of this battle, it was believed, made it less likely that Britain and France would intervene on the side of the Confederacy. Gould writes, "As the corrosive effects of the war on slavery as an institution became more apparent, Lincoln concluded that freeing the slaves would strengthen the Union with European nations . . . and [undermine] the economic

---

5   Gould, 28.

base of the South."[6] The Emancipation Proclamation of 1863 did not free any enslaved persons beyond Union control, but it set the North on an unalterable course of changing the status of Black Americans. "A return to slavery became impossible."[7]

After adoption of the proclamation, Lincoln increasingly looked to the passage of a constitutional amendment outlawing slavery, thereby banishing it from American life forever. This was motivated by the desire to ensure that slavery was politically dead. Should Southern Democrats rejoin the country after the Civil War and one day gain political success, a congressional majority could not legislate a return to slavery. The Thirteenth Amendment resolution quickly passed the Senate, but on June 15, 1864, it failed to achieve the requisite two-thirds vote in the House, where a strong Democratic vote thwarted the Republican majority. However, after Lincoln's reelection in November, the two-thirds vote was achieved on January 31, 1865. Lincoln signed the amendment resolution shortly thereafter, and it was sent to the states.

Lincoln was nominated for a second term in Baltimore in June 1864. As the Republicans anticipated a close contest, given war-weariness and the continuing strength of the Northern Democrats, the delegates temporarily adopted the name "National Union Party" to appeal to a broader spectrum. Gould writes, "The desire to present a broad front against the Democrats and their probable candidate, General George B. McClellan, led to a fateful decision in the convention."[8] That was replacing Lincoln's vice president, Hannibal Hamlin of Maine, with Andrew Johnson of Tennessee, a Democrat who had served as military governor of his state. Gould writes:

> No one inquired about Johnson's views of African Americans, his possible style as president, or his character as a politician.

6   Gould, 29.
7   Gould, 29.
8   Gould, 31, 32.

[He] hated the Confederacy and its leaders and spoke in harsh terms about those who waged the rebellion. Yet he really did not oppose slavery as such.[9]

The decision to choose Andrew Johnson proved to be a terrible one. Once he succeeded the assassinated Lincoln and the South was defeated, Johnson introduced a process to provide amnesty for Southern men and ignored any provision for Black suffrage. He believed—and said outright—that the United States was a country for White men.[10] Johnson's impact was antithetical to all that the Republicans had fought for during the war. Sympathizing with the South, he locked the pseudo-slavery of Jim Crow into place there for the next hundred years—until the Civil Rights Movement, with the support of the Kennedy and Johnson administrations, challenged it. Andrew Johnson had looked away while the Democratic South began to reassert control over its Black population with the Ku Klux Klan and Jim Crow policies.

The Republican Party of Andrew Johnson was not what our Founders would have wanted. It was decidedly not what our "second Founder," President Lincoln, or his government wanted. As a result (at least in part) of the selection of Andrew Johnson, America is still fighting the Civil War as far as principles and policies are concerned. There has been considerable progress, yes—but victory, no. Today's version of the Slave Power is seen in the advent of Donald Trump and in the billionaire class powered by dark money.

President Andrew Johnson essentially sided with the South, although he did back the Thirteenth Amendment banning slavery and asked regional leaders in the South to support it. With the new president largely repudiating Lincoln's program for the future, Congress decided it would have to take the lead. Gould describes its leadership as resulting in three important pieces of legislation: (1) the renewal of

---

9 Gould, 32, 33.
10 Gould, 36.

the Freedmen's Bureau, which helped newly freed persons deal with the new world they now lived in, offering assistance in dealing with such necessities as contracts and leases; (2) a civil rights bill to clarify and expand the rights of Black Americans, particularly the formerly enslaved; and (3) the Fourteenth Amendment, which became, over time, one of the most important parts of the Constitution in advancing liberty and equality.[11] It is described by Lewis Gould as "a separate amendment to the Constitution that wrote the principles of the civil rights legislation into the fundamental law of the nation . . . what became, in effect, the peace terms of the Civil War."[12]

With regard to the Reconstruction process, Southern leaders were recalcitrant and uncooperative. Johnson did not press them to act otherwise. Johnson vetoed the Freedmen's Bureau bill, and his veto was sustained, although a substantially watered-down version subsequently passed. His veto of the Civil Rights Bill was overridden. Johnson violently opposed the Fourteenth Amendment and urged Southern governors and legislatures not to ratify it, although Congress had made its ratification a condition for seceded states to return to the Union. Johnson urged those who opposed the amendment to fight hard in the 1866 midterm election. He assured Southern leaders that, if the Democrats prevailed, the Lincoln/Radical Republican measures could be repealed and Johnson's Reconstruction plan adopted.

Rather than denouncing violence in the South, his stance, according to Heather Cox Richardson, was essentially, "Welcome back." Indeed, President Johnson egged the violence on. Northern voters were outraged by this, and in 1866 they voted congressional Republicans back into power with a two-thirds majority in both houses. This Republican Congress could override any veto they wanted to.[13] Even though Republicans held a congressional majority, however, Reconstruction was not a success because Southern leaders and the president opposed it.

---

11 Gould, 38–39.
12 Gould, 38.
13 Richardson, *To Make Men Free*, 64.

The Lincoln reformist Republican Congress delivered its last great piece of legislation, the Military Reconstruction Act, in 1867. The act divided the ten Southern states still outside the Union into five military districts in which Reconstruction could be managed. It adopted the principle of universal male suffrage and required the ten states overseen by the administrators of the act to guarantee Black suffrage and ratification of the Fourteenth Amendment. The act represented the culmination of the Lincoln program delivered by the Republican Party for the country.

The Military Reconstruction Act was of great significance. Richardson writes, "With it, Republicans asserted that all men, poor and underprivileged as well as rich and educated, should have a say in America's government." [14] The legislation included Black men as well as White. It signified not only an end to slavery but also the desire for an end to racial discrimination.

> [It also] committed the nation to a system of government that funded individual prosperity and promoted education. Both elements—prosperity and education—were required, and if either fell through, voters would be swayed by economic dependence on demagogues, and the Republicans would fall.[15]

Free labor, both Black and White, would ensure prosperity, and a freely elected government would provide education. The Founding Fathers, through the framework of the Declaration of Independence, had implicitly sought these objectives when they declared that all men have an inherent right to "Life, Liberty and the pursuit of Happiness." They reaffirmed them with the Constitution and Bill of Rights. They looked to future generations to fill out this framework. The Military Reconstruction Act and the Thirteenth and Fourteenth Amendments largely did that. Richardson writes, "The effect produced by [the act]

---

14 Richardson, 66.
15 Richardson, 66.

was far-reaching and radical. It changed the political history of the United States."[16] Sadly, indeed tragically, "the Military Reconstruction Act of 1867 was the last gasp of Lincoln's Republican Party. Over the next five years, party members would abandon this commitment to equality [so valued by our Founders and Abraham Lincoln] and become the party of big business."[17]

In 1867, Sens. Ben Wade and Charles Sumner, both Radical Republicans, demanded stronger Reconstruction measures—among other things, compelling plantation owners in the South to donate land to freedmen. Their proposal was bottled up in committee. Sumner publicly attacked many Republicans for the failures of Reconstruction policy. He criticized many prominent Republican members of Congress, including Roscoe Conkling of New York, soon to move up to the Senate. Conkling never forgave Sumner, and their feud over the future direction of the party severely weakened it and ultimately resulted in the party's abandoning its commitment to equality for Black Americans—indeed, for the South. Republicans were to become the party of business, not of reform.

In 1867 Republicans attempted to impeach President Johnson and drive him from office. They came within one vote of doing so in the early months of 1868 at the conclusion of his trial in the Senate. Perhaps the principal reason conviction was not achieved—although it was a very near miss—was that a significant number of Republicans did not want to make Radical Republican Ben Wade president of the United States. The previous year he had been elected president pro tempore of the Senate, and the law then designated that the president pro tempore of the Senate succeed the president if there were no sitting vice president. (Today the successor would be the Speaker of the House.)

In the Republican convention that year, Ben Wade sought the

---

16 Richardson, 66.
17 Richardson, 66.

nomination, as did the unpopular incumbent, President Andrew Johnson. The name of the moderate Gen. Ulysses S. Grant came forward. Sumner was not happy with the prospect of a Grant nomination. He did not see much chance for the Radical program under Grant, although Grant had chosen as his running mate Speaker of the House Schuyler Colfax. Though a Radical, Colfax was far more moderate than Sumner's ally Ben Wade. As the election of 1868 neared, it became clear that only one candidate could gain the nomination—General Ulysses S. Grant. In the end, because of soldiers' support and general popularity, Grant won every vote in the convention.

The real contest was for vice president. Although Wade assured himself of his own victory for the post, late in the process the governor of New York, Reuben Fenton, threw his votes to Schuyler Colfax, making him the vice presidential nominee. Later in the year Wade lost his Senate seat.

To oppose Grant, the Democrats nominated Horatio Seymour, a former governor of New York, and Francis Blair of Missouri. They accused the Republicans of "subjecting the Southern states, 'in time of profound peace, to military despotism and negro supremacy.'"[18] The pair took the position that they were defenders of the views of former Illinois senator Stephen Douglas, who in the late 1850s, ten years earlier, had favored "a government by white men, of white men, for white men."[19]

For their part, the Republicans for the first time waved the "bloody shirt." A party orator held up the bloodstained shirt of a Union veteran and urged the crowd to vote the way they had shot in the war. The following is an example of "bloody shirt" rhetoric—this one from Indiana governor Oliver P. Martin in 1866.

> Every man who labored for the rebellion in the field, who murdered Union prisoners by cruelty and starvation, who conspired to bring about civil war in the loyal states . . . every

---

18 Gould, *Grand Old Party*, 44.
19 Gould, 44.

officer in the army who was dismissed for cowardice or dis-loyalty calls himself a Democrat . . . every wolf in sheep's clothing, who pretends to preach the gospel but proclaims the righteousness of man-selling and slavery; every one who shoots down negroes in the streets, burns negro school-houses and meeting-houses, and murders women and children by the light of their own flaming dwellings calls himself a Democrat. In short, the Democratic party may be described as a common sewer and loathsome receptacle, into which is emptied every element of treason North and South, and every element of our inhumanity and barbarism which has dishonored the age.[20]

Each side used the war as a political tool. The Republicans used "bloody shirt" oratory nearly to the end of the 19th century, well after the party had become the party of big business. The Democrats responded by extolling the glory of the Confederacy, a theme the Democrats in the South used with great effect into the 1920s and which some would say their ideological descendants are still using today in the furor about removing statues of Confederate generals.

General Grant won the election, earning 53 percent of the popular vote. One way of looking at the election results is that, while the Democrats won a majority of the White vote, the newly enfranchised Blacks gave Grant the victory. The Democratic Party was far from chastened, as former Confederate states began to be readmitted, gathering strength with their increasing number. Before Grant was inaugurated, the Republican Congress passed its third constitutional amendment, the Fifteenth Amendment, which guaranteed universal male suffrage for all races. Republicans reasoned that the amendment would enable Black voters to offset the majority of Whites supporting the Democrats.

---

20 Gould, 45.

Grant, while supporting the civil rights of Black Americans, longed for peace after the horrible violence of the Civil War. Instead of peace, Grant and the Congress encountered the reality of the Ku Klux Klan. The Klan was founded in the South as a paramilitary terror organization. It used intimidation and violence to keep Black Americans, most of them formerly enslaved, from voting or holding office. Grant was warned by a North Carolina Republican that "an organized conspiracy is in existence in every County in the State, and its aim is to control the government."[21] In response Congress passed the Ku Klux Klan Act of 1871. Grant had his attorney general and the newly created Justice Department pursue the Klan with vigor. This led to hundreds of trials and conviction of many of the Klan's key leaders. According to Gould, the Klan was at least temporarily driven back into the shadows of society. The suppression of the Klan was one of Grant's most important achievements.[22]

Grant remained popular with the Republicans, but among the Radical leaders Grant's term in office was intolerable. The Republican governments established in the South were highly corrupt. Radical Republicans were offended by the perceived failure of Reconstruction. They wanted to leave the issues of the Civil War behind and benefit from the new industrial society. "Reconstruction and slavery we have done with," penned the editor of *The Nation*, a publication supportive of the Radical cause. "For administrative and revenue reform we are eager." There was only so much that the president and the remaining Radicals in Congress could do to stem the shift of national attention away from the issues of Reconstruction and toward the emerging questions of an industrial society.[23]

In the 1868 election, President Grant lost New York and, as a result, won the presidency by a somewhat closer margin than he might have

---

21 Gould, 50.
22 Gould, 51.
23 Gould, 47.

done. He didn't want that to happen again, so he befriended Roscoe
Conkling, the most powerful politician in New York. According to
Richardson's account, this relationship became an alliance as a byprod-
uct of Grant's first foreign policy venture. Grant's primary political
goal was economic growth, and as part of the effort, he wanted to
annex Santo Domingo, a part of the island of Hispaniola that is now
the Dominican Republic, to help establish markets for US goods in the
Caribbean. Grant used his private secretary, Orville Babcock, to nego-
tiate the treaty. He did not inform the chairman of the Senate Foreign
Affairs Committee, Charles Sumner, the leader of the Radicals in the
Senate, until Babcock was safely back in Washington, signed treaty
in hand. This slight caused a permanent break between Grant and
Sumner, resulting in a disastrous split in the party and, ultimately,
the end of its role as a reformist, liberal political organization. But
given that Conkling had very poor relations with Sumner as well, the
emerging close friendship between Grant and Conkling had positive
results for Grant in New York. Sumner blocked the treaty annexing
Santo Domingo in the Senate later in 1870 and it never came into
force. After this, Grant gave up all hope of ever working with Sumner
and his friends and turned regularly to others such as Conkling for
political support.[24]

Sumner's campaign against Grant following the treaty debacle
began to have the effect of turning Republican-oriented newspapers against Grant. Horace Greeley's *New York Tribune* was the first.
Greeley's attacks on Grant, after a time, became hysterical. Many
journalists across America had been trained by Greeley and venerated
him. Greeley's views carried weight because he was a former leader of
the abolitionist cause. His bashing of Grant caused many journalists to
join the Sumner camp. There was now powerful opposition to Grant
and a major split in the Republican Party that would change it—

---

24 Richardson, *To Make Men Free*, 82, 83.

indeed, degrade it. This was no longer the party of Lincoln. Sumner repeatedly made public attacks on Grant, describing him at one point as an "ignorant puppet of designing men." [25]

Grant, for his part, began removing men who had been appointed to government at Sumner's request. A year later, when the 42nd Congress convened in March 1871, the Republican caucus removed Sumner from his chairmanship of the Senate Foreign Affairs Committee at Grant's instigation. Grant was pleased at this heavy blow to Sumner's career. He thought Sumner's blocking of the treaty and refusal to support the administration deserved punishment. Sumner's response was in kind, and the country was treated to the spectacle of a man who had built his career as an abolitionist, the country's self-styled chief defender of the rights of Black Americans, destroying the republic's efforts to establish a fair system of free labor in the South and pushing the Republican Party away from its commitment to equality—away from Lincoln's and the party's fundamental principles. The Ku Klux Klan and Jim Crow policies, not objected to by congressional Republicans, virtually reestablished much of the slave system.

In support of Sumner's vendetta against Grant,

> Greeley begged Republicans to abandon Grant before the 1872 presidential campaign. [After all, Sumner] had been a driving force behind opposition to the Kansas-Nebraska Act in 1854, and no one had forgotten—or *could* ever forget—that he had been beaten almost to death on the floor of the Senate as he stood up for Republican principles. Greeley's attacks on the president began to shift Republican principles away from the defense of equality. The former abolitionist abruptly abandoned the idea of a free labor system in the South, vilifying the administration's defense of ex-slaves in order to turn votes against the president . . . the mercurial

---

25 Richardson, 84.

editor was willing to abandon Black Americans if it meant he could score points against Grant."[26]

In 1871, a resurgent Ku Klux Klan was gradually becoming the dominant power in South Carolina. The governor beseeched the president to help him. Grant sought authorization from Congress to deploy the army against the Klan. Greeley strongly opposed this, persuading other journalists to follow him. He said that Grant had no right to interfere with the South in this way. Greeley and his allies—journalists and politicians—assailed Grant's free labor policy in the South, arguing that Grant was using uneducated, illiterate, and second-class people—the formerly enslaved—to become a powerful political force in the South and, among other things, to redistribute the wealth of educated, upper-class Whites into the hands of an irresponsible rabble, the newly freed Black Americans.

Greeley and his allies also argued that the administration was doing the same thing in the North with its free labor policies: redistributing wealth into the hands of an uneducated, undisciplined underclass. These, they said, were communist policies, advocated by Karl Marx and exemplified by the horrendous Paris Commune of 1871, which for two months in Paris ruled with progressive, anti-religious, anarchist policies such as the workers' right to take over businesses. Increasingly such rhetoric was attributed to the Democratic Party, North and South, and was said to be supported by Grant.

To prevent Grant from being reelected, the Sumner/Greeley group formed what they called the Liberal Republican Party and held a separate convention. To the astonishment of some, the New York delegation unexpectedly gave their votes to Greeley, a choice anathema to all except the Sumner faction whose meeting this was. When the authorized Republican Party held its convention, there was a general sense that despite difficulties, Grant was likely the only

26 Richardson, 91.

eligible candidate who could win the general election. The Liberal (actually the Radical) Republicans advanced an economic agenda that would eventually help Grant and further draw Republicans away from their original principles. Given the economic strength of the South, bankers and businessmen had generally backed the Democrats before the war. However, during the war, business had benefited greatly from Republican policies. After the war, the business community became uneasy at the rise of the Sumner group, the so-called Liberal Republicans, because of their rhetorical support of Southern Democratic positions. Also, the Democrats as a whole—Northern and Southern—made no secret of their intention to dismantle the Lincoln economic policy which had benefited business so much.

The Liberal Republicans planned to defeat Grant by destroying "the political power of African Americans and organized workers, who, they thought, elected politicians to pass laws that would redistribute wealth."[27] This way, they could purify the Republican Party from what they saw as the corruption of Grant and his followers. Thus they destroyed Abraham Lincoln's program of free labor, which, instead of redistributing wealth as they charged, served to level the playing field between rich and poor, giving all laborers a chance to earn the fair wages they were entitled to. The Liberals and the Democrats called Lincoln's labor program corrupt mobocracy in the South and communism or socialism in the North. As a result, "the opposition of the business community to the Democrats pulled the Republican Party into its orbit, and Republican ideology continued to drift away from its original focus on equality."[28] With their readiness to undercut policy aimed at providing for the common good through accusations of "communism" or "socialism," Liberal Republicans and their Democrat allies appeared right-wing and reactionary.

The Republicans at their convention touted such accomplishments

---

27 Richardson, 96.
28 Richardson, 99.

as freeing the slaves, establishing universal male suffrage, giving land to settlers, and passing a protective tariff. They pointed to their record of protecting both Black and White workers. In the election, Grant was reelected—this time by a landslide. He carried New York, the state with the most electoral votes, due in part to the machine politics of Roscoe Conkling and in part to contributions by Wall Street and other business centers to his campaign war chest. The Democrats saw Greeley as their best chance to defeat Grant, and they too nominated him as their candidate. The parties adopted identical platforms.[29] Democrats couldn't stomach Greeley and he got little support from them, nor did he get support from administration Republicans.

But the split in the Republican Party had profound effects for the future of the party and the future of the nation. Mainstream Republicans adopted some of the rhetoric of the attacks by the Liberal Republicans. Summarizing changes to the Republican Party, Richardson writes:

> Ironically, in their quest to preserve the principles of Lincoln's Republican Party, the Liberal Republicans doomed these very principles. In order to take down President Grant, [they] had adopted the language of Democrats who opposed Republican ideals in general. Liberal Republicans had tarred administration Republicans as corrupt demagogues who promised wealth distribution to lazy African Americans in order to keep themselves in power. . . .
>
> The confluence of events of 1871 turned Northerners against ex-slaves, and they also determined that the maturing Republican Party would not champion organized workers. When Liberal Republicans went after ex-slaves as lazy schemers they opened the door to attacks on New York City immigrants and eventually to a blanket condemnation

---

29 Gould, *Grand Old Party*, 52.

of workers as a separate interest attacking the harmonious system that guaranteed American prosperity.

By refusing to adapt their ideas to the realities of postwar industry, the Democrats pushed businessmen firmly into the Republican Party. Most industrialists and financiers were determined to prevent the return of power to the Democrats, whose postwar economic policies they abhorred.

The Liberal Republicans delegitimized the argument of the Civil War Republicans that a strong national government should promote general prosperity by creating economic opportunities. . . . After 1872, administration Republicans argued just the opposite. They tended to deride any effort to use tax money for programs that helped society in general as "communism" or "socialism". . . . Lincoln's policy of helping every man work his way up had been jettisoned by his own party after only 12 years.[30]

The party that turned away from Lincoln has remained today's Republican Party, slavishly supporting wealth and big business, rigging tax laws on behalf of business and the wealthy, and rejecting most attempts to improve, strengthen, or liberalize the country. There have been exceptions: James Garfield, the last Lincoln man, assassinated after a few months in 1881; the great reformer and environmentalist Teddy Roosevelt; General Dwight David Eisenhower; and the two men who ended the Cold War, Presidents Ronald Reagan and George H. W. Bush. All of these men, to a greater or lesser extent, attempted to return the Republican Party to the principles of Lincoln. Some succeeded for a time. Such exceptions did not erase the party tendency to turn a blind eye to Jim Crow and the Ku Klux Klan—the tendency that reestablished a social order not dissimilar to the former Southern slaveocracy. Had Civil War Northerners earned

---

30 Richardson, *To Make Men Free*, 106, 107.

the "bloody shirt" in vain? When Richard Nixon succeeded to the presidency on the basis of his Southern strategy—explicitly replacing Southern Democrats as the Republican "new" Old South—he only made overt existing changes in the Republican Party, changes that dated back a century.

How diminished today's Republican Party seems in the light of the vision Abraham Lincoln articulated for our nation—that it maintain "in the world that form and substance of government, whose leading object is, to elevate the conditions of men—to lift artificial weights from all shoulders; to clear the path of laudable pursuit for all; to afford all, an unfettered start, and a fair chance, in the race of life." [31]

---

31 John Lewis Gaddis, *On Grand Strategy* (New York: Penguin Books, 2018), 244.

CHAPTER 3

LINCOLN REVIVED; BIG BUSINESS, ENSUING CATASTROPHE

THE ELECTION TO SUCCEED President Grant put the final nail in the coffin of Lincoln progressivism in Republican Party leadership. Grant had been Lincoln's general, and his administration did reflect some of Lincoln's priorities, including free labor in the North and South, voting rights for Black Americans, and at least the temporary destruction of the Ku Klux Klan. In the 1870s, such positions were opposed by the Liberal (Radical) faction in the Republican Party. As noted above, this faction—once known as the party Radical wing—followed Charles Sumner in conducting a personal vendetta against Grant. Sumner had been personally offended by Grant and was determined to force him out of the presidency. Horace Greeley and other journalists influenced by Sumner followed him in abandoning Lincoln's principles and adopting many positions of the slaveholding South.

While the Republican Party evolved into the party of big business, it had to balance the wishes of the Grant supporters as well as those of the Liberal (Radical) wing in selecting its next presidential candidate. The party settled on Rutherford B. Hayes, governor of Ohio, after passing up James G. Blaine, perhaps the leading Republican politician, because he had become tainted by scandal. Hayes was neither corrupt, nor was he a reformer who would make business interests uncomfortable. He would be easy on the South. The Democrats chose Samuel B. Tilden, governor of New York, which was the principal swing state in national elections during this period. Because Democrats had control of the House for the first time since before Lincoln and had elected a governor of New York for the first time since the 1850s, the Democrats were given a chance to win the White House.

Although Tilden won the popular vote by 264,000, he did not become president.

On election night, Tilden was clearly running ahead. As morning neared, it became clear that Tilden had won in 16 states with 184 electoral votes, one short of a majority in the Electoral College. Hayes had 165 electoral votes from the 18 states that he carried. There were three Southern states where the outcome was still unresolved: Florida, Louisiana, and South Carolina. These three states possessed 20 electoral votes, enough for Hayes to win by one vote if he carried all three. The three state electoral boards—controlled by Republicans, with federal troops in those states being part of the control—declared Hayes the winner. They sent their electoral lists to Washington. The Democrats sent their own electoral lists to Washington, declaring all three states for Tilden.

The Constitution provided no clear solution to a case of competing electoral lists. Congress received the conflicting vote totals, debated the matter, and established a commission to resolve the case. There were to be seven Republican members, seven Democratic members, and one independent member—Supreme Court justice David Davis of Illinois. It was assumed he would cast an objective, non-party-line vote if a seven-to-seven tie resulted from the other members' votes. However, shortly after the commission was formed, Davis became a senator from Illinois when the state legislature elected him to oust the incumbent Republican. Subsequently, a Republican justice was appointed to the commission in place of Davis. A series of eight-to-seven votes followed, and Hayes was declared the winner. Although Tilden won the popular vote by a sizable margin, Hayes won the decisive Electoral College by one vote, 185–184. Gould reports that Tilden won a majority of the White vote in Florida, South Carolina, and Louisiana. And, despite the impact of Ku Klux Klan terrorism, it's not unreasonable to think that a majority of the Black vote might have gone to Hayes.[1] In the event, Democrats called this outcome a fraud.

The decision of the Electoral Commission had to be approved by Congress. The Democrats began a filibuster.

> As the inauguration date of March 4, 1877, approached, intense bargaining ensued. . . . Southern Democrats sought railroad subsidies and other economic concessions in return for the acceptance of Hayes as president. But both parties realized that the larger issue was the end of Reconstruction. Hayes made it clear that he would not continue to support Republican regimes in the South using military power.[2]

As Hayes told Carl Schurz, a Republican senator, "There is to be an end of all that, except in emergencies which I do not think possible again." The Senate Democrats abandoned their filibuster and Hayes became president on March 4, 1877. Gould writes:

> Once in office, the new chief executive took federal troops out of politics in Louisiana and South Carolina . . . indicating that Reconstruction was over. Black Americans were now on their own, and commentators predicted that their fate would cease to be a factor in national politics.[3]

---

1 Gould, *Grand Old Party*, 59.
2 Gould, 59.
3 Gould, 59.

These commentators were largely correct until the Civil Rights Era some 75 years later.

After Hayes was inaugurated, he did his best to defuse the political situation. It seemed to many that the Republicans and their supporters were determined to control the government—especially the White House—without regard for the will of the people. Grant had said during the four-month period before the inauguration that he would oppose any violent protests with martial law. To some Tilden supporters it seemed as though the American republic was being destroyed by an economic oligarchy that called itself the Republican Party—backed by the military power of the state.

Hayes announced that several important posts in his cabinet would be given to Democrats and also that the federal military would no longer support Republican state governments in the South, which began to be controlled by Democrats. Heather Cox Richardson writes:

> But Democrats held onto the idea that the Republicans had perpetrated the "Great Fraud of 1876" to perpetuate their political empire. . . . Beginning to electioneer for the midterm election even before the 1876 election was settled, Democrats insisted that Republicans had stolen the presidency and were determined to never give up power.[4]

If the public believed that the Republicans intended to run the country exclusively for their benefit and that of their rich constituents, this view seemed to be confirmed by the Great Railroad Strike of 1877. The strike began when the Baltimore and Ohio Railroad cut wages by 20 percent. Violent strikes spread all down the line; mobs destroyed millions of dollars of property. About 100 people were killed. Strikers hoped that this was the opening shot against the economic oligarchy controlling the country with the help of the Republican Party. Republicans saw it as a reprise of the Paris

---

4   Richardson, *To Make Men Free*, 115.

Commune of 1871. Richardson writes, "Albert Pinkerton, the founder of the strike-breaking Pinkerton Detective Agency, claimed that the strike offered proof that 'we have among us a seditious communistic spirit.'"[5] Hayes used the military to break the strike just months after Grant had threatened martial law.

In response the Democrats introduced the Posse Comitatus Act, which would prohibit the president from using the army within US borders without the consent of Congress. Some of the Republicans in Congress, including most notably James G. Blaine in the Senate, were outraged. The act passed anyway. At the time the Democrats controlled the House and the Republicans had a narrow majority in the Senate. The *Chicago Tribune*, a voice of the Republicans, expressed horror, declaring resolutely that no troops "shall be used to protect colored voters of the South . . . or to crush our communist riots in the North."[6] Republican outrage was undercut somewhat by the agreement settling the 1876 election, which had made it clear that Republicans would no longer protect Black voters in the South. Under Hayes, Black citizens had been left to the tender mercies of the Ku Klux Klan and the administrators of Jim Crow policies.

The Republican Party realized that the country was beginning to slip away from their leadership. They needed to do something to regain voters.

Grant Republicans, their ally Roscoe Conkling, and the machine politicians believed that they needed to mobilize their pro-business wealth machine and renominate Grant. Others supported Sen. James G. Blaine. But, at the convention, the nomination swung to dark-horse candidate James Garfield, then an Ohio representative and House majority leader. Garfield was perhaps the last Lincoln Republican to grace America's political stage and likely would have made an excellent president, having been a general in the war and a supporter of

---

5   Richardson, 115.
6   Richardson, 116.

Black rights. His running mate was Chester Arthur, a man from the Conkling machine, undoubtedly a servant of the economic oligarchy. The Democratic candidate Gen. Winfield Scott Hancock made the Great Fraud of 1876 his campaign centerpiece.

Garfield and Arthur won the 1880 election narrowly in the popular vote but easily in the Electoral College. Richardson explains:

> The terrible end of this interparty struggle came in July 1881, when a deranged office seeker from the Conkling wing of the party shot and mortally wounded President Garfield at the Washington train station. "I am a Stalwart [meaning from the Conkling wing] and now Arthur is president!" he shouted. . . . The big business wing of the Republican Party, to which the assassin belonged, had so corrupted the meaning of government that he had felt justified in killing the president to get a job. Surely, voters thought, this was not the Republican government for which soldiers like Garfield had died only twenty years before. Just as surely, they thought, the Republican Party, controlled as it was by the big business wing, must no longer govern the country.[7]

Recognizing the damage Garfield's assassination had done to the public's view of Republicans, President Arthur kept a low profile. Congressional Democrats tried to scale back some of the negative steps that previous Republican administrations had taken. To prevent Republicans from controlling the country through patronage, Congress passed the Pendleton Act in 1883. This act established a nonpartisan procedure for filling civil service positions. The object of the law was to get politics out of the business of filling jobs in the civil service bureaucracy, removing the risk of a one-party political system. This was a real risk, given the dominance of the Republican Party fueled by Gilded Age money.

---

7   Richardson, 118.

Republicans, for their part, looked upon the Democratic resurgence as a threat to the very existence of the nation, or the part of the nation to which they were beholden—the robber-baron economy, which concentrated the wealth of the nation in the hands of a few. The Republicans naturally felt threatened by the ascendance of a system controlled by the Northern Democrats. By this time the South was Democratic again and gave the Northern Democrats its support as long as it was left alone. More and more, the Northern Democrats became the party where labor had a home. This system would replace an economic structure organized to support big business and economic royalty with one set to adopt measures to aid and protect workers. Republicans felt that those who did not want to protect business must be socialists or, perhaps, communists. In short, Republicans reacted similarly to kings being threatened by peasants.

At the 1884 Republican National Convention, the Grant/ Conkling/big business coalition remained in control despite the presence of a faction that wished to reclaim the original principles of the party—those enunciated by Abraham Lincoln. The latter stayed with the party but voted for the Democratic nominee in the election. One of these breakaway Republicans declared, "We are Republicans but we are not slaves."[8] As it turned out, Grover Cleveland, the reform Democratic governor of New York, won the election because of public outrage over the influence of big business and corrupt money in politics. The Democrats, while ignoring their Southern Democratic allies, became a reform party dedicated to supporting the working man— ironically, advancing the very reforms that Republicans had supported under Lincoln.

The Republicans had transformed themselves. Their positions were like those of the conservative Democrats of pre–Civil War days—a combination of those advocated by Stephen Douglas of Illinois and John C. Calhoun of South Carolina. This wasn't the self-perception

---

8   Richardson, 121.

of the old guard Republicans—as the big-business-supporting Republicans came to be known. Richardson explains:

> Only a generation after the Republican Party had formed to make sure that all hardworking Americans could rise, its members had replaced that principle with a defense of big business that looked perilously close to antebellum slave owners' defense of their society. And, as in the 1850s, most Americans in 1884 thought their nation should stand for the opportunity of every man to rise as long as he worked hard.[9]

Republicans who manipulated the political system on behalf of big business, Richardson says, realized some short-term gains but lost their strength in the long term.

Republicans argued that "the Democrats were simply unworthy to govern and incapable of doing so."[10] The Democratic Party was the same in character and spirit as when it sympathized with treason, they believed. The Republicans lost in 1884, with Grover Cleveland riding the wave of popular anger into the White House. It would take a new generation of Republicans to try to reform the party and restore Lincoln's principles.

After the 1884 election, the Republicans acquired a new nickname. During the 1870s some newspapers had taken to calling the Republicans "the Grand Old Party" to show support. In 1884 a typesetter at an Ohio newspaper ran out of spacing and used the initials "GOP." The shortened name stuck.

The Republicans, desperate to succeed in 1888, turned to a new kingmaker named Mark Hanna. He succeeded in reorganizing Republican electoral efforts and won the House back in 1886. In 1888 the Republicans pulled out every stop to elect their candidate, Benjamin Harrison. The Republicans prevailed in the struggle to control the

---

9   Richardson, 122.
10 Gould, *Grand Old Party*, 90.

House and Senate, and Harrison eked out a victory over Cleveland by somehow carrying the swing state of New York. Harrison, a religious man or at least an observant one, commented to Hanna after the election that, given the closeness of the election, "Providence has given us this victory." Hanna later responded, "Providence hadn't a damn thing to do with it. [A] number of men were compelled to approach the penitentiary to make him president."[11]

Cleveland ran again in 1892 and, once more creating a tidal wave of public anger—this time at the vast sea of corruption that had engulfed the nation under Harrison—was returned to the White House. In 1896 Cleveland retired, and the Democrats put up a new candidate they hoped would succeed him—a spellbinding orator from the Middle West named William Jennings Bryan. The Republican candidate, however—Ohio governor William McKinley—would prevail.

The country had been in economic crisis, referred to as the Panic of '93, since shortly before Cleveland was elected for his second term. The Republicans, with only weeks left in Harrison's term, had refused to act to alleviate the crisis, preferring to hand it to Cleveland for the second time. Republicans had foisted on the country a slaveholding-type economy, and the robber-baron culture had produced its fruits. By 1896 the crisis was acute. A few large "trusts," as they were called, held controlling stock positions in many companies and dominated the economy. The most prominent of the robber barons were four men: J. P. Morgan, John D. Rockefeller, Andrew Carnegie, and Jay Gould. Between them, they controlled the American economy. By the late 1890s, no one could stand against them—certainly not the president or Congress.

It was not until the rise of Theodore Roosevelt and the new men who came with him that the problems of an economic oligarchy would be addressed. Roosevelt had been elected governor of New York in 1898 and was McKinley's running mate in 1900 for his second term.

---

11 Richardson, *To Make Men Free*, 123.

Some months after he was reelected, McKinley was shot by a political extremist during a reception at the 1901 Pan American Exposition in Buffalo. Roosevelt took office after McKinley's death approximately a week later. Things began to happen. Roosevelt made a serious attempt to bring back Lincoln's principles within the party, with some lasting success. But the Republican establishment, the old guard, was not happy. As Mark Hanna said, "That damned cowboy is president!" [12]

After McKinley's assassination, Roosevelt spoke to a joint session of Congress as president. In his speech he made clear that reform was coming but also that he was not anti-business. He wanted to regulate and provide rules for business, to make it strong. He wanted to further strengthen business, not tear it down. It was a conservative speech. The old guard was somewhat mollified, but the truce didn't last long. The old guard saw that many younger men coming into power believed that reform and a return to Lincoln's principles was imperative.

Henry Cabot Lodge was the first of these. He had been elected to the House in 1886 and moved on to the Senate in 1893. When early on he met Roosevelt, they had become close friends and political colleagues. Sen. Albert Beveridge of Indiana and Gov. Robert La Follette of Wisconsin were other important, like-minded colleagues. After his command of the Rough Riders contingent during the Spanish-American War and his subsequent election as the reform governor of New York, Roosevelt had become the leader of this group. His programs of reform as president were supported by these men and by other young Republicans, who saw in Roosevelt the embodiment of a new America.

One of these young supporters said to the *New York Times* that Roosevelt would demonstrate to Americans that "there is a higher and nobler ideal than the acquisition of fortune, and that service to one's country is the first duty of patriotic citizenship." Roosevelt's imperialist zeal would maintain "the country's honor against the mewing

---

12 Richardson, 153.

advocates of surrender, national effacement, and 'peace at any price.'"
Roosevelt's insistence, like Lincoln's, that all Americans, regardless
of race or class, could successfully work their way up was wishful.[13]
The system as it existed was biased against wage earners and farmers
in favor of the old guard. In the South it was biased against Blacks
in favor of the former slaveholding elite. Jim Crow laws enforcing
racial segregation and lynching had increased significantly in the late
19th century. As Richardson notes, "Still Roosevelt had reclaimed
Lincoln's ideological language, if not his inclusive vision. The government should stand behind any man who worked hard. No longer
would it be held in thrall to corrupt old ways of doing business."[14]

The young Republicans coming to power in place of the old
guard were motivated by a different vision. They were committed to
Lincoln's principles and wanted them restored. They believed that an
economic system benefiting only the few at the top was dangerous
to the country as a whole. They put the welfare of the people ahead
of the vested interests of the old guard. They believed in Lincoln's
ideas about equality and free labor. This was so even though many of
them were from the top echelons of society, including Henry Cabot
Lodge and certainly their leader, Theodore Roosevelt. On the other
hand, they embraced imperialism, which they believed went hand in
hand with a vibrant democracy based on principles of freedom. Why
shouldn't the American system of democracy, the best form of government for humanity, be spread all over the world? They favored
annexation of Hawaii and intervention on the side of the rebels against
Spain in Cuba and in the Philippines. They also favored the annexation of Guam and of the part of the Samoan Islands that would, in
1911, become American Samoa.

By contrast, the old guard was anti-imperialist and preferred to live
well by continuing to fleece the American people. They were afraid

---

13 Richardson, 146, 147.
14 Richardson, 147.

that going abroad might eventually be unfavorable for the successful—but shaky and corrupt—domestic economic empires they supported. Roosevelt and his followers looked at the sweatshops, tenements, exhausted mothers, and grinding poverty—the conditions in industrial America—and worried that uneducated, already working, and undernourished children raised in such appalling conditions could never grow to be healthy, vigorous, and "fitted for the exacting duties of American citizenship."[15] The need to have strong citizens for a strong America went together with the young Republican commitment to imperialism.

To cure the ills that the young Republicans at that time saw in American industrial society, they intended to return the country to the principles of Abraham Lincoln. As he had, they opposed the concentration of wealth in the hands of the few, which blocked those outside of the old guard hereditary structure from rising. Lincoln had believed that every man should have equal opportunity to rise in a free society, and so did this new class of Republicans. The extremely wealthy upper class, supporting and supported by the old guard, should not control the country. As Lincoln also did, this new class of Republicans called for a strong middle class. They pronounced themselves "liberals" in support of the concept of American liberalism, based on the ideas of Thomas Jefferson and the Enlightenment philosopher John Locke.

Following such principles, Roosevelt became more and more the Republicans' liberal leader—similar to but also different from the Liberal Republican Party, formerly the Radical Republicans, of the post-Lincoln period. But Lincoln was the lodestar. As Richardson writes, "Roosevelt insisted that Lincoln held the rights of property sacred, but less important than the rights of men. He was 'for both the man and the dollar, but in case of conflict, the man before the dollar.'"[16] Upon McKinley's death and his ascension to the presidency,

---

15 Richardson, 149.
16 Richardson, 150.

Roosevelt did as Lincoln did—he supported every American. Over objections in the South, he invited the famous Black educator Booker T. Washington to lunch with him at the White House. Roosevelt thus emphasized that all American citizens prepared to work hard and contribute to society should be treated equally by the government. Lincoln had invited Frederick Douglass to the White House in 1863 to make the same point.

By contrast, the old guard facilitated those who would have put the economy of America in a very few hands—supporting a financial oligarchy. They put control of many businesses in a particular industry into a single trust controlled by a few men and repeated this tactic in other industries. The case of the Northern Trust is an example of the practice. In February of 1901, J. P. Morgan combined businesses representing two-thirds of the nation's steel companies into the U.S. Steel Corporation. The combined company was capitalized at $1.4 billion, three times the annual budget of the US government. Then, in November, Morgan combined all the principal railroad companies into his Northern Securities Company, a holding company. Morgan was attempting to put the nation's steel interests and the railroad industry under his personal control. This step also effectively circumvented existing antitrust laws. The Republican *Chicago Tribune* exclaimed, "Never have interests so enormous been brought under one management."[17] Midwestern legislatures sought ways to undo this flagrant assault on American laws and equal-opportunity principles. As Sen. Albert Beveridge of Indiana had stated a few years before, such actions by the business community required "rebuke, regulation, and retirement."[18] The response to the legislative criticism of the Northern Securities action, Richardson notes, was that officials of the company announced that they would keep all business transactions and operations secret.[19]

---

17 Richardson, 152.
18 Richardson, 150.
19 Richardson, 152.

Building conglomerates to purposefully evade antitrust laws was, of course, beyond outrageous. It was contrary to the quintessential American notion—expressed by the nation's Founders and repeated by Abraham Lincoln—that all have opportunity for "the pursuit of happiness." The concentration of the country's economic power into fewer and fewer hands was a direct blow at liberty and was deeply un-American. Roosevelt was furious. He expressed the hope in late 1901 that Congress would clean up this direct threat to the economic health of the country. When it became clear that Congress—still under the control of the old guard—would do nothing, he took action. He moved beyond his view that big business needed only regulation. Recognizing the lengths to which J. P. Morgan and his associates were prepared to go, he decided that super-large organizations like the Northern Trust represented a threat to the nation's freedom and must be dealt with. He made a breakup of the trusts—and barring the formation of new trusts—a central theme of his presidency. The financial abuse engendered by the robber barons and the GOP would be echoed in that pursued by the Republican Party in the 1920s and also in the late 20th and early 21st centuries through manipulation of the tax laws and violation or circumvention of campaign finance laws. But there has been no Teddy Roosevelt, no Republican president like him, in the White House since his time.

In early 1902, the state of Minnesota sued Northern Securities for violation of Minnesota law. As the Republican-dominated Supreme Court did not take action on the case, Roosevelt's attorney general, Philander C. Knox, told newspapers that the administration believed that the organization of the Northern Securities Company had vi-olated the Sherman Antitrust Act. Members of the old guard were horrified, both by the Justice Department action and by the fact that Roosevelt hadn't consulted first with Wall Street. In response the president indicated that was the whole point—no more cozy deals with government for Wall Street. Richardson relates how Morgan responded to Roosevelt:

"If we have done anything wrong send your man [Knox] to my man [one of his lawyers] and we can fix it up." The president indicated that he would not do that. "We don't want to fix it up," explained the attorney general. "We want to stop it."[20]

Trust-busting, which could often be a long process, was what President Roosevelt became best known for. Roosevelt laid out the battle plan and had a few early successes. Many more monopolistic combinations were dismantled by his successor, President William Howard Taft, who did little else in terms of progressivism. The enormous Rockefeller Standard Oil Trust wasn't broken up by the courts until 1911, pursuant to a government suit in 1906, toward the end of the Taft years. But Roosevelt's actions, also implemented by Taft, effectively removed a huge threat to the liberty of the American people. Future generations have been and should remain grateful.

To be sure, the old guard continued to strengthen itself in the Congress—if not in numbers, at least in the leadership. Richardson describes how four senior senators—Nelson Aldrich of Rhode Island, John Spooner of Wisconsin, Orville Platt of Connecticut, and William Allison of Iowa—worked closely with Mark Hanna, the Republican Party chairman and soon a senator, to boost the interests of Wall Street. Aldrich, leader of the group, became very rich through the manipulation of street railways and politics. His only daughter had married John D. Rockefeller's only son. He was not well known publicly, but he exercised considerable power on behalf of the old guard. As recipient of much of the campaign financial support large corporations provided, he had additional influence with fellow senators. Aldrich and his associates held tightly to protectionism—a high tariff on many products—as the cornerstone of American prosperity. Illinois representative Joseph Cannon, known as "Uncle Joe,"

---

20 Richardson, 155.

was made Speaker of the House. He ruled the House with an iron fist on behalf of the old guard.[21]

There was more to Theodore Roosevelt's progressivism and his commitment to the principles of Lincoln than his assault on trusts. Roosevelt offered the American people a "square deal"—for everyone. He was wildly popular, was renominated easily in 1904 despite old guard opposition, and was reelected in a landslide. The Republicans also won a significant majority in the House that year. With the mandate his election gave him, Roosevelt proposed such progressive measures as federal oversight of labor and business, railroad safety laws, and slum clearance. Congress ignored them all.

The people had had enough. Resistance to Aldrich's gang and the old guard became evident. Wisconsin sent its governor, the progressive leader "Fighting Bob" La Follette, to the Senate. Publications exposing the outrages of big business began to appear, the most influential of these being Upton Sinclair's book *The Jungle*. Even with the Republican majority in the House, the tide began to turn in 1906. That year the following measures were passed by Congress, all in the single month of June, over the old guard's strong protest:

> The Hepburn Act gave the federal government power to set maximum rates for the railroads. The Pure Food and Drug Act made it illegal to make, sell, or transport adulterated or fraudulently labeled food or drugs. The Meat Inspection Act gave the federal government power to regulate and inspect factories that packed meat for shipment across state lines. This trio of laws marked an epochal change in the power of the federal government to protect individuals against the abuses of industrial capitalism. The *Chicago Tribune* noted that these laws were "a radical departure from previous governmental methods."[22]

---

21 Richardson, 160.
22 Richardson, 162.

But Roosevelt wanted much more. The very idea that before the Pure Food and Drug Act was passed it was perfectly legal to sell bacteria- or toxin-laden food in the market was abhorrent. Hundreds or thousands might die without penalty to the manufacturer in such "free market" capitalism—the economic philosophy dear to the heart of the dominant wing of the post-Lincoln Republican Party. Of course, irresponsible market capitalism is not really free when it amounts to hard-hearted, harmful behavior, of which Republicans should not be proud. The old guard were less the GOP (Grand Old Party) and more the GOS (Grand Old Savages) in that era of squeezing the vulnerable for every dollar. Teddy Roosevelt fought to return the party to the principles of Abraham Lincoln, but the old guard, their associates, descendants, and heirs, using corrupt money and means, prevented it from happening.

Completely fed up with the old guard, Roosevelt no longer sought compromise; he sought their defeat. He referred to these men as "malefactors of great wealth." In this Industrial Age, he feared a workers' rebellion if these malefactors were not reined in and the government led as Lincoln had said it should be led. As Richardson writes, "He wanted stronger regulation of big business, an inheritance tax, and an income tax."[23] But his successors would have to make this happen. He had announced, after reelection in 1904, that he would not seek another term.

His successor was William Howard Taft. A somewhat lackluster presidential campaign nonetheless resulted in a considerable progressive presence in Congress after the 1908 election. Taft did as he had promised and continued a vigorous trust-busting campaign, bringing some 90 lawsuits by the government, compared with 44 brought under Roosevelt. But beyond this he did little else except golf, sleep, and eat.

Although he was conflict-averse, he did call a special session of Congress early in his tenure to revise the tariff downward. This was

---

23 Richardson, 163.

an issue that had been lurking for years. Since before the Civil War, Democrats had believed that tariffs should be used to raise money and not for other purposes. Progressives wanted lower tariffs. Republicans liked higher tariffs for their protectionist effect, so that some less well-managed firms—as well as others—wouldn't have to compete with more efficient foreign enterprises. Since many businessmen wanted to protect their companies, the old guard were able to get help from the Democrats to pass a House bill significantly raising, not lowering, tariffs. The same thing happened in the Senate, even though the progressives led by La Follette made a strong case against the bill. Taft decided to sign on with Aldrich on this, once calling the revised tariff "the best bill that the Republican Party has ever passed."[24]

The bill caused a profound split in the Republican Party. Differences over the tariff and the failure to do anything new for the progressive cause were reasons that led Roosevelt to accept the nomination of the Green Party, of which Senator La Follette was a prime mover, when the old guard blocked him from attending the Republican National Convention in 1912. This move split the Republican vote and resulted in the election that year of the Democrat reformer Woodrow Wilson.

In 1910, while still contemplating running in the 1912 election, Roosevelt had given a speech at a John Brown celebration in Osawatomie, Kansas, in which he opened both barrels at the Republican old guard. Prominent in the audience were Civil War veterans. Before them, Roosevelt claimed the mantle as Lincoln's heir:

> In Lincoln's day, the threat to government had come from the Slave Power; in 1910, it came from business interests. America was currently governed by "a small class of enormously wealthy and economically powerful men, whose chief object is to hold and increase their power." This must stop or the country was doomed. . . . He, like Lincoln, believed

---

24 Richardson, 166.

that every man deserved a chance to work hard and rise. To permit a special interest to dominate the economy and reduce everyone else to virtual slavery would destroy the country.[25]

Roosevelt went on to say, anticipating the welfare state far into the future, that an active government must ensure a level economic playing field—as Lincoln had done.

> For the good of the country, the government should regulate both big business and the terms of labor. Roosevelt called for transparency in corporate operations, regulation of business, and abolition of corporate funding of political campaigns. To prevent the accumulation of huge fortunes, he called for both graduated income taxes and inheritance taxes. He insisted that the government must protect natural resources for future generations rather than permit industrialists to grab them all. To guarantee that all men could rise, he called for minimum wage and maximum hours measures, as well as for far better factory conditions. And to make sure that future generations grew up healthy and sound, he called for the regulation of child labor and women's work.[26]

He had called his plan the New Nationalism.

Theodore Roosevelt's stance was very similar to Lincoln's and that of our Founders. Even though the Republican Party has turned its back on this vision, the country should not. We all should be committed to follow the lead of our Founders, their brilliant disciple Abraham Lincoln, and Lincoln's heir Teddy Roosevelt. To keep our country safe, we must fight for our founding principles and never, never give them up.

President Woodrow Wilson attempted to carry on Roosevelt's reforms. One would think that, at least to some extent, the Republican

25 Richardson, 167.
26 Richardson, 167, 168.

Party would have supported this. Not at all. The party, back in the hands of the old guard, attacked Democrats as the traitors they had been 60 years in the past. Wilson was dubbed a Confederate *and* a socialist—the latter epithet earned because he followed Roosevelt's reform policies. The same policies in Republican hands were perhaps not as socialist as they were in Democratic hands, and the old guard was primed to attack them in these terms.

As Gould points out, "When the Democrats enacted an income tax in 1913, they permanently changed how government revenues were created."[27] The passage of this legislation meant that the government would no longer be funded with tariffs but with personal and corporate graduated income taxes. Wilson's administration also passed legislation to establish the Federal Reserve in 1915. The new Democratic tariff cut rates from roughly 50 percent to 25 percent. Henry Cabot Lodge attacked this as being destructive of business, but it wasn't too many years before the Republicans adopted free trade and ceased protecting American business as a matter of general policy. The old guard found that this policy didn't hurt their profits at all. In 1914, the Wilson administration was able to get the Clayton antitrust bill passed, which "outlawed price fixing and interlocking corporate directorates and made corporate officials personally responsible for illegal actions of the entities they oversaw."[28]

World War I ended with the Treaty of Versailles, which included the Wilson-sponsored League of Nations, designed to prevent another world war. Republicans believed that they now had another weapon with which to strike the Democrats. They argued that the League of Nations was part of the world communist movement exemplified by the Bolshevik Revolution in Russia. If the United States joined it, America would be destroyed. Heather Cox Richardson explains how one Republican official articulated the essential party line:

---

27 Gould, *Grand Old Party*, 131.
28 Richardson, *To Make Men Free*, 175.

"Conjure in your mind, if you can, a world without the Declaration of Independence, without the Constitution and free institutions, without our proclamation of emancipation of races and of nations, without this nation itself" and you have a world with the League of Nations. Internationalism was, [Henry Cabot] Lodge pointed out, the goal of communism. One senator saw a more direct communist link: Wilson was a professor and a government of professors would ultimately lend to Bolshevism.[29]

The US did not join the league, the treaty being rejected by the Senate. Republican opposition made the advent of World War II much more likely but convinced some Americans for the longer term that international cooperation would destroy the America they knew. Better, those thought, to rely on our military.

Republican antagonism toward the League of Nations had some effects on US politics into the 21st century. It also led to a decisive victory for the Republicans in the 1920 election. Thus the Republican Party began a 12-year period of governance—12 years with the old guard and "big money" ruling the nation without interference by Congress, reformers, or anyone. The 1920s would be a glorious ride to prosperity led by the superrich. Just keep the power in the hands of the Republican rich elite, the old guard, and all would be well! Republicans would oversee joyous prosperity into the indefinite future. That was the message. Republicans ignored historical experience and spurned the principles upon which this nation was founded. While the twenties roared, speculation kept driving up the stock market, and speakeasies with illegal mafia liquor kept fueling high times. Americans remained asleep to the coming terrible retribution such "parties" invite.

Warren J. Harding of Ohio—a man who looked like a president,

---

29 Richardson, 178.

although his skill set unfortunately stopped there—was elected president. With a "back to normal" sentiment running strong, Republicans saw Harding as the perfect choice in 1920. In contrast to Wilson—the creative, passionate, intellectually connected professor—Harding was the nice guy who would keep an eye on your house while you were away. He was undistinguished and indistinguishable. The *New York Times* called him "a very respectable second-class politician."[30] His job during the campaign was to keep his mouth shut and look presidential.

The real attention-getter on the ticket was the vice presidential candidate, Massachusetts governor Calvin Coolidge, the man who had broken the Boston police strike. Harding was there because he was part of the old guard and could carry Ohio, where he was a sitting senator. Coolidge would protect the nation from the Bolsheviks.

Harding began his term by doing nothing—as he had been intended to do. He turned the government over to business, who set about to get from it what they could. Harding spent his days drinking and playing cards with a circle of friends known as the Ohio Gang. Fairly early during the Harding term, Secretary of the Interior Albert B. Fall, a member of the Ohio Gang, in exchange for money (in one case, a suitcase filled with $100 bills), leased government lands at Teapot Dome, Wyoming, and Elk Hills, California, to oilmen who were also members of the Ohio Gang, Edward L. Doheny and Harry Ford Sinclair. Other members of the Ohio Gang were taking kickbacks from liquor deals—liquor, of course, now being contraband. Suspicion of the Ohio Gang began to grow, and two of its members, fearing exposure, committed suicide.

Scandal rapidly closed in on Harding himself. In July of 1923, as the scandals were breaking, Harding and his wife took a trip to Alaska and the West Coast. He was accompanied by some Ohio Gang members. Commerce Secretary Herbert Hoover—whom Harding,

---

30 Richardson, 184.

between card games, had earlier selected for the post—was along too, though he was soon sorry to have accepted the invitation. Harding saw that he was not being greeted by crowds as usual. For that reason, he spent most of his time at the bridge table with those Ohio Gang members who had accompanied him. On July 27 Harding dropped a page while making a speech. Shortly after, he began to deteriorate and was rushed to the hospital in San Francisco. He died in his hospital bed, probably of a heart attack, though the cause of death was never confirmed. Of Harding, Alice Roosevelt Longworth, Teddy's daughter and oldest child, said afterward, "Harding was not a bad man, he was just a slob." [31]

Now Calvin Coolidge, the bulwark against Bolshevism, was president. Andrew Mellon had Coolidge's ear. He spent much of his time making the case for reducing the very high World War I–era tax on income earners in the highest brackets so as to persuade wealthy men to invest in the economy: "The government is just a business, and can and should be run on business principles." [32] In addressing the postwar slump, Hoover, a growing influence in the government, was strongly opposed to government aid to unemployed workers. He did not see the government as having a duty to care for the public, of which unemployed workers are a part. Coolidge did not disagree with this view. It was clear that Mellon and wealthy businessman friends were not going to help carry out Coolidge's duties as president by helping the poor. Mellon himself, the richest of the rich, asked the head of the Internal Revenue Service for tips on how he could reduce his taxes.

As Heather Cox Richardson writes, "Coolidge had gone down in history as a do-nothing president who worshipped business almost as a religion. This is largely true, and if Republicans were right, nothing was precisely what a good president should do." [33] Republicans warned

31 Richardson, 186.
32 Richardson, 188.
33 Richardson, 190.

the electorate in 1928 that to elect a Democrat could bring on a depression, ignoring the fact that the Panic of 1893 had begun under the Republicans well prior to their handing over the government to the Democrats. President Harrison's refusal to do anything about the economic situation in 1893 had given Republicans a good issue to hit President Cleveland with, but in the event, it wasn't fear of the return of a now 30-year-old economic crisis, safely buried in history, that influenced voters in 1928. Americans didn't need encouragement to vote for Hoover as Coolidge's successor. They had been convinced by the irresponsible excesses of preceding years. Despite scandal and corruption of a major sort, they believed Republicans had discovered the secret of how to create and maintain a booming economy. Hoover won in a landslide over the Democrat Al Smith, governor of New York, and was sworn in as president in early March 1929. Shortly after Hoover's election, the stock market experienced a "victory boom," with five million shares changing hands.

What the Republicans did not see in the happy days of early 1929 was that the economic success they were experiencing

> was based on two terrible fallacies. First, the rising living standards getting so much attention in the media were not widespread; they affected primarily white, middle-class, urban Americans. And second, 1920s prosperity rested on a speculative bubble, not on solid economic growth. When the bubble burst, there was an explosion the likes of which the world had never seen, proving that the very fundamentals to which the Republican Party had held since the mid-1880s were breathtakingly wrong.[34]

The elitist money-obsessed model that the Republicans had followed since they gave up on Lincoln principles and opted for advancing big business was proved criminally, catastrophically wrong.

---

34 Richardson, 193.

The Lincoln model, which Teddy Roosevelt had tried to revive, was shown to have been overwhelmingly right. The market crash of 1929 has in it a lesson for the early 21st century.

The Republicans turned their backs on Black Americans, leaving those in the South to suffer from the de jure racial segregation of Jim Crow laws and those in the North to be oppressed by de facto segregation. They did not invite Black leaders to important forums or to the White House. They turned against immigrants. They refused to help the poor or provide jobs with potential to anyone except Whites from established families. An economy based heavily on racial, ethnic, class, and even religious bigotry was not sustainable. "When an ill wind blew, the entire edifice collapsed,"[35] and the Republican Party in the early 1930s went down with it.

In his inaugural address, Hoover told the audience that the problem was not how to avoid sliding back but how to progress forward to even higher levels of success. That was in March 1929. Early 1929 had seen a huge rush to speculate in stock. New investment vehicles were being created almost every day. Richardson writes:

> On October 17, Irving Fisher, a renowned professor of economics, cheered that stock prices had reached "what looks like a permanently high plateau." Within a few months he expected to see the stock market "a good deal higher than it is today." October 24, a Thursday, was the beginning of the end. Heavy trading in the morning made the ticker tape that recorded stock trade prices run behind. Fearful of getting caught with overvalued stock as prices dropped, brokers sold more and more heavily.[36]

Bankers intervened to stabilize the market, and by afternoon most of the morning's losses had been made good. A remarkable number of

---

35 Richardson, 196, 197.
36 Richardson, 198.

shares had changed hands during the day—12,894,850. This was an incredible total for the 1920s.

The market appeared to recover on Friday and Saturday, but Monday, October 28, saw more losses. The Dow Jones Industrial Average was down 49 points. Bankers, no longer confident, were in a state of high tension. The next day was Tuesday, October 29, known to history as Black Tuesday. On market opening, there was immediate, heavy trading—all of it downward. Huge blocks of stock came on the market with no bidders at all. Brokers pleaded for bids—of any amount. But not one bid came—not even small amounts—nothing. When the ticker finally caught up with the trading, nearly 16½ million shares had changed hands. Losses continued on virtually a daily basis. By mid-November the market overall was 50 percent of its high in October. Brokers called in margin loans, thereby effectively wiping out most investors, who, counting on a permanent rising stock market, had bought on margin. The stock market crash did enormous damage beyond the market itself; throughout the country many institutions and individuals had used stocks as their store of value. The market crash triggered the Great Depression.

When Franklin Roosevelt was elected president in 1932, taking office in March of 1933 after four years of an ineffectual, do-nothing Hoover and a comparable Republican Party, he found that he had a true economic catastrophe facing him. It was somewhat like (though much worse than) the one President Obama faced in 2009 after the third—or fourth—economic collapse engineered by the Republicans, depending on whether one counts the 1987 stock market crash and the savings and loan crisis. As Richardson writes:

> Republican leaders might have been able to explain the crash
> as a normal correction in an inflated market, but the de-
> pression that followed it convinced most Americans that the
> modern Republican economic vision was wrong. Since the
> 1880s [for nearly 50 years], Republicans had been saying that

enacting their program of hard money, high tariffs, low taxes, and no regulation would create endless American growth and prosperity. In the 1920s, they put that vision into place. When the result was a depression of unimaginable depths and duration, it deeply undermined Americans' faith in the Republican Party.[37]

37 Richardson, 199.

CHAPTER 4

MODERATE VERSUS ISOLATIONIST

THE 1932 ELECTION was an unmitigated repudiation of the Republican Party and everything it stood for. Roosevelt won the election with 58 percent of the vote, and the situation went downhill for the Republicans from there. During the interval between election and inauguration, Hoover and Roosevelt could not agree on what actions to take in an atmosphere of swelling unemployment. So nothing was done. Thus, when Franklin Roosevelt took office on March 4, the banking system and, with it, the economy stood right on the edge of a precipice. The New Deal, as Roosevelt called his promise to the American people, took off with considerable vigor from a nearly moribund Hoover administration.

The Republicans found themselves in a difficult situation. After implementing their vision of national policy and economy, they had demonstrated they had no idea how to run the country for the benefit of the American people. All they knew was how to fix things so that much of the money generated by the economy could be funneled into the hands of the rich—primarily the hands of the very rich. Republicans envisioned an authoritarian oligarchy for the country, not a democracy. This had been rejected by the American people. Republicans had no other vision to offer. Lewis Gould writes:

> Conservatives argued that the best and most intellectually honest course was to oppose the New Deal and all its works from the start. As an Ohio senator told Herbert Hoover, "I would rather be defeated in antagonizing this program of economic absurdities than to have been elected either by advocating them or sneaking in as noncommitted."[1]

Thus, true to their name, the Republican old guard held to their failed vision in 1933. But other Republicans in the Northeast did not like this position for the party. In this sense the Northeastern Republicans were closer to the voters. Gould notes, "A New Yorker observed, 'It is no longer good political strategy to abuse and denounce everyone and everything without regard to the facts or the temper of the times.'"[2]

The New Deal program launched itself with the effort to save the banking system and find jobs for the huge number of Americans who, after the Republican collapse, had none. The level of public support and the widespread support in the Congress was such that many of the early New Deal programs passed the Congress without opposition. The New Deal went on to roll out Social Security, support for labor and minorities, and the Tennessee Valley project, which led to the Tennessee Valley Authority.

As 1933 turned to 1934, some Republicans expressed opposition to certain programs, but instead of trying to stop them, they sought to improve them. For example, Sen. Arthur Vandenberg pressed for a law requiring federal insurance for bank deposits, which was included in the Glass-Steagall Act of 1933 and proved to be "one of the most im-

---

1   Gould, *Grand Old Party*, 193.
2   Gould, 193.

portant parts of the early New Deal because it introduced stability into the financial systems."[3] No matter how Republicans acted during the 1934 legislative session, however, the tide continued to turn against them. Democrats held majorities in both houses. Headed into the elections of 1934, Republicans held 117 seats in the House. The 1934 elections brought the number to 104. That year they lost another ten senators, retaining only 25 Republican senators with whom to oppose the Democrats in the Senate.

After this election, the Democrats passed the Social Security legislation, the Wagner Act to strengthen organized labor, the Public Utility Holding Company Act, and the Banking Act of 1935. They also introduced legislation to raise taxes on the rich. In Congress, Republicans fought a rear-guard action. As Gould lays it out, they strongly opposed Social Security, for example, asserting they saw "no compelling reason" for dealing with repairs until economic recovery had been achieved. By contrast, Democrats argued that government support for citizens in their old age was necessary. With respect to the Wagner Act, Republicans opposed the "closed shop," which would require all employees to either join the union or leave if a union by majority vote ruled that a particular business would be open only to union members.[4] All in all, President Roosevelt was seen by Republicans as a "socialist" out to destroy free enterprise and individual freedom to boot.[5]

The Republicans chose Kansas governor Alf Landon as their standard-bearer in 1936. The anti–New Dealers were in control of the Republican Party. Opposing the New Deal across the board, they argued that Roosevelt's policies threatened freedom and individual rights. The Republicans had no alternative to the New Deal except a return to the old guard right-wing policies suppressing people's civil

---

3   Gould, 192–193.
4   Gould, 194.
5   Richardson, *To Make Men Free*, 205.

and economic rights to further enrich the very rich. They touted the same policies of the Gilded Age and the 1920s—the very ones that had caused the greatest economic calamity in the nation's history.

Fascism was spreading around the world—in Mussolini's Italy, Hitler's Germany, and militarized Japan. The United States had its fascistic voices as well: Huey Long, with his dictatorial reign in Louisiana, and hugely popular radio personality Father Charles Coughlin, the Catholic priest whose early support for FDR had migrated to a violent anti-Semitism, fanatical nationalism, and fascism. For a long time, the old guard policies of the Republican right had appeared to be oligarchic in nature. All was for the benefit of the class at the very top, somewhat like Mussolini's Italy.

Alf Landon himself was immutably anti–New Deal. He considered it wasteful, stifling to business, and he was no fan of labor organizations. As Richardson points out, "Even Landon, though, was willing to accept the idea that 1920s Republicanism could not reign unchanged, and he grudgingly endorsed some mild adjustments in Mellon's values."[6]

In November 1936, Landon carried only Maine and Vermont.

> Roosevelt did achieve a landslide of seismic proportions. . . .
> He won nearly 28 million popular votes to almost 17 million
> for Landon. The Republican candidate actually increased
> the party's total over Hoover in 1932, but Roosevelt gained
> almost 5 million votes over his previous showing as well.
> The electoral vote tally was 523 for Roosevelt and only
> eight for Landon. The Democrats controlled the Senate 80
> to 16. There were only 89 Republicans left in the House of
> Representatives. The Republicans seemed to have reached
> such a low ebb that there was talk of their imminent demise
> as a party.[7]

6   Richardson, 208.
7   Gould, *Grand Old Party*, 197.

Deal Democrats in the White House. In the end, FDR's New Deal established a coalition that won five of the next seven presidential elections and dominated American politics for a generation. The New Deal coalition only fell apart when the Southern Democrats became the Republican Dixiecrats in the late 1960s.

The five consecutive nomination victories for Republican liberals began with the nomination of Wendell Willkie. A former Democrat, he found a significant part of the New Deal program acceptable and was no supporter of Republican 1920s-type policies. He was also an internationalist. When delegates gathered in Philadelphia in June 1940, Thomas E. Dewey could be said to have been a leading candidate, though there was no clear front-runner. According to Richardson's account, Dewey and his faction approved: government action to regulate business; New Deal policies that had employed 8.5 million people whose paychecks stood between them and starvation; the construction of 650,000 miles of highway; the building or repairing of 120,000 bridges; the construction of 125,000 public buildings; and a social safety net firmly in place. Taft and his faction opposed all this. Dewey favored intervention in World War II on behalf of Britain and France; Taft and his supporters were isolationists.[9] These two intraparty factions—relatively liberal versus conservative, East versus West—fought each other for 25 years. After this there was a gradual complete takeover by first old guard conservatives and then even more radical conservatives known to some as movement conservatives.

As the 1940 presidential contest approached, Republicans believed their fortunes were reviving, what with Dewey's distinguished tenure as district attorney and his subsequent showing as a contender for the governorship. Dewey won a couple of primaries over Taft and Sen. Arthur Vandenberg and thus, as the June convention opened, he appeared to be ahead. Willkie at this point was a dark horse candidate, known to only 5 percent of Americans. He had registered as a

9   Richardson, 210–11.

Republican only in November 1939 and had become a candidate just months before the convention. He announced that he was opposed to Taft's isolationism and criticized inconsistencies in Dewey's stump speeches.

> Everyone who was there [in the 15,000-seat Philadelphia convention hall] remembered the galleries packed with supporters of Wendell Willkie, chanting "We want Willkie". . . . Rep. Charles Halleck, a Willkie supporter from his home state of Indiana, asked the crowd as he placed his man's name in nomination, "Is the Republican party a closed corporation? Do you have to be born into it?" The galleries rocked with the response: "No, no". . . . The shouts from the gallery continued: "We want Willkie!" After six tumultuous ballots, the Willkie supporters got their wish. The new candidate told them he would wage "an aggressive fighting campaign." As he left the podium, the organist played "God Bless America," and the delegates sang in unison as the convention ended.[10]

Improbable, yes. Seemingly impossible, yes. But a popular upset could still happen in the America of 1940. Although Willkie was an attractive candidate, he was never more so than the day he was nominated. It was all downhill from there. He refused to attack Roosevelt's sale of 50 old destroyers to Britain in exchange for long-term leases of British bases and territories in the Caribbean—after all, he supported Britain and France against Hitler. But as the campaign proceeded and his fortunes continued to decline, he moved increasingly to the right and to isolationism. His campaign was not well organized, and he lacked a strategic vision. Although he could be said to have run a creditable race, he lost to Roosevelt by about five million votes. He certainly did better than Landon had.

After the campaign was over, the European war moved closer as a

---

10 Gould, *Grand Old Party*, 190.

threat to the United States. By November 1940, France and virtually all of Europe had fallen to Hitler and his ally Mussolini. Franco, the fascist dictator of Spain, kept his distance from Hitler. Only Britain stood for democracy, a large part of the credit going to its incomparable leader Winston Churchill. Britain was successfully weathering the Battle of Britain but now was in extremis given the substantial losses of its transport ships to Germany's submarines and the continual bombing of London by the Luftwaffe.

In 1941, Roosevelt moved openly to the side of Britain. The Lend-Lease Act—making supplies available to Britain and allies—was passed. Willkie, as a patriotic American, testified in Congress in favor of lend-lease. He helped Roosevelt in other ways, as most American Republicans and Democrats increasingly thought they should.

> The lend-lease program . . . sharpened the divisions. Willkie and his friends saw the United States as tied to the fortunes of the global conflict. Senator Taft and the isolationist wing believed that the country must not be drawn into Europe's battles. The idea of making war supplies available to Great Britain during the fighting and receiving payment only after the war was won seemed fiscally unsound and, worse yet, a blatant violation of neutrality. As Taft told a friend in January 1941, "I feel very strongly that Hitler's defeat is not vital to us, and that even the collapse of England is to be preferred to participation for the rest of our lives in European wars."[11]

When read from the perspective of 2021, this statement seems truly shocking. But perhaps in the heated ongoing debate between the isolationists and those who wished to support the British, it did not seem as extreme. The United States was not yet in the war, but its government, through the Lend-Lease Act, was taking sides, an action contrary to the Neutrality Act, which had been on the books

---

11 Gould, 207.

for years. In final passage of the Lend-Lease Act, Senator Taft had led 17 Republican senators to vote against it; ten supported the administration. Republican obstacles against US preparedness to enter the war if necessary continued to be placed in the administration's path by the Republicans, largely led in this by Senator Taft, despite the support of the ten Republican senators for lend-lease.

In August of 1941, four months before Pearl Harbor, the manpower draft under the Selective Service Act came up for renewal. Republicans voted overwhelmingly against it and expressed such strong opposition to using selective service to draft young men into the armed forces that it became very difficult for Speaker Sam Rayburn to get the act to a vote. In the end, it passed by one vote.

The Japanese attack on Pearl Harbor on December 7, 1941, ended all debate over US participation in World War II as an active belligerent. Partisan lines largely disappeared, and almost all Americans supported the war effort against two implacable foes. Willkie was no exception, though he remained a committed Republican.

The fact that the US had been attacked and ultimately had to lead a worldwide coalition in the war significantly undermined the doctrine of Republican isolationism. But "the impulses that isolationism embodied did not easily die." [12]

Willkie's tragic death from a heart attack in 1944, when he was only 52, removed a capable moderate politician from Republican Party leadership. He was missed in the next few years. The Republican candidates in 1944 were Dewey for president and Governor Bricker of Ohio for vice president. After Dewey had beaten Willkie in the Wisconsin primary, he had dropped out of the race. With Willkie out of the competition, Dewey was able to win the presidential nomination. Bricker, a favorite of the right, was chosen for the number-two slot.

Roosevelt and Dewey truly disliked each other, and the campaign

---

12 Gould, 208.

became bitter. In a Texas speech, Bricker argued that the Democratic Party had become for all intents and purposes the Communist Party, with Roosevelt as its leader. Speaking in Boston near the end of the campaign, Dewey said, "The communists are seizing control of the New Deal, through which they aim to control the government of the United States." [13]

Roosevelt won the election for his fourth term in a heavy turnout with 53 percent of the vote and a 3.5-million-vote margin. This was the closest of Roosevelt's four elections. Tragically, Roosevelt died of a cerebral hemorrhage some five months after reelection. His vice president, Harry S. Truman, moved into the White House as the next Democratic president.

The Republican presidential candidate in 1944 had been a moderate who supported important sections of the New Deal. But Senator Taft effectively controlled the Senate, and his politics were essentially those of the 1920s or indeed the late 19th century—those of the old guard. The years before 1942 had seen nine new Republican senators elected to replace Democrats, giving the Republicans 37 and—through their pact with the Southern Democrats, negotiated by Senator Taft in the late 1930s—operational control of the Senate. So the two wings of the Republican Party that had appeared in 1901, under the leadership of Teddy Roosevelt, and that had disappeared after Hoover's defeat only to reappear in 1936, were still there in 1945.

With the death of the architect of the New Deal in April 1945, the split in the Republican Party, which had been simmering since 1936, came to the fore as an important part of national policy. Taft and his followers wanted to eliminate as many of the New Deal measures as the public would allow, while moderate Republicans wanted to keep

---

13 Alonzo L. Hamby, "FDR, Dewey, and the Election of 1944," *Presidential Studies Quarterly* 43, No. 2 (n.d.): 307. Quoted in Gale Academic OneFile, https://go.gale. com/ps/i.do?id=GALE%7CA331168540&sid=googleScholar&v=2.1&it=r& linkaccess=abs&issn=03604918&p=AONE&sw=w&userGroupName=oregon_ oweb&isGeoAuthType=true.

the popular and workable elements of the Roosevelt programs while trimming unnecessary bureaucracy. Regarding the role of America on the world stage, there was a difference of view as to whether the United States should retreat into Taft-style isolationism or continue to play a leading role in the world. As Gould writes, "The era of Roosevelt was over. The Cold War was beginning." [14]

In 1945, the Republicans did yield to what the American people wanted; they supported the GI Bill. One of the most influential legislative acts in American history, it was designed to help servicemen and servicewomen return to civilian life. There was a concern that the Depression, which had ended with the onset of World War II, might return. Instead, the GI Bill became the agent of vast postwar economic growth and social changes. All who had served in the war were eligible for financial assistance under the bill, and while the financial assistance went mainly to White men, the expansion and social changes that accompanied the bill ended up helping all.

An enormous baby boom took place. Dormitories and apartments were built to house the student-veterans and their families as 7.8 million veterans went back to school. Many skilled workers were added to the workforce: 450,000 engineers; 180,000 medical professionals; 360,000 teachers; 150,000 scientists; 240,000 accountants; 107,000 lawyers; and 36,000 clergymen. Providing housing and substantial educational benefits to returning veterans entirely transformed America. Richardson writes:

> Millions of Americans vaulted into the middle class and enjoyed a standard of living unimaginable before the war. Initially forced into supporting the GI Bill by veterans' groups, Republicans helped to resurrect the vision of the original Republicans, who in 1862 passed the Homestead Act and the Land Grant College Act to provide poorer

---

14 Gould, *Grand Old Party*, 216.

Americans with the means to fund homes and get an education. In doing so, they laid the foundation for an economic boom of astounding proportions.[15]

The end of the war was initially a shock to the American economy. Pent-up demand drove up prices, causing inflation. Economic problems were aggravated by workers striking for higher wages. These problems pushed Truman's popularity down to so low a level that Republicans swept the 1946 elections. Both House and Senate fell under Republican control for the first time since 1928, delighting Senator Taft and his partisans. Taft's followers began to work extensively with Southern Democrats to dismantle the New Deal. Essentially, they tried to revive the disastrous Republican policies of the 1920s. They said Truman wanted to "tax Americans for the support of a huge government, to destroy individual enterprise, to ruin 'home rule'—this was a veiled reference to Southern racial laws—in short, to become a dictator."[16]

In addition, the 1946 Republican Congress—over Truman's vetoes—enacted a large tax cut, using the 1920s argument that tax cuts are good for business; passed a law to permit railroads to collude in setting rates free of antitrust constraints as long as the Interstate Commerce Commission approved; and passed the Taft-Hartley Act, which undermined the Wagner Act, a centerpiece of the New Deal. This act substantially weakened the power of organized labor. Republicans also attacked "communists" in government, which was what they had called FDR during the 1944 election.

The House established the Committee on Un-American Activities, popularly known as the House Un-American Activities Committee or HUAC, which became the legislative arm of Taft's attempt to brand Democrats as communists. The hearings of the committee, particularly its attack on the movie industry, sharply divided America. Some

---

15 Richardson, *To Make Men Free*, 214–15.
16 Richardson, 216.

in the movie industry supported the charge that Hollywood was a Soviet instrument for spreading communist propaganda in America. Others, such as Henry Fonda and Katharine Hepburn, regarded the committee's smears as trampling on the right to free speech. Many actors and actresses were summoned to testify. Ten refused to appear and were subsequently blacklisted in the industry. The Republican committee members branded as disloyal anyone who argued that the committee's actions interfered with Americans' rights to speak freely and defend themselves in court. Once the campaign to root out communists in the movies was underway, the Screen Actors Guild began to require its officers to swear that they were not communists. The guild's president, a young actor named Ronald Reagan,

> testified before Congress that there were indeed communists in Hollywood but they couldn't gain much ground. He gave similar information to the FBI—although he was in no position to know anything that wasn't already public—but at the same time he had a reputation in Hollywood as being kind, fair, and caring of the actors in his union.[17]

Because of his role in all these initiatives, Taft thought he was going to be the next president. He was heartbroken when the Republican National Convention, meeting in Philadelphia in June, considered his Washington activities staged, old-fashioned, and too full of 1920s ideas that would never triumph in New Deal America. The convention nominated Dewey again for president and Gov. Earl Warren of California for vice president. The Republicans believed that they had a great advantage: the Democrats had split into three parts—the regular party, the progressives under former FDR vice president Henry Wallace, and the Dixiecrats led by Sen. Strom Thurmond. All the polls and many newspapers predicted a Dewey victory, but they were just as wrong as Taft was. Truman won and it wasn't even close. He

---

17 Richardson, 238.

took 49.5 percent of the national vote, with Thurmond and Wallace emerging as also-rans. Richardson writes, "Taft and his followers had been wrong. Americans liked their New Deal reforms—especially those that defended laborers—and did not want them expunged." [18]

Taft was convinced that Truman's reelection in 1948 had resulted from Republican candidates' willingness to support parts of the New Deal. These were "me too" candidates. Dewey had lost because he was that type of candidate; he, Taft, would not be. Taft saw all Republicans who were not ideologically 1920s Republicans as communists, bent on using government to redistribute wealth. He saw Roosevelt and Truman as communists too. Republicans had worried about communism and forced redistribution of wealth all the way back to the 1870s and the Paris Commune. They feared that Black workers in the South and White workers in the North might try to redistribute wealth as had activists of the Paris Commune. Ever since that time, the Republican Party leadership—the old guard and its successors— had opposed as communist every government initiative to level the playing field between worker and employer. Those who proposed a social safety net were thus the enemy. During the 1920s, Republicans embracing these ideas had engineered the Great Depression.

Already concerned that supporters of the New Deal were domestic communists, Taft Republicans received a huge boost from the junior senator from Wisconsin, Joseph McCarthy, when he announced that he had a list of "205 card-carrying communists" working in the State Department. He charged that Secretary of State Acheson was protecting these men and that President Truman was doing the same. Taft Republicans jumped on board. Dewey Republicans pushed back against such an accusation. Margaret Chase Smith, the highly respected senator from Maine who later served for 15 years as chair of the Senate Armed Services Committee, issued a "Declaration of Conscience" on June 1, 1950, in which she said she opposed the actions

18 Richardson, 219.

of McCarthy and his allies "as a Republican . . . as a woman . . . as a United States senator . . . and as an American." Though Smith wanted the Republicans to prevail in the upcoming elections, she opposed the party gaining such a victory through McCarthy's methods: "I do not want to see the Republican Party ride to political victory on the Four Horses of Calumny—Fear, Ignorance, Bigotry, and Smear. As an American, I condemn a Republican 'Fascist' just as much as I condemn a Democrat 'Communist.' They are equally dangerous to you and me and to our country." [19]

Smith's declaration was not just an attack on the evils of the Senate Republican demagogue Joseph McCarthy; it was as a statement for all times, all Americans.

McCarthy was not intimidated by Dewey Republicans. He continued his terrible attacks through the 1952 presidential elections and beyond with the blessings of the Taft wing of the party. Once again, Senator Taft, believing that Americans wanted old-fashioned, 1920s-style Republican politics, expected to be his party's standard-bearer. Once again, he was disappointed, this time by the political debut of the victorious World War II American general Dwight D. Eisenhower.

Both parties had asked Eisenhower to run for president on their tickets after the war—believing that the American military should stay out of and above politics, he had never been consistently partisan in casting his own vote—but he had refused, instead accepting an offer to serve as president of Columbia University. This was because he believed strongly in the importance of education for those who would play a role in politics or government. As university president, he had gathered a think tank of educated and wise leaders from various fields to discuss the domestic and international problems facing the United States.

The June 1950 invasion of South Korea by North Korea, however, pulled Eisenhower more directly into public affairs. After the inva-

---

19 Richardson, 228.

sion, Truman immediately ordered American troops to join a United Nations force being formed to stop the invasion. Some Americans believed that this was a Soviet feint to draw US support away from Western Europe, making a planned conquest there easier. Truman asked Eisenhower to come on board and assess conditions in NATO, which had been established the previous year. Eisenhower found Europe—including NATO—wholly unprepared to fend off a Soviet attack. Upon his return to America to report to the president, he searched for support to help improve the situation at NATO.

Hoping to find support for the immediate strengthening of NATO, Eisenhower met with Senator Taft, considered the odds-on favorite for the Republican nomination in 1952, an idea that horrified Eisenhower.

> [Eisenhower] tried to enlist Taft's support for NATO, but Taft wanted to cut all foreign aid, not increase it. . . . Eisenhower saw Taft's isolationism as catastrophic. He promised Taft that if the senator would back NATO, Eisenhower would not challenge him for the presidency. Taft refused. Eisenhower seemed to have no choice but to yield to those insisting that he run for President.[20]

So Eisenhower did.

The Republican National Convention met in Chicago in July. Taft, through the machinery of the Republican Party, had most of the delegates he needed to win. Eisenhower, however, had huge national support—far beyond any Taft could imagine—as the man who had led the US to victory in the field against Nazi Germany. Eisenhower was also vigorously supported by the Dewey Republicans. The two factions engaged in a mighty struggle, one that featured very strong language and even fistfights. Eisenhower finally emerged the winner. He agreed to the selection of a fierce anti-communist, Richard Nixon,

---

20 Richardson, 230, 231.

as his vice president to placate the Taft forces—an attempt that was only marginally successful. The bitterness would continue for decades. Some Taft followers put it about that they had been defeated by an international conspiracy to spread communism. This attitude by the Taft partisans had a very deleterious effect on the party over the years, as Taft supporters continued to argue that only those who followed their principles were fit to govern the country.

In the general election, Eisenhower's enormous popularity carried the ticket to victory, despite a mini-crisis involving political funding gifts to Nixon, from which Nixon extricated himself by means of a speech on the new medium of television. Nixon said that no matter what his detractors said, he planned to keep the little cocker spaniel given to the family, which his six-year-old daughter had named Checkers. The Republican ticket took 55 percent of the vote versus Adlai Stevenson's share of 44.5 percent. The Republicans were back in the White House again after 20 years. Importantly, Eisenhower was the last Republican nominee from the Eastern establishment wing of the party.

Eisenhower fully subscribed to Lincoln's vision of an activist government supporting the development of a strong middle class, and he made Lincoln's concept modern by extending it to the entire world. A world with such governments would have lasting peace and prosperity. The Eisenhower administration strove for what the president called "a middle way between untrammeled freedom of the individual and the demands for the welfare of the whole nation."[21] He sought peace primarily through humanitarian aid rather than through amassing weaponry. He spoke about how producing a weapon that was not needed could mean that a needed schoolhouse would not be built.

It may seem strange that a man so known for his military accomplishments was so often an agent for peace, but it was part of an ongoing effort by Eisenhower to stop the developing arms race and

---

21 Richardson, 234.

seek peace with other nations, making war unnecessary. Interestingly, he had urged Truman in 1945 not to use the atomic bomb against the Japanese. In late July of that year, he had also tried to persuade Secretary of War Henry Stimson not to do so. In *The Making of the Atomic Bomb*, Richard Rhodes quotes from Eisenhower's diary entry regarding the Stimson meeting:

> [Stimson] asked for my opinion, so I told him I was against it on two counts. First, the Japanese were ready to surrender and it wasn't necessary to hit them with that awful thing. Second, I hated to see our country be the first to use such a weapon. Well . . . the old gentleman got furious . . . Stimson abhorred bombing cities. . . . As soldier and cabinet officer he repeatedly argued that war itself must be restrained within the bounds of humanity. . . . Firebombing was "a kind of total war he had always hated." He seems to have conceived the idea that even the atomic bomb could be somehow humanely applied.[22]

As president, Eisenhower had many crises to deal with in Europe, Indochina (Vietnam, Cambodia, and Laos), Korea, and Iran. Most went as well as they could, with perhaps the exception of the Iran problem. US support of a 1953 coup to overthrow the democratically elected prime minister, Mohammad Mosaddegh, and replace him with the autocratic shah, who had fled the country, had most unfortunate long-term effects.

Eisenhower was not a fiscal hawk. He wanted a progressive America with a strong and inclusive social safety net. There were only two years of Eisenhower's eight years in office during which the Republicans controlled Congress, but he worked well with Democrats. Famously, under his leadership the 1956 Federal-Aid Highway Act was passed,

---

22 Richard Rhodes, *The Making of the Atomic Bomb* (New York: Simon and Schuster, 1987, 2021), 933, 1002.

which set the foundation of the vast US interstate highway system. He also was instrumental in the establishment of the International Atomic Energy Agency, which supports peaceful nuclear power around the world.

> Eisenhower's Middle Way worked. Between 1945 and 1960, the gross national product (GNP) grew from $200 billion to $500 billion—a jump of 250 percent. The new prosperity was widely shared as newly educated former soldiers joined a rapidly expanding middle class. . . . For the rest of the century, politicians would work to bring back the economic prosperity of the Eisenhower era.[23]

In his farewell address this great man said, among other things:

> As we peer into society's future, we—you and I, and our government—must avoid the impulse to live only for today, plundering, for our own ease and convenience, the precious resources of tomorrow. We cannot mortgage the material assets of our grandchildren without risking the loss also of their political and spiritual heritage. We want democracy to survive for all generations to come, not to become the insolvent phantom of tomorrow. . . . In the councils of government, we must guard against the acquisition of unwarranted influence, whether sought or unsought, by the military-industrial complex. The potential for the disastrous rise of misplaced power exists and will persist. We must never let the weight of this combination endanger our liberties or democratic processes.[24]

---

23 Richardson, *To Make Men Free*, 238.
24 "President Dwight D. Eisenhower's Farewell Address (1961)," https://www.archives.gov/milestone-documents/president-dwight-d-eisenhowers-farewell-address.

CHAPTER 5

GLORY AND RADICALISM

AFTER THE FAILURES of Sen. Robert Taft and other old guard Republicans in the late 1950s, the Republicans gradually fell away from the plan to accomplish their goals through the system established by the Constitution. They gradually shaped an economic and political ideology, with ideas about freedom or the lack thereof, into a nation-alistic creed that a citizen might blindly champion. In the face of resistance by those who believed in the Declaration of Independence, the Constitution, and the Bill of Rights, they slowly progressed. They came to believe that anyone who did not intellectually and emotionally adopt the Republican pseudo-religion could not be a true American. In its initial years, the movement within the party was called by some "movement conservatism."

In opposition to the vast consensus supporting Eisenhower, the Taft Republicans stood angry and aloof, even after the senator himself died in the early 1950s. At first it seemed as though they were a van-ishing breed, but then a young college student by the name of William F. Buckley rejuvenated the Republican right. Buckley adopted McCarthy's fascist techniques and converted them into principles that he argued all should follow. In his book *God and Man at Yale*, written and published while he was a student there, Buckley hearkened back to the Republicans of the 1920s, arguing that government intervention in the economy was socialism. Socialism, of course, was close to communism, which was represented by the Soviet Union, which the United States was fighting worldwide. Buckley argued that courses supporting individualism and Christianity should be taught in US universities and that left-wing, demonic thinkers like John Maynard Keynes should be spurned.

The Republican right rejected the government's response to the school desegregation crisis in Alabama and Little Rock, even though that response was led by a Republican president. Eisenhower put the power of the federal government behind the law articulated in the Supreme Court's 1956 landmark decision *Brown v. Board of Education*. He sent federal troops to support the end of segregation and to desegregate Central High School in Little Rock, Arkansas. Buckley's new political magazine, the *National Review*, reasserted the old guard Republican view of the link between the federal government's aid to Black Americans and communism, with its evil redistribution-of-wealth agenda. The quest by Black Americans for redistribution of wealth had been a recurring dread of the Old South, the Republican Party old guard, the robber barons, and the 1920s and Taft Republicans. The Old South and the old guard Republicans had argued for well over a century that the Constitution prohibited this. That was why opposing equality for Blacks was, in Buckley's view, following a strict and appropriate interpretation of the Constitution.

After Little Rock,

> in a response to an equation straight out of the 1870s—that an active government would use tax dollars to help Black people—[some] Americans fell back on their ancestors' solution. In a revision of Republican ideology more thorough even than that of the 1890s, movement conservatives by 1960

rejected the worldview of Abraham Lincoln in favor of an explicit echo of James Henry Hammond's.[1]

The Republicans of 1960 wanted a strict construction of the Constitution, which they argued had been intended by the Founding Fathers to "protect rich men from 'the tyranny of the masses,' from those who demanded wealth redistribution. America's founding principle was not equality, movement conservatives asserted, but the protection of property."[2]

The threat, in their view, was more than a national conspiracy against men of property; it was an international one as well, not far removed from an alliance with international communism. They thought that the United Nations, with its support of desegregation, had served as a wedge to open America to subjugation by international communism. This widely held belief of Taft Republicans was absorbed by movement conservatism, which insisted that America should have nothing to do with so dangerous an organization as the UN. Sen. John Bricker of Ohio, the Republican vice presidential candidate in 1944, following in the footsteps of Taft, claimed that, under the present state of affairs, the entire government of the United States could be overthrown by a treaty with a foreign nation. So, in 1953, he proposed an amendment to the Constitution that shifted treaty-making power to the Senate.

Eisenhower strongly opposed this change, saying that it would return the United States to the days of the Articles of Confederation, 1781–89. He saw that shifting treaty-making power to the Senate would remove foreign policy from the purview of the federal executive. Control of foreign policy by the federal government had been the avowed objective of George Washington and his political allies and had been achieved by the adoption of the federal Constitution of

---

1   Richardson, *To Make Men Free*, 240.
2   Richardson, 240.

1787. The Bricker Amendment was defeated in the Senate, but many Americans even beyond the Taft wing of the Republican Party had been unsettled and unnerved by the arguments made by the senator. In 2021, there remains a large coterie of Americans who don't like the United Nations or indeed any multilateral organization—for example, the International Criminal Court—except perhaps such organizations as those with our allies, like NATO.

Increasingly, Bill Buckley became the public voice of Republican conservatism, and members of the Taft wing became movement conservatives. Buckley, far from the party elite, was not able himself to put the movement conservatives in control of the Republican Party. That required a secret organization, the John Birch Society, founded by a businessman named Robert Welch in 1958. He published a book on the life of John Birch in which, along with other crazy conspiracy theories, he alleged that Birch, a young clergyman in China at the end of World War II, had uncovered the communist plot to take over China. Birch, Welch said, had wanted to make the wider world aware of this oncoming danger, but he was prevented from doing so by the US State Department because they secretly sided with the communists. As Richardson points out, "With the John Birch Society, Welch linked racial fears and anti-communism and turned them into a grassroots organization to oppose Eisenhower Republicanism"[3] and promote the ideology of Bill Buckley. Thus Welch drew on the oldest trope of them all, rooted in the antebellum South. Welch argued that it was quite proper to oppose the Civil Rights Movement since it was the same as opposing creeping communism in the federal government. Civil rights and communism, he believed, both had the same objective: desegregation and the redistribution of wealth to Black Americans as an atonement for slavery.

Welch was quite successful. In its early days the John Birch Society was supported by wealthy businessmen and spread through-

---

3 Richardson, 252.

out the South and West among conservatives. After all, hadn't Taft Republicans believed largely the same thing? As the John Birch Society grew, so did the media pressure it exerted. The society helped expand movement conservatism within the Republican Party, not because all conservatives were persuaded by its views—although many were—but because its energy pushed Buckley's intolerant ideology more and more to the fore. Within a few years, the Republican Party leadership again turned traditional, embracing old guard, 1920s, Taft-style Republican principles. These, as mentioned above, were ideas that went back to those of the Old South and bypassed the views of Lincoln, Roosevelt, and the Eastern establishment Republicans (the last of whom could be said to have been Eisenhower, although Presidents Nixon, Ford, Reagan, George H. W. Bush, and George W. Bush were definitely not movement conservatives).

Although Buckley provided the ideas absorbed by the John Birch Society, more and more Sen. Barry Goldwater provided impetus and political leadership. In the early 1960s, Ronald Reagan emerged as a spokesman. The movement Republicans promoted Goldwater for president in 1960, but Vice President Nixon won the Republican nomination. This was because his strong anti-communism aligned his rhetoric with that of the movement conservatives—although he was a moderate at heart. Goldwater was essentially backed by wealthy men. Nixon had a somewhat broader appeal in 1960. And as the incumbent vice president, Nixon fairly early on established himself as the unbeatable favorite for the nomination. "The future direction of the GOP on race," Gould writes, "was still in flux."[4] Race, of course, was an essential issue for the movement-type Taft Republicans. Gould writes, "William F. Buckley and his *National Review* were skeptical of a pro–civil rights stand. As Buckley's father told Strom Thurmond, his son was 'for segregation and backs it in

---

4   Gould, *Grand Old Party*, 241.

every issue.'" [5] The eventual candidate Nixon lost very narrowly to Sen. John F. Kennedy. With Eisenhower out and Nixon defeated, the door was now open to a movement-type Taft Republican takeover of the Republican Party in 1964.

The primary campaign was largely between Nelson Rockefeller, governor of New York, and Goldwater. Goldwater had said that the United States was losing the battle against communists because American liberals were afraid to stand up to the Soviet Union. He also was suspicious of the United Nations. On civil rights his views were consistent with what had always been the position of old guard conservatives in the Republican Party:

> If the senator endorsed, as he did, states' rights and the power of the people of the South and Southwest to make segregation the law in those states, Goldwater believed that the freedom of whites to do so was of higher value than black equality. . . . Goldwater had once said that in seeking votes the Republicans should go hunting "where the ducks are." Southern whites, particularly male, would be a key element in the new Republican electoral coalition.[6]

So, in other words, the Republican Party was again controlled by the old guard allied with movement conservatives. They also had kinship with the Dixiecrats. This alignment has not changed to the present day, although the next four Republican presidents selected were not from the radical wing.

Following a successful primary campaign, Goldwater had a lock on the nomination, and his campaign machine took over control of the party machine. Goldwater became the party's next presidential candidate after a stirring nomination speech by Ronald Reagan. However, he lost the 1964 election to incumbent President Lyndon

---

5   Gould, 241.
6   Gould, 248.

B. Johnson, who had received a huge sympathy vote in the wake of the assassination of President Kennedy on November 22, 1963, as well as the votes he would have normally received. Following the election, Johnson obtained the passage of sweeping civil rights legislation—so sweeping that Southern Whites could no longer pass segregation laws. To a degree, the legislation revolutionized the South, leading to Black mayors, members of Congress, and so on.

In 1968, Nixon again gained the Republican nomination, embracing the traditional Republican platform as all candidates were required to do. This time, however, in contrast to 1960, he also embraced the Goldwater Southern strategy. He did not, however, align himself with the Goldwater states' rights position and all that it meant. He indicated he was opposed to segregation but also opposed busing to achieve racial balance. And he assured Southern leaders privately that he would not appoint liberal activist judges like some who then sat on the Supreme Court. Strom Thurmond helped him in the campaign.

This time Nixon won the election, over Vice President Hubert Humphrey. He accomplished many good and progressive things during his tenure—for example, the passage of the Clean Air Act and the opening to China in 1972. However, he became involved in the severe electoral scandal known as Watergate and in mid-1974 was forced to resign, the first president to do so. His vice president, Spiro Agnew, had also been forced to resign, largely because of corruption during his term as governor of Maryland. Nixon had appointed in Agnew's place Gerald R. Ford, the House minority leader. When Nixon resigned, Ford became president. Among Ford's first words as president, speaking to a joint session of Congress, were a play on the names of cars and on the name of our greatest president: "I am a Ford, not a Lincoln."[7] A brilliant statement, it summed up the situation and calmed the nation.

---

7 "Gerald R. Ford Quotes," BrainyQuote, https://www.brainyquote.com/authors/gerald-r-ford-quotes.

It is perhaps anomalous that, working under a party leadership in the hands of a mix of movement conservatives and old guard Republicans, three outstanding, essentially moderate leaders later took office: Presidents Ford, Reagan, and George H. W. Bush. These men were not great on the order of Washington, Lincoln, and the Roosevelts—although a case could be made for Reagan—but all three were near-great presidents. They all accomplished much for the country. The circumstance of a presidential trio of this moment serving nearly 16 years within a 20-year span had happened only once before, and while not equal to Washington, Adams, and Jefferson's terms, it was similar. President Carter was good as well, if not quite at the level of these three. All these men helped stabilize the nation, and their service was a reaffirmation of the principles that should guide us. Let us hope it is not the last time we will have such a group of leaders.

In his brief tenure of two and a half years, President Ford was confronted with several problems, the first of which was what to do about a disgraced and resigned president. Nixon, when he resigned, had admitted no wrongdoing, simply saying that he no longer had the support in Congress needed to lead the country. He had also blamed the media for being "out to get him." This explanation was looked upon with favor by conservatives, whose paranoia had fed into his own and crippled his presidency. Conservative Republicans were now more and more movement conservatives, but many old guard types remained, and they clung even more tightly to their extreme-right, hard-edged policies.

At the end of his first month, Ford decided to pardon Nixon for all crimes he might have committed while in office. In Ford's view, putting the former president on trial could have been extremely divisive for the country, perhaps leading to something close to a civil war. There were defensible reasons to believe that a trial would have been volatile, but the Ford administration never tried to make the case for this. They just announced the pardon and that was that. After a firestorm of criticism, Ford dropped over 20 percent in the polls, from

71 percent to 50 percent. Ford's heroic act of setting public welfare above his private interest was, of course, supported by the conservative Republicans, as they had always opposed Nixon's impeachment.

Ford's planned policies were pushed aside by the need to manage what Nixon had set in motion. Nixon had terminated US military action in support of South Vietnam in 1973, in the wake of the Paris Peace Accords. In December 1974, North Vietnam invaded the South, and in early 1975, Congress refused further support aid. Ford had to try to manage a panic-stricken retreat during which Americans were treated to the sight on television of huge helicopters heavily laden with Americans and their allies departing from the rooftop of the US embassy in Saigon.

Nixon had also pumped up the economy to support his reelection, and Ford had to deal with the resultant inflation—not an easy task. "How goes the economy?" is often the issue the American voter will focus on when a president seeks reelection—and the economy wasn't doing well. Ronald Reagan decided that this was the time for him, but he was defeated in the primary in a very close vote, and President Ford went on to lose the general election, also by a very close vote. Ford had dropped Rockefeller as his running mate and replaced him for the 1976 campaign with the far less moderate Sen. Robert Dole, thinking that would draw more active support from movement conservative and old guard Republicans. All in all, Ford had done an outstanding job of putting the nation back together in difficult times. But, in the post-Watergate climate, he could not save himself.

Jimmy Carter, governor of Georgia, became the next president. He did reasonably well in the South because of his being a Southerner and having a sincere commitment to the Baptist Church. He was, however, an avowed liberal and thus unattractive to most Republicans.

Inflation in the economy continued to be toxic, and the Carter administration and the country looked ineffectual and weak in the abortive attempt to free the 52 American embassy hostages seized after the 1979 Iranian Revolution—contrary to international law, of course—by radical supporters of the Khomeini Islamic government. After initial hesitancy, the effort to free the hostages was backed and implemented by the government. The US sent a secret expedition into Iran to accomplish this, but it was forced to withdraw. Then, in late December 1979, the Soviet Union invaded Afghanistan to oust the mujahideen Islamic movement there that had overthrown this pro-communist government on their borders. Initially the Soviets seized all the Afghan cities, and it looked as though the Soviet Union was truly on the march. In the end—with strong mujahideen resistance fighting from the mountains, fueled by American arms, particularly the Stinger missile, which could shoot down Soviet attack helicopters—the Soviets were forced to withdraw in 1989, a development that was a major cause of the collapse of the Soviet Union in 1991.

With America evidencing a loss of status on the world stage and economic woes at home, movement conservatives

> blamed these crippling indicators on Buckley's banes: over-regulation of the economy, godless liberalism, and an almost criminal neglect of national defense. The solution to the economic troubles, they believed, was for the government . . . to cut taxes. Wealthy people would invest their accumulating money, inspiring new businesses that would hire more workers. The principles of the 1920s had come back to life, but this time they seemed to carry the authority of economic science. . . . This old vision of the American economy also got a new academic-sounding name—supply-side economics— for it promised to fix the economy not from the bottom, the demand side, but from the top, the supply side.[8]

Ronald Reagan began his 1980 presidential campaign with a stronger base of support. Movement conservative Republicans had developed a strong link to the growing Christian evangelical movement.

---

8   Richardson, *To Make Men Free*, 289.

President Reagan's allegiance to the evangelical movement made it a permanent asset to Republicans. In 1979, traditional Republicans had persuaded Jerry Falwell, leader of the Moral Majority, an important evangelical organization, to directly enter politics on their side. His support had made a big difference.

Movement conservative Republicans took up the accusation—made since the days of Eisenhower—that American weakness had led to advances by the Soviet Union and the spread of communism. The Soviets had just added a new puppet state to their empire—Afghanistan. This the movement conservatives erroneously blamed on Carter's budget cuts, insisting on a lie, as often this part of the political spectrum does. Carter had increased defense spending to the highest point ever. Movement conservative Republicans, with their new Christian evangelical allies, argued that "as long as the government cut taxes, people believed in Jesus, and Congress properly funded the military . . . prosperity and calm would return." [9]

After Reagan easily won the Republican primary over George H. W. Bush, he asked him to be his running mate. While conservative, Bush was definitely not either an old guard Republican or a movement conservative Republican. He was a moderate like Gerald Ford in many ways. Reagan, also like Bush, Ford, and Nixon, was a moderate at heart even though he rode the wave of movement conservatism. As his foreign policy leadership in dealings with the Soviet Union showed, he had the most insightful and effective policies toward the Soviet Union—indeed, the most liberal—of any president.

In the general election, Reagan defeated Carter solidly if not by a landslide. He took office in 1981 and promptly put economics in the hands of David Stockman at the Office of Management and Budget. Stockman was also a proponent of supply-side economics, explaining that it was just a new term for the old Republican pre–New Deal policy of "cutting taxes for the rich and letting the good effects 'trickle

---

9   Richardson, 290.

down' to everyone else." [10] But supply-side economics made no more sense than the 1920s policy had; it was simply the same recipe for economic inequality with a new name. Supply-side economics was a fraud and a failure, as it had been in the 1920s when Hoover, Coolidge, and Mellon were promoting it. Though Reagan delivered on the tax cuts, he left a large deficit for his successor.

Several months after taking office, President Reagan spoke to the National Association of Evangelicals in Orlando, Florida. Heather Cox Richardson writes of his speech:

> [He said] there was sin and evil in the world. . . . Communism was godlessness, and god-fearing Americans must never come to an accommodation with it. America was engaged in a titanic struggle between "right and wrong and good and evil." The Soviet Union was the "evil empire." [11]

In June of 1988, during his last year as president, Reagan visited Moscow to exchange instruments of ratification of the Intermediate-Range Nuclear Forces Treaty (or INF Treaty, as it is generally known) with Soviet leader Mikhail Gorbachev; the two leaders had signed the treaty in Washington in December. The Cold War was finally ameliorating and, although its end would be implemented on President George H. W. Bush's watch, much of the credit belonged to Ronald Reagan (as well as to Gorbachev, of course). In Reagan's first meeting with Gorbachev in Geneva in 1985, he and Gorbachev had agreed that "a nuclear war cannot be won and must never be fought." [12] At the remarkable meeting at Reykjavik, Iceland, the two attempted the incredible feat of eliminating nuclear weapons worldwide. The INF

---

10 Richardson, 294.
11 Richardson, 296.
12 "The Reagan-Gorbachev Statement: Background to #ReaffirmOurFuture," European Leadership Network, November 19, 2021, https://www.european leadershipnetwork.org/commentary/the-reagan-gorbachev-statement-background-to-reaffirmourfuture/.

Treaty was important. But of enormous effect on Reagan was his living through perhaps the most dangerous nuclear weapon crisis of the Cold War, probably the crisis during which general nuclear war was the closest: the Able Archer crisis of 1983. Even the existence of this near destruction of civilization was not made known to the broad public until 2016, some 33 years after the event. (Nate Jones's *Able Archer 83 Sourcebook*, published by George Washington University's National Security Archive in 2016, contains a formerly highly secret history of this crisis.) It was a very different Reagan who arrived in Moscow in June of 1988 than the one who spoke to the evangelicals in 1981.

Soon after he arrived in Moscow and was greeted by Gorbachev, Reagan attended the exchange of the instruments of ratification that brought into force the INF Treaty. As it was a mild day, he and Gorbachev took an arm-in-arm stroll through Red Square afterward. A Western reporter who happened to be in Red Square at the time saw them, approached Reagan, and asked him whether he still believed that the country he was now visiting remained the "evil empire." Looking directly at the reporter, Reagan replied, "No, that was another time, another place."[13] The Cold War is not generally recognized as ending until the dissolution of the Soviet Union in December 1991, but this was the real end.

Presidents have strengths and weaknesses, but in this kind of all-important policy arena Reagan had no peer.

Vice President Bush was Reagan's successor after a moderately easy primary campaign and a somewhat more difficult general campaign. He initially had a large voter deficit to overcome, but with the leadership of Treasury Secretary James Baker, who would later be Bush's secretary of state, Bush was able to gain ground and achieve a reasonably decisive victory. During his presidential campaign, he was

---

13 Lesley Kennedy, "How Gorbachev and Reagan's Friendship Helped Thaw the Cold War," History, October 24, 2019, https://www.history.com/news/gorbachev-reagan-cold-war.

forced to pledge that he would implement no new taxes and famously prefaced this promise by saying, "Read my lips."

Toward the end of the Reagan administration, the ideology of the movement conservative Republicans evolved, as did the means of propagating it. Starting with the beginning of the electronic media era, the Federal Communications Commission had required radio and then television stations to present all issues fairly, balancing different views. The ideologues associated with the movement conservative Republicans placed this "fairness doctrine" in their sights, claiming (as had Buckley) that it was simply a device to promote liberal views. In 1987, the rule was abandoned by the FCC. Freed from a requirement to balance different views, organizations like Fox News became well-funded propaganda machines. These organizations bear the principal responsibility for the divisiveness and bitterness that pervades our politics today.

Republicans began to spend their large war chests in media markets where the FCC "fairness doctrine" no longer provided restraints. Soon liberals, Democrats, and even moderate Republicans labeled as RINOs (for "Republicans in name only") became not just the opponents but *the enemy*. Grover Norquist, the leader of the anti-tax movement, contributed much to traditional Republican ideology. According to Richardson, he began to recruit evangelical Christians into his organization Americans for Tax Reform, but the sought-after coalition between Christians (Southern and Western) and big business proved an uneasy alliance. In 1989 the evangelical leader Ralph Reed, a friend of Norquist, solved this problem by turning evangelicals into a permanent pressure group, the Christian Coalition, which rallied behind the Republican Party.[14] The Christian Coalition began to be a factor in the buildup to the 1988 election.

By 1987, it was clear that relaxing the rules governing savings and loans banks had permitted speculation and downright

---

14 Richardson, *To Make Men Free*, 301.

theft that had allowed wealthy men, including Vice President Bush's son Neal and a number of congressmen from both parties, to emerge wealthy from the wreckage of people's retirement accounts. . . . Then, in October 1987, the booming stock market crashed, revealing the underbelly of the Reagan economy. Perhaps, naysayers noted, supply-side economics didn't work at all. Perhaps the whole idea was just what Stockman had admitted in 1981: a justification for the age-old trick of gaming the system to benefit the rich. . . . But movement conservatives saw it differently. The problem with Reagan, they thought, was simply that he didn't cut government enough.[15]

After the Reagan years, the GOP became tightly controlled by the ideology adopted by movement conservatives, a party advocating a government that embodied the ideas of Sen. James Henry Hammond, the spokesman for the Old South. These Republicans claimed they were simply trying to reduce the government to a manageable size. In truth, they were trying to destroy the New Deal and replace it with a larger government based on 1920s-style big business, replete with regulatory and financial breaks from government for business, religion, and the military. The Republican Party leadership had become the Old South in modern dress.

The moderate wing of the Republican Party was disappearing, leaving the party largely a conservative organization of the far right, composed of movement conservatives and old guard Republicans. The two groups had the same views on most issues except that the movement conservatives wanted to merge the Republican Party with the evangelical Christian movement and make Republicanism itself into a pseudo-religion. The future of the party was largely theirs.

George H. W. Bush was never too popular publicly because of his

---

15 Richardson, 306.

patrician ways, but he tried to give the party people what they wanted during the campaign. Once elected, Bush had to do something about the debt and annual deficits. Reagan had tripled the national debt and greatly increased the annual deficit. Bush faced an annual deficit of $171 billion, made worse by the need to clean up the savings and loan mess. The problem was worse for Bush than it had been for Reagan because a 1991 law required 40 percent across-the-board reductions in federal spending if the deficit was not effectively addressed. Bush told his diary, "I'm willing to eat crow. But the others are going to have to eat crow. I'll have to yield on 'Read My Lips,' and they're going to have to yield on some of their rhetoric on taxes and on entitlements."[16] But, as Richardson recounts, in the fall of 1990, Bush underestimated his enemies. Bush made a deal with Democrats for deep cuts in federal expenditures, with the agreement that future spending would be paid for in new taxes, and he called for "$134 billion in new taxes."[17] Even while conservative Republicans signed off on the agreement in private, in public they broadly attacked their president, calling his actions an affront to economic growth, the common people, and Reagan.

To Rep. Newt Gingrich, now leader of the movement conservative ideologues, Bush said:

> "You are killing us, you are just killing us." That was exactly Gingrich's intention. . . . Gingrich believed he could put the Republicans in control of Congress for the first time since 1954. To do that he took a hard . . . line, accusing anyone who stood against him of elitism, socialism, or corruption—either personal or in the traditional sense of corrupting the body politic by representing "special interests."[18]

In the buildup to the Iraq war, Bush's popularity in the polls soared to 89 percent, and he achieved all the goals of the first Gulf War.

---

16 Richardson, 310.
17 Richardson, 310.
18 Richardson, 310.

But this success didn't matter at all to the movement conservatives. They took the position that anyone who had voted for the 1990 tax increase must pay at the polls. As a bloc, in 1992, they voted for the independent candidate, Ross Perot, who siphoned off 19 million votes. This broke the Bush campaign and elected the Democratic governor of Arkansas, Bill Clinton, and his running mate, Al Gore, president and vice president. In the meantime, Gingrich was paving a road that led directly to Trump.

But before leaving our consideration of George H. W. Bush and walking further down that Contract-with-America road to Trump, we should acknowledge Bush's contribution. A war hero, he left college to fight for his country, was shot down in his fighter aircraft over the Pacific, and spent days floating in his life raft before being picked up. Though he was from a prominent family, he left the East to make his fortune in Texas. He attained success as a businessman, sold his company, and entered politics. He had his ups and downs—won a House seat, lost a Senate race, was appointed UN ambassador and later Republican national chairman by President Nixon and then ambassador to China and CIA director by President Ford. President Reagan chose him as his running mate. He was vice president for eight years and was elected president in 1988. Trying to balance the country's debt, which had been accrued by another, he was viciously attacked by those who had done nothing—at least nothing good—for their country.

In foreign policy, fulfilling the president's very important job to keep the country safe, Bush was beyond outstanding. He successfully negotiated four treaties on weapons of mass destruction. No other president has achieved more than one such treaty. He ended the Cold War peacefully—when it could have led to nuclear war—and presided over the conclusion of the treaty formalizing its end. He prevailed in the Gulf War. He kept us safe. He was as American as anyone could be, a true American hero. He was treated disgracefully by men and women much his lesser. He gave his all for his country. Before

Gingrich started us down the dark road, we could see in Bush what an American should be: a man or woman of principle, decency, honesty, and ability.

CHAPTER 6

A LONG, SLOW DIVE TOWARD THE BOTTOM

GINGRICH WENT ON PURSUING his objectives, and his Contract with America was announced with much fanfare in 1994.

> It is a clear crisp day in Washington as 300 Republican members of the House of Representatives and GOP congressional candidates assembled on the steps of the Capitol on September 27, 1994. Behind them was a large blue sign that read, "Contract with America." . . . The architect of the event, Newt Gingrich of Georgia, the minority whip and the presumed next Speaker of the House, came forward to present the message that he had been perfecting for 15 years.[1]

Gingrich had timed his movement well. That November, Republicans gained 123 seats and the majority, giving Gingrich the potential power to realize his goals.

---

1 Gould, *Grand Old Party*, 304.

He sought, a Gingrich friend said, "to squash tax-and-spend liberalism which had dominated our politics for 60 years" . . . the Democrats represented a set of ideas that history had rendered obsolete. . . . Once in power, Gingrich and his allies had an even longer vision. With their Contract with America enacted, they would move forward to recapture the presidency, implement the conservative opportunity society of Gingrich's dreams, and make the nation Republican for a generation or more.[2]

The Contract with America nicely brought together those committed to movement conservatism (transmuted by Bill Buckley and his followers into Republican ideology) and followers of the anti-tax movement headed by Grover Norquist. Perhaps one should use the designation "radical conservative movement" as more apt, because the movement in control of the party at this juncture was in fact neither Republican nor traditionally conservative. It had a radical, right-wing ideology that bore little in common with the political views of Lincoln, Teddy Roosevelt, Eisenhower, Reagan, and George H. W. Bush, all of whom were certainly Republicans—indeed, elected party standard-bearers. The frequently stated objective of this radical ideology was the destruction of the socialist system its proponents saw as gripping America. They would do so by eliminating the taxes that paid for it.

Gingrich was part of this radical conservative movement—and the Contract with America was its banner. Drawing on Rush Limbaugh, the extremist radio commentator who had supported Republican radicals running for Congress, the Contract with America said that the Congress must "begin an emergency dismantling of the welfare system, which is shredding the social fabric."[3] The number of lobbyists in Washington vastly increased as more of the representatives embracing this radical conservatism relied on lobbyists employed by

---

2   Gould, 304.
3   Richardson, *To Make Men Free*, 315.

movement conservatives or monied interests such as the Koch brothers rather than their own independent staffs. In 1998, it was reported that there were over 10,000 registered lobbyists spreading $1.45 billion to influence members of Congress.[4]

What Gingrich had perhaps not anticipated was that the Clinton administration would be so successful and so popular with many Americans. The economy boomed under Clinton, recovering from its poor performance in 1991–92. Per capita income improved rapidly, ultimately climbing 3 percent a year beginning in 1997. Unemployment dramatically fell, and inflation was crushed. This economy permitted Clinton to expand healthcare for poor children, provide tax credits, and cut the capital gains tax almost in half. This made the radical conservative group all the more determined to stop him.

> If the Democratic program worked, Americans would continue it. . . . The country would be right back where it had been when William F. Buckley Jr. had despaired that people could not be trusted to choose the right thing: a government that worked hand in hand with business and religion.[5]

At Grover Norquist's urging, Gingrich's initial effort was adding a balanced budget amendment to the Constitution. Norquist termed the effort "the containment strategy." "Defunding the government is defunding the left," he said.[6] This went nowhere. The Gingrich group tried several far-right efforts against Clinton, including an attempt to defund Medicare, which they had hated for a long time. Some bills passed the House, were watered down in the Senate, and fell to a Clinton veto.

Ultimately, Gingrich went too far when Clinton refused, in 1995, to sign the Republican budget, which contained significant cuts to Medicare, the environment, and education. Gingrich rejected any

---

4   Richardson, 318.
5   Richardson, 320.
6   Richardson, 316.

compromises. Therefore the federal government shut down all non-essential activities for 28 days in November and December 1995. The national parks were shut down, government contracts were suspended, and no visas or passports were approved, among other things. The Republicans thought their refusal to compromise would show and increase their strength. The American public didn't agree; they blamed the Republicans. Clinton's poll numbers climbed steeply.

Eventually, Gingrich had to back down. "The Contract with America, announced with such fanfare, withered; by March 1996, Republicans themselves were ignoring it."[7] Clinton was easily re-elected in 1996 over the Republican candidate, Sen. Robert Dole.

Only a few weeks before the 1996 election, the Fox News Channel, backed by the radical conservatives, had been launched, with Rupert Murdoch as founder and Roger Ailes as CEO. Unquestionably aimed at the further enriching of the few and the destruction of democracy (if by "democracy" we mean the freedom of all to participate in the "pursuit of happiness"), Fox News dedicated itself to lies and demagoguery to make money, while correcting what Republicans believed was a liberal bias in the media. The repeal of the FCC's "fairness" doctrine under Reagan had opened the way. Murdoch announced that Fox News would be "fair and balanced," noting that conservative views had been often attacked by "leftist and anti-American" news outlets.[8] When founded, Fox purported to have as its purpose the promotion of fairness in American politics. It has of course done the opposite, spreading poison with its lies throughout the American political system.

The midterms took place two years later in 1998. That year, it was made public that President Clinton had lied about and covered up an extramarital affair with a young intern, Monica Lewinsky. As it turned out, some movement leaders, including Gingrich, had had their

---

7   Richardson, 316.
8   Richardson, 318.

own extramarital affairs and other ethics violations. Political leaders of these radical conservatives had, in the past, taken the position that their venal sins didn't matter. Still, the radical conservatives made the most of the Lewinsky scandal. With the midterms approaching, Gingrich promised Republican gains of 10 to 40 seats. But the economy was leaping ahead, and the American people believed that a politician's (in this case Clinton's) venal sins didn't matter but that his capital successes, such as a strong economy, did.

The result—to Gingrich's disappointment—was a pickup of five seats in the House for the Democrats and an even hold in the Senate. So positive an outcome in the sixth year of a presidential term was almost unheard of in American politics. It had last happened in 1822. Gingrich was disgraced by the outcome. The Contract with America was dead, and Gingrich resigned from the House.

Party power then appeared to flow to the House majority whip, Tom DeLay, an evangelical Christian who threatened primary challenges against anyone who opposed him. He himself was later exposed as being involved in serious ethics violations, some of which were criminal. Nevertheless, he got his way when, on December 19, 1999, the House impeached Clinton for the Lewinsky affair. The Senate took up the case in January, called no witnesses, deliberated in private, and acquitted Clinton on all counts.

Clinton's poll numbers remained high, and he went on to a glorious final year as president, including highly successful foreign policy initiatives. He came within a whisker of a Mideast peace agreement in January 2001. Clinton could truly say when he left office that America was at peace and the economy was very sound, with nothing but annual surpluses as far as the eye could see into the future.

The radical conservative movement at the time moved on to spinning conspiracy theories and designing new radical right-wing websites.

With the onset of the 2000 election, the obvious distrust of the American people for the Gingrich "contract" and parts of the radical conservative movement would seem to have suggested that the Republican Party should move back toward the center of the political mainstream. But radical politicos said there was no such thing as a moderate Republican. And the movement was in control of the party. Bill Buckley, the intellectual founder of the radical conservative movement, had once said that anyone who accepted any part of the New Deal was a socialist. There was no middle ground.

The party platform and the nomination came down to a fight between Texas governor George W. Bush and Sen. John McCain. McCain was seen as somewhat suspect to radical conservatives because, among other issues, he supported campaign finance limits. Bush actively sought the support of the radical conservative movement coalition and Norquist's anti-tax organization. Bush's adviser Karl Rove helped him in the critical state of South Carolina by spreading rumors of McCain having fathered an illegitimate Black baby; in actuality, McCain and his wife Cindy had added to their family an adopted daughter from South Asia.

Bush ultimately won the nomination and then the 2000 election in a faceoff against the sitting vice president, Al Gore. During the campaign Bush promised to privatize Social Security and never to raise taxes—in fact, he promised to enact a large tax cut.

The election of 2000 bore a distinct relationship to the Tilden-Harrison race and election of 1876. Bush was four votes short in the Electoral College; Harrison had been 19 votes short in the Electoral College, with three states submitting competing elector slates that added up to 20 votes. In 1876, an electoral commission composed of eight Republicans and seven Democrats had been established. The commission had voted 8–7, awarding the 20 undecided votes to Harrison, who then won the presidency in the Electoral College by one vote. Like Harrison, Bush had been several hundred thousand votes behind in the popular vote—truly a minority president—but he would win the Electoral College vote. In 2000, it was Florida (where Bush's brother Jeb was governor) and its 25 votes that were undecided.

After a struggle that lasted some six weeks, the Florida Supreme Court ordered a machine recount. Throughout this struggle, some Republicans fought no-holds-barred for Bush, as they still believed they were the only legitimate party. The Democrats had been traitors since 1860.

After the Florida court decision, the Supreme Court (at Republican request):

> stepped in, announcing that recounting the votes would create "irreparable harm" to Bush and the country by "casting a cloud upon what he claims to be the legitimacy of his election." Although this seemed to suggest that the court thought Gore would win if there were a recount, in a five-to-four decision, the Supreme Court upheld Bush's election.[9]

All somewhat suspect.

> Rather than seeing his weak support as a sign that he needed to steer a moderate course, Bush appeared to believe—as Benjamin Harrison had under similar circumstances—that God had eked a surprise victory for him and that he should take a stronger, not a weaker, stance because of it. As soon as he took office, he pushed the agenda of movement conservatives aggressively.[10]

Bush took several actions against legalized abortion. He established a faith-based-initiatives office in the White House, designed to help religious charities acquire federal funding. Because labor had endorsed Gore, he overturned many regulations protecting labor.

The new Bush administration had designs against such safety-net programs as Social Security and Medicare. Indeed, Bush had himself wanted to privatize Medicare for years. But since these programs were

---

9   Richardson, 324, 325.
10 Richardson, 325.

popular, Bush decided not to move against them in a direct way. With whatever expediency, the administration certainly intended to follow the radical conservative route, straight from the Bill Buckley playbook. Bush, with Democratic help, enacted a huge tax cut, and enormous deficits returned after they had been eliminated by the administration of his father and Bill Clinton through long and difficult work.

In the first months of his presidency, Bush's poll numbers slid steadily downward, but then came 9/11. The World Trade Center towers were brought down by hijacked airliners; a third struck the Pentagon, causing considerable death and damage; and a fourth destined for the Capitol crashed in Pennsylvania when passengers revolted and brought it down. Bush visited the World Trade Center site and pronounced that "you are either with us or against us" in the worldwide campaign against terrorism. Workers came from all over the country to repair and rebuild New York. Bush's approval rating in the polls shot up to stratospheric heights as America got behind its president.

Because of a general disdain for Clinton's staff, whom they saw as amateurs, Bush's team had been dismissive of warnings by Richard Clarke, Clinton's White House coordinator on terrorism, who had advised Bush administration officials to pay close attention to al-Qaeda and bin Laden. Clarke knew worldwide terrorism to be a real threat. He was paid no heed. The White House and other parts of the administration cared about (1) building missile defenses and (2) attacking Iraq. To ensure that North Korea would remain the poster boy for the need for missile defense, the Bush White House tossed out the nearly complete arms limitation, nuclear weapon control, and peace deal with North Korea that Clinton had almost completed by fall 2000.[11] By summer 2001, George Tenet, the holdover CIA director, informed the administration that the agency's entire detection system was "blinkin' red," suggesting an attack was likely. In August, Tenet

---

11 Thomas Graham Jr., *The Alternate Route: Nuclear-Weapon-Free Zones* (Corvallis: Oregon State University Press, 2017), 183.

personally visited Bush at his ranch in Texas and presented him with a brief with a headline indicating that bin Laden intended to strike in the US. This was ignored by the president. In fact, the administration almost went out of its way to avoid being warned.

The result, as everyone knows, was a terrible blow to the United States and resulted in more than 3,000 Americans dead. Lewis Gould writes, "Bush defenders contend[ed] that there was no way the attacks of September 11, 2001, could have been prevented, and that the intelligence failures that led to them should not be attributed to incompetence."[12] But this was not true. As Ambassador Jack Matlock, a distinguished adviser on the Soviet Union to President Ronald Reagan and an ambassador to the Soviet Union, said in his book *Superpower Illusions*:

> The attacks on the World Trade Center in New York and the Pentagon in northern Virginia on September 11, 2001, could have been prevented. They very likely *would* have been prevented if a competent, alert administration had been in office in Washington. That was not the explicit conclusion of the bipartisan commission established by the Congress and the president to investigate the terrorist attacks on the United States. But few people knowledgeable about the manner in which most presidents and their national security assistants react to intelligence warnings can escape the conclusion that President George W. Bush [and his staff] . . . were inexcusably negligent when they were warned repeatedly of an impending attack by al-Qaeda.[13]

Matlock detailed several not-particularly-expensive steps that could have been taken to cause the hijack attacks to be canceled or,

---

12 Gould, *Grand Old Party*, 333, 334.

13 Jack F. Matlock, *Superpower Illusions: How Myths and False Ideologies Led America Astray—and How to Return to Reality* (New Haven: Yale University Press, 2010), 188.

if not canceled, to fail: there could have been instructions to pilots to keep doors closed and locked during flight, with the doors reinforced; knives of any size could have been banned on planes, with airport screeners directed to watch for them along with other dangerous objects; and the number of US marshals assigned to flights could have been significantly increased. Airline executives might possibly have objected to some of these measures, but "in fact, if the news of these measures had leaked, as it undoubtedly would have, al-Qaeda might have had to abort the mission because its chances of success would have been seriously diminished." [14]

Following 9/11, the Bush administration did not set out to unearth the facts behind the attacks, as the Roosevelt administration had done after Pearl Harbor. Nor did they expend excessive time commiserating with the American people about their terrible losses. Rather, they held meetings to decide how best to gain political advantage from the attacks. President Bush made two decisions: to destroy the Taliban and al-Qaeda, capturing—killing, if possible—Osama bin Laden, and to make the defeat of Saddam Hussein a principal military priority. The administration hoped to find a link between terrorism and both Iraq and Afghanistan—one that would justify an immediate attack. They were confident they would find a plausible link—whatever the reality.

The political advantage in engaging with Iraq was that it would address a lingering doubt Republicans had. After Desert Storm, Republicans had questioned whether the weapons of mass destruction (WMDs) had really been eliminated by Democrats, as they were supposed to have been. After all, Democrats could not be trusted in international security matters; during the Civil War, they had betrayed the nation. Also, eliminating Saddam Hussein would greatly please the Israelis. If Bush could find evidence of weapons of mass destruction in Iraq, Republicans could finger the failure of Democrats in this regard and justify another war.

---

14 Matlock, 189–90.

No credible cache of WMDs was ever found.

But the US did invade Afghanistan with a massive attack on October 7, 2001. The Taliban was quickly crushed, and bin Laden fled into Tora Bora in the mountains bordering Pakistan. The United States nearly got him, but he and several aides escaped into a frontier province of Pakistan. After a few months the frontline American forces left Afghanistan, even though the Afghan people very much wanted the US troops in force to stay and help them build a democracy. The US forces left Afghanistan in the hands of warlords, against whom the Taliban had revolted in the first place and whom the Afghan people did not want. The US left a small residual force behind, but it failed to prevent the Taliban from regrouping and rebuilding so that, in a few years, the Afghanistan war was unwinnable for the US. The Taliban simply decided to wait us out, and they did. A real tragedy.

The Bush administration wanted their first-line forces to return to prepare for the Bush administration's long-desired attack on Iraq—always the first priority and one endorsed by a major segment of the Republican Party, led by a group called the neoconservatives or neocons. Neocons were highly talented national security experts, but they were nevertheless impervious to key facts about Iraq. Supposedly they were pushing for an attack on Iraq because Iraq still had many weapons of mass destruction, and these chemical, biological, and maybe a few nuclear weapons threatened America and the world. In fact, Iraq had none of them.

In reality the neocons didn't actually care about the weapons; the existence of WMDs was simply the excuse for war. "We settled on the one issue that everyone could agree on, which was weapons of mass destruction as the core reason" to justify war, said Paul Wolfowitz, then deputy secretary of defense.[15] Once more, the Republicans could charge the Democrats with being implicit allies of America's enemies by not eliminating these weapons, again making the loyalty of

---

15 Gould, *Grand Old Party*, 335.

Democrats uncertain. Also, America could demonstrate that the US did rule the world. Said senior Republican leader Karl Rove:

> That's not the way the world really works anymore. We're an empire now, and when we act, we create our own reality. And while you are studying that reality—judiciously, as you will—we'll act again, creating other new realities, which you can study too and that's how things will sort out. We're history's actors . . . and you, all of you, will be left to just study what we do." [16]

The Iraqi oil fields, among the richest in the world, would be ours, and a defeated Saddam would please the Israelis.

Shortly before the invasion of Iraq in 2003, Sir Richard Dearlove, then chief of the British foreign intelligence agency MI6, had one of his best agents conduct a series of meetings with the chief of Iraqi intelligence. According to journalist Ron Suskind, Dearlove asserted that Saddam Hussein had destroyed his nuclear and chemical weapons programs in 1993 and the last biological weapon had been destroyed in 1996, but Saddam had kept this information secret to avoid an appearance of weakness in the eyes of the Iranians. As a matter of routine, this information was shared with appropriate recipients in the White House. After the meetings had concluded, Dearlove came to Washington in person and presented it all to CIA director George Tenet. But Washington ignored it; they wanted the war. [17]

So, in late March 2003, the Bush administration directed the US military to invade Iraq, knowing that their publicly stated reason for a war that would place our troops in danger was false. The Republican administration plunged ahead with the war, believing the conquest

---

16 Ron Suskind, "Faith, Certainty and the Presidency of George W. Bush," *New York Times Magazine*, October 17, 2004, https://en.wikipedia.org/wiki/Reality-based _community.

17 Ron Suskind, *The Way of the World: A Story of Truth and Hope in an Age of Extremism* (New York: Harper Collins, 2008), 192–93, 362–67.

would be short and the aftermath shorter—thereby enhancing the president's reelection chances. They were right about the invasion, but much less so about the aftermath. As General David Petraeus, later the commander in both Iraq and Afghanistan, kept asking members of the media riding with him into Iraq on that first day in his armored vehicle, "Tell me how this ends." [18] Of course, no one could.

The invasion was short; Baghdad was soon captured. In just a few weeks, the president appeared on the deck of a US aircraft carrier in front of a banner announcing, "Mission Accomplished." But a dark future lay ahead. Compounding the initial mistake of invading Iraq, whose government had demonstrably had nothing to do with 9/11—as had been demonstrated by the failure of a vigorous Republican attempt to establish a link between Saddam Hussein and bin Laden—was a mistaken follow-through. Paul Bremer was made civilian administrator of the Coalition Provisional Authority appointed to oversee the occupation of Iraq in 2003. He fired all the senior officials of the Iraqi government and most of the armed forces as well. The result of these actions was twofold. First, it assured a completely incompetent government for Iraq, as Republican loyalists from various states would now be in a Baghdad with high US salaries administering a complicated part of the Iraqi government, handling scores of ethnic and religious troubles in Iraq. Some of these US officials spoke no Arabic, had never studied Islamic or Middle Eastern history, barely knew where Iraq was, and had little administrative experience. Second, when thousands of capable Iraqi government bureaucrats and trained Iraqi soldiers were dismissed, they were turned out into the streets with no job prospects except joining the growing insurgency. Join they did and grow it did.

The rosy picture the Bush administration had of seizing Iraq and successfully converting it to a democratic ally soon faded. Instead of

---

18 David Petraeus, "Tell Me How This Ends," Government Affairs Institute at Georgetown University, https://gai.georgetown.edu/tell-me-how-this-ends/.

the vindication of finding weapons of mass destruction or, failing that, seeing democracy emerge, the American public saw videos of US forces standing by under orders, doing nothing, while gangs looted the world-famous Iraq Museum in Baghdad of many or most of its irreplaceable antiquities. Some of these antiquities have been recovered over the years, but certainly not all. Although Defense Secretary Donald Rumsfeld had been warned many times before the war about the need to protect these antiquities, an inestimably valuable record of human civilization, he failed to do so. The US military stood by and watched, without orders to do anything.[19]

Bush's high poll numbers during the Iraq invasion helped his re-election campaign in that, once again, Republicans could denounce Democrats as terrorists—allies of Saddam. Facing such accusations, the Democrats could hardly push for withdrawal from Iraq in the midst of the campaign. In the longer term, the public's view of the Bush administration was not positive. Bush had recklessly, without serious provocation from Iraq and with disastrous civilian management of our own, led America into a limitless, catastrophic sinkhole from which there was no apparent escape and nothing but loss for America. The American people turned on this folly with a vengeance: not of course on the soldiers, who had done a wonderful job, but on the incompetent politicians. The effect of American dissatisfaction was strongly felt in the campaign of 2008.

As the 2004 contest neared, Bush's poll numbers were not what they had been even a year earlier. Bush expanded Medicare coverage to prescription drugs, knowing that such a move would be popular among senior voters, a very high percentage of whom usually voted. This measure would add $40 billion a year to the deficit—some $400 billion over ten years. It was a hard sell in a conservative Congress, even from an administration that considered itself part of the movement

---

19 "Liberation and Looting in Iraq," Human Rights Watch, January 13, 2003, https://www.hrw.org/news/2003/04/13/liberation-and-looting-iraq-0.

wing of the party. As Gould writes, "Getting the measure through a conservative Congress required extraordinary tactics, including an almost three-hour roll call vote before the House went along, 220 to 215."[20]

The 2004 presidential race was a close one again. John Kerry did well in his three debates against Bush and won 251 electoral votes to Bush's 286. This time Ohio and Florida decided the election. However, for the fourth consecutive election, the Republicans failed to get 300 electoral votes—not since Reagan have they achieved that. The Republicans gained seats in the House and Senate, however.

Not long after the election, George W. Bush decided he would try to place his mark on the presidency. He would take on Social Security.

> With favorable majorities in the House and Senate, it seemed possible to address the centerpiece of the Democratic legacy and the New Deal and achieve "reform" as Republicans envisioned it. If he could dismantle the structure of the welfare state and reorient popular thinking toward what he called an opportunity society, he believed his greatness as a domestic president would equal his foreign policy triumphs since September 11.[21]

A desire to reform Social Security had been a consistent theme throughout George W. Bush's political career. He mentioned it when he ran for Congress in 1978. His objective in 2005 was to privatize Social Security in the stock market and then let people manage their retirement money. Since he lived in a world where the Dow Jones always continued to rise in value, making him and his family richer, he thought everyone would like such a plan. But he was wrong. The Democrats believed he had deceived them on Iraq, and they resented the savage attacks on their candidate in 2004. Why should he be

---

20 Gould, *Grand Old Party*, 237.
21 Gould, 337–38.

trusted on Medicare? The American people generally mistrusted this proposal and emphatically wished to keep Social Security just the way it was. A complete failure, the Bush proposal to reform Medicare was dead by mid-2005.

Then came Hurricane Katrina, completely devastating New Orleans and damaging Bush's reputation further. If the Federal Emergency Management Agency had been as well-staffed as under Clinton, it could have effectively mitigated Katrina's worst effects. But Republicans—particularly movement conservatives—had staffed smaller agencies like FEMA with less-able loyalists. FEMA's director was Republican loyalist Michael Brown, formerly a breeder of Arabian horses—perhaps not the best training for combating the effects of large killer hurricanes. The result was a major disaster, another one in which Bush showed little personal interest or involvement. There were pictures of him gazing out a plane window at devastated New Orleans as he flew over. He didn't visit those on the ground.

> He had appointed incompetents and had not hurried back to the capital to guide the federal disaster response. A friendly aide later recalled, "Katrina to me was the tipping point. The president broke his bond with the public. Once that bond was broken, he no longer had the capacity to talk to the American public." [22]

For decades, indeed generations, many Republicans have regarded Democrats as disloyal Americans, unworthy of leading. Likewise, Republicans have felt they were the nation's rightful leaders and that they are constantly being undermined by illegal or unworthy immigrants and (especially) by Black people. Any measures, they feel, are justified to halt unjustified efforts to keep the Republicans from holding leadership offices. The Republicans have, they believe, the right and the duty to block such un-American efforts. As a result, the

---

22 Gould, 339.

Republican Party has engaged in voter suppression efforts for many decades and has often alleged voter fraud—fraud which was almost never based on fact. Efforts at voter suppression in the Bush administration were no exception.

"The majority of Republicans did not want to vie for the votes of the blacks." [23] Most Black Americans' ideas about civil rights and social welfare programs conflicted directly with Republican ideology, particularly radical conservative ideology. Gould writes:

> Especially in the South there was historical residual but intense reluctance to contemplate an approach that would diminish white dominance of policy and governance. With Blacks and Hispanics voting in ever larger percentages relative to whites, a strategy of voter suppression based on a rationalization of voter fraud emerged as the preferred Republican response. . . . In 1982, Sen. Christopher "Kit" Bond of Missouri told his colleagues that "a major criminal enterprise designed to defraud voters" was part of Democratic strategy. That widespread voter fraud existed was "an attitude of religious faith" for Republicans, a Texas party member said in 2007. . . . [But] the difficulty with voter fraud as a rationale for measures to lower minority participation was that there was so little of it to root out. [24]

In Congress, Republicans played by their own set of rules and enforced another set for Democrats. Appointments to the federal bench were handled in a way that stripped Democrats of privileges that Republicans had previously insisted on for themselves. In February 2016, Senate Majority Leader Mitch McConnell blocked a hearing being called on the nomination of Judge Merrick Garland to the Supreme Court on the grounds that Supreme Court nominees

---

23 Gould, 340.
24 Gould, 340, 341.

shouldn't be considered in a presidential year, whereas in 2020, he would push for and ensure Amy Coney Barrett's nomination to the court a few weeks before the November election, when votes were already being cast in some states.

As for corruption, the Republican Party took a back seat to none, even besting its own historical record. During the Bush years, a lobbyist of great skill named Jack Abramoff worked with Republican House Minority Leader Tom DeLay—later indicted and convicted (as was Abramoff)—and other representatives to arrange more corrupt deals than anyone had ever witnessed before. This in the face of a historic record including Watergate, Teapot Dome, and those of the latter President Harrison years—some of the greatest scandals of American history.

In 2008, the Republicans nominated John McCain, who was a truly great man and one unassociated with movement conservatism. McCain wanted Connecticut senator Joe Lieberman—a Democrat somewhat alienated from his party—to serve as his running mate. But evangelicals, eyeing Lieberman's pro-choice record, threatened to block him on the floor. At the last moment, McCain chose the governor of Alaska, Sarah Palin, who proved to be an unfortunate choice. She sometimes seemed out of control. She could dazzle Republican audiences but often wasn't in sync with McCain. As she was from Alaska—a state McCain was certain to carry—her selection had not been strategic from that point of view. Some wondered what was in John McCain's mind when he chose her.

Barack Hussein Obama beat out former senator Hillary Clinton for the Democratic nomination and then chose Sen. Joe Biden from Delaware as his running mate. Obama offered voters a chance to make history by electing America's first Black president. The 2008 general election started out in Obama's favor, but the McCain-Palin ticket gained ground in August. Then a major financial crisis hit the country and rapidly spread worldwide. This was widely regarded as the greatest financial crisis since the Great Depression—also, of course, brought to us by movement conservative Republican policies similar to those of the 1920s. Experts feared that in 2008 there could be a collapse of the entire world economic order.

The Glass-Steagall Act had been adopted by the Roosevelt administration in 1933 to halt reckless speculation by large banks and investment houses in the stock market of the 1920s—speculation that had led to the crash of 1929 and the Great Depression. With the repeal of the Glass-Steagall Act in 1999, large banks could again also act as investment banks and mortgage underwriters. It wasn't long before Wall Street was once again embracing speculative practices like those of the 1920s. The dangerous speculation now involved real estate investments—packaging subprime mortgages with sounder real estate investments, then selling them as investments and/or using them as collateral throughout the financial world. Huge profits were made by the banks. When the housing market went into a sharp decline, largely because of the subprime mortgages, the chaos that followed threatened the entire banking industry as well as the many people living in homes purchased with subprime mortgages. With the September 2008 failure of the giant banking firm Lehman Brothers, the stability—even the survival—of other large banks was in question. Soon the economy was in a major recession. Depression loomed.

Senator McCain suspended his campaign and returned to Washington to participate in a major meeting on what to do about the economic crisis. The Democrats chose Senator Obama as their representative at the meeting. Obama was well briefed; Senator McCain was neither well briefed nor effective. After this event McCain's poll numbers took a downward turn. When General Colin Powell publicly supported Obama, the McCain-Palin ticket lost more support, and Obama-Biden pulled away to a very solid victory in early November. This time the Republicans chose not to contest the election; Obama had won with 365 electoral votes to McCain's 173.

But the Republicans continued to question Obama's legitimacy as president, denying that he had been born in the United States, as required by the Constitution, at least according to some interpretations. It is documented that Majority Leader McConnell met with other senior Republicans after the election and said that the primary—maybe the only—objective of the Republican Party for the next four years was to ensure that Obama would be a one-term president.[25] This strategy became clear in the early days of the administration, with the Republicans using tactics that they would have disavowed as un-American if applied to a Republican president—filibustering nominees and blocking any cooperation with the administration. Gould writes:

> At the start of the decade that began in 2001, Republicans had credible claims that they were a party of mature adults who could govern the United States with an effectiveness and authority the Democrats could not match. Bush promised "a spirit of cooperation" once it was clear he had prevailed in 2000. Eight years later they had on their record a devastating surprise terrorist attack, an unpopular war, a blundering response to a natural disaster, and governmental policies that had led to a near collapse of the national economy. An election defeat then followed.[26]

In the first years after Barack Obama's victory, the Republican Party devoted most of its considerable energy to limiting him to a one-term presidency. In 2010, the Republicans regained the House by organizing a new wave of radicals known as the Tea Party. Republicans continued to operate on the principle that truth was whatever they said it was. Their principal legislative activity was aimed at repealing the

---

25 Glenn Kessler, "When Did McConnell Say He Wanted to Make Obama a 'One-Term President'?" *Washington Post*, September 25, 2012, https://www. washingtonpost.com/blogs/fact-checker/post/when-did-mcconnell-say-he-wanted-to-make-obama-a-one-term-president/2012/09/24/79fd5cd8-0696-11e2-afff-d6c7f20a83bf_blog.html.

26 Gould, *Grand Old Party*, 348.

Affordable Care Act, which had been spearheaded by the Obama administration and was popularly known as "Obamacare." The House sent some 40 or so measures with this goal behind them; all were blocked in the Senate.

The 2012 Republican nominee, Mitt Romney, was able and backed by considerable financial resources. Polls consistently showed Obama in the lead, but the Republicans, who believed that Obama was weak, incompetent, criminal, and illegitimate, asserted that most of the pollsters were Democrats and that Romney was headed for a decisive triumph. When he lost, Republicans fell back on their usual internal analysis: votes had been bought by the Democrats, there had been widespread voter fraud favoring the Democrats, and, as a result, the election that the Republicans should have won had been stolen.

As has been the practice of the Republican Party in facing past defeats caused directly or derivatively by their extreme politics, they rejected the idea of moving toward the center, doubled down on their radicalism, and told themselves they would win next time. The problem with this strategy, in 2013, is that they were already so far right that movement rightward took them over the cliff into fantasyland. Moving toward the extra-constitutional, they shut down the government. They played with defaulting on the national debt and thereby discrediting US currency as the backbone of the world financial system. They didn't seem to care about that. As Gould writes:

> For Republicans, scorched earth seemed to be the appropriate response to the presence of a pretender in the White House who pursued the collapse of the American republic. There no longer existed between Republicans and Democrats a rough consensus about the purpose of the United States. The rank and file of the Republican Party believed that Barack Obama was illegitimate and evil; that the fabric of society was being torn apart by gays, blacks, Hispanics, and liberals; and that meeting these threats by any means available was the urgent

duty of all true patriots. In this worldview global warming was a hoax, evolution was against God's will, government menaced freedom, and liberals and Democrats were instruments of evil.[27]

How could a party have reached this pass? How intelligently hold such views? How endorse views so completely at odds with the Constitution, the Bill of Rights, the Declaration of Independence, George Washington (the founder of our country), and Abraham Lincoln (the founder of the Republican Party)? Views more extreme than those of the founders of the Confederacy? Apparently, the divisions that erupted into the Civil War have never been resolved. And, ironically, the party that fought the Civil War to free the slaves and bring liberty to the South has ended up taking the place of the South in politics while still regarding the Democrats as having been sympathetic to the Southern cause and therefore traitors. The party that now represents the political position of the antebellum South can somehow claim that the Democrats are traitors because they sympathized with the cause that Republicans now champion.

The Republican Party today is not the party of liberty—they are the Dixiecrats. When viewed through the lens of history, our perceptions of the two parties are perverse: Republicans repeatedly act as though, because of the Democrats' behavior during the Civil War, the Democrats cannot be trusted to lead and only the Republicans have a right to govern. As Lewis Gould writes, "Republicans were destined to be in charge and the Democrats to occupy a position of perennial deference."[28] Or in other words: the party that is the modern equivalent of the Slave Power—not the party that represents fealty to the Constitution, the Bill of Rights, and the Declaration of Independence—is destined to rule the country.

---

27 Gould, 350.
28 Gould, 351.

In this era of traditional values being shattered, the Republican allegiance to democratic practice wavered and then collapsed. . . . Americans could not really have elected Barack Obama and put his party in control of the destiny of the nation. Such an outcome must be illegitimate. And what is the remedy for illegitimacy, treason, and godlessness? How the Republican Party answers that question over the coming decades will reveal whether the Republican conviction about Democratic illegitimacy, introduced into the American bloodstream so long ago, proves fatal to what Abraham Lincoln once called "the last best hope on earth."[29]

And then there was Trump.

---

29 Jeff Wright, "Is America the Last, Best Hope of the World?" Libertarian Christian Institute, September 8, 2021, https://libertarianchristians.com/2021/09/08/last-best-hope/.

CHAPTER 7

REACHING THE BOTTOM

THE REPUBLICAN PRIMARY PROCESS in 2016 was a sad and disgraceful affair. Mitt Romney and Paul Ryan had been the ticket in 2012; both declined to run in 2016. According to political scientist William Mayer's account, no candidate was able to reach 20 percent early on in 2015. Jeb Bush initially seemed attractive, but it became clear early in the process that, after George W. Bush's presidency, most Republicans did not want to support any more Bushes.[1] Even with Jeb Bush's established name recognition, he never polled over 20 percent. Two other possibly attractive candidates were Ohio governor John Kasich and Florida senator Marco Rubio, but Kasich never seemed to be able to move past his Ohio base and Rubio made several major mistakes early on.

Then, on June 16, 2015, Donald Trump announced that he was in the race. Immediately his poll numbers began to rise.

Donald Trump had wanted to be president for a long time. He was convinced that, if he ran as a candidate, he would win, and he

---

1 Mayer, "The Nominations," in *The Elections of 2016*, ed. Michael Nelson (Thousand Oaks, CA: CQ Press, 2017), 36.

had been saying so since the late 1980s. That Trump had nothing but contempt for the law—and, likely, minorities—had been public knowledge right along. In the 1980s, Trump had weighed in on the widely condemned arrest and charging of five Hispanic teenage boys for the rape of a female jogger one night in New York's Central Park. Trump took out a full-page ad in the *New York Times*, declaring that all five of the boys should get the death penalty despite their youth. All the boys were convicted and duly sentenced to prison. On appeal, the case was overturned and dismissed because DNA evidence had become available that proved conclusively that the boys could not have committed the crime. None of the convicted boys' DNA was found in the victim's body, while DNA from unknown assailants was present. When asked about this development in the case, Trump said the five should get the death penalty anyway. Because they were suspected, but not actual, rapists? Such gratuitous violence belongs in the non-rational world of *Alice in Wonderland*!

In 2011, Trump had teased his candidacy by publicly pronouncing that he was a "birther," that is, someone who believed that President Obama had been born in some country other than the United States and was, therefore, an illegitimate president. His family having spent a lot of time in Indonesia when he was very young was also seen as problematic. Trump would eventually force Obama to produce his birth certificate, which showed that he had been born in Hawaii after it became a US state.

The issue of Trump's possible candidacy came up at the White House Correspondents' Dinner that year. With President Obama on the dais, comedian Seth Meyers quipped, "Donald Trump has been saying that he will run for president as a Republican. Which is surprising because I thought he'd be running as a joke."[2] Obama himself

---

2   "Meyers Fires at Trump at Correspondents' Dinner," Associated Press, accessed on YouTube, May 1, 2011, https://www.youtube.com/watch?v=0oT_4RJx4G0.

piled on.[3] Sadly, four years later, the American people found out that Trump's candidacy was no joke.

Trump announced his entry into the primary race in a heavily scripted event in 2015, descending to the first floor of Trump Tower (a debtor's dream) and announcing that he would be a candidate for president the following year. We don't know about what went through Trump's mind before he made that announcement, but it might have gone something like this: "If I just repeat the standard, conservative positions of the Republican Party with a little more bite and profanity and refuse to back off when the media or other politicians tell me to back off, I can win this. By saying what close to half of Americans want their candidate to say—if not actually do—I can easily win the nomination. The general election is chancier. But if you have the nomination, who knows? And even if I lose, I would establish myself as a national figure whose voice counts for something. I could start my own TV network and make a *huge* amount of money."

Speculating further on Trump's nascent reasoning: "Old guard Republicans have always, at least since the 19th century, opposed immigration. Haven't they hated Blacks, Hispanics, Asians—indeed anyone who is not (or does not look) White and northern European? Haven't they always referred to Democrats as traitors for their link to the Confederacy? Haven't they called them socialists, communists, Bolsheviks, whose main objective is weakening the country by re-distributing wealth from financially successful Republicans to lazy, worthless bums who come from shithole countries around the world? Don't they believe that this is a Christian nation and that people of other religions don't belong here (except perhaps the Jews, who can stay because they are pre-Christian)? Aren't the Republicans the only legitimate political party in this country whose decisions are right?

---

3 "Watch Obama Dig into Trump at the 2011 White House Correspondents' Dinner," CNN, accessed on YouTube, April 28, 2016, https://www.youtube.com/watch?v=HHckZCxdRkA.

The answer to all these questions is yes. So I'm practically a winner already." Again, sadly, he wasn't wholly wrong.

And so the Republican primary race began in earnest. For a time, Ted Cruz was a contender against Trump, prevailing in the Iowa caucuses, the first primary. But as often happens, the outcome wasn't the same in New Hampshire. The electorates in the two states are very different, with the Iowa Republican electorate being dominated by very conservative evangelicals and New Hampshire's by far more mainstream conservatives. Trump won the second primary and 16 out of the next 19 primaries, including the highly important Florida primary. By late July he was the undisputed front-runner, a position he held—except for a few days at the end—until the close of the primary season. Although Trump essentially had the nomination, he finished the primary race having won only 45 percent of the Republican votes, the lowest for any Republican winner since the primary system had been established in the 1970s.[4]

Many Republican leaders made clear their negative views of Trump, though some would backpedal after the election. When the Republican National Convention took place in July in Cleveland, Ohio, a substantial number of Republican leaders, including the home-state candidate Gov. John Kasich and all the living presidential nominees except Bob Dole, were notably absent. This was, of course, unprecedented. In the face of Trump's commanding lead, Ted Cruz chose not to endorse him "but instead only recommended that voters 'stand, and speak, and vote your conscience, vote for the candidates up and down the ticket who you trust to defend our freedom and be faithful to the Constitution.'"[5] At this point there still seemed to be hope for the GOP.

Looking back at his campaign, we ask how it is that Trump, with very little initial support from Republican Party leaders and despite

---

4   Mayer, in *Elections*, 52.
5   Mayer, 57.

a highly negative opinion of him by most Republicans at that time, could come from nowhere; dominate a race that included four or five seasoned politicians, senators, governors, and popular national figures; and then go on to win the nomination and subsequent general election?

One factor was certainly his complete and utter domination of the national news cycle. There never had been a candidate like this, who, from the time he emerged as a candidate for the Republican nomination, was recognized both as politician *and* entertainer—the latter having been established through his long-running, successful TV show. The media loved him as a figure for news coverage even though many members of the journalistic community came to hate him. The terrible things he said and did and his extreme lack of the qualities essential to becoming an actual president and a leader for the country did not mean he wasn't entertaining; the media eagerly booked him on their various shows whenever possible.

Trump was largely a media creation. He earned considerable money for the various media organizations, and in return they gave him unlimited coverage and built him up as much as they could—to the detriment of other candidates.

> As CBS president Les Moonves said in a moment of candor, "It may not be good for America, but it's damned good for CBS. . . . The money is rolling in and this is fun. . . . It's a terrible thing to say. But bring it on, Donald. Keep going."[6]

Although many media commentators were negative, they made Trump a media star by granting him unlimited coverage. Coverage of Trump by the media amounted more to free promotion than to free press. The media (as well as their dark star) must bear a considerable part of the blame for what Trump did to America.

Even at the end of 2021, when Trump had been out of office almost a year, practically his every move was still being covered. For

---

6   Mayer, 38, 39.

Fox News and others in the right-wing media, interviewing Donald Trump was like talking with a purveyor of holy scripture. For some media figures, so intense was their abhorrence of Trump that they and their public couldn't stop talking about him. Only Twitter (in an act of great civic courage, and joined in this at least temporarily by Facebook) challenged the tsunami of Trump media coverage. Because whatever Trump as candidate said or did became fodder for media, earning them money as noted above, it almost didn't matter what he said or did. This condition, to a degree, carried over to the general election. The media response to Trump was not undercut by his winning the nomination in 2016 with the lowest percentage of the vote since the primary system was established, nor by his not-too-dissimilar showing in the general election.

All this media exposure meant that Trump got out his message more easily and more strongly than the other candidates. And many Republicans liked what they saw and heard from him. They thought that Trump was saying what needed to be said. They were tired of political correctness. It is true that much of the substance of what Trump was saying in the campaign had been long-standing traditional conservatism, but to those traditions he added big lies and a good measure of personal attack. His campaign distortions of Republican views were not always recognized as such, and they were appreciated by the extreme Republican right wing, the movement conservatives, and the old guard supporters, all of whom comprised perhaps 25 percent of the voting public.

Many Republicans said that Donald Trump shared their values; they liked what he was selling. They wanted a candidate who would "bring change." They didn't seem to understand change can be bad as well as good. Mayer points out:

> After eight years of George W. Bush's big government, pro-
> immigration conservatism, followed by eight years of Barack
> Obama's unabashed liberalism, many Republicans wanted

someone who would approach the federal government not with a surgical scalpel but with a sledgehammer. Trump convinced such voters that he was the person most likely to do this. . . . [He would] "tell it like it is."[7]

In the end, it didn't matter really what Trump said; he was bashing the federal government, liberals, and the liberal media. He was also denouncing foreigners; even in his 2015 introductory speech, Trump included a reference to Mexican immigrants as "rapists."[8] He and his followers were angry with, or contemptuous of, the same people. So—whatever—he was the right man.

It soon became clear that, to a certain percentage of the electorate, Trump could do—and say—no wrong. During the general election, Trump continued his all-out, falsehood-filled, unprincipled attacks on everyone who opposed him in any way: some elements of the media, the Republican establishment, the Democrats, supporters of immigration, foreigners, women, and even war heroes. In July 2016, Trump said about John McCain that he was a war hero only because he had been captured and that "I like people who weren't captured."[9] Politicians didn't attack war heroes. They especially didn't attack McCain, in view of his years of suffering on behalf of his country. But Trump did.

A few months later Trump verbally lashed out at the father of Capt. Humayun Khan, a Pakistani American who was killed in Iraq. Captain Khan's father had denounced Trump's ban on travel to the United States for citizens of half a dozen Muslim states. No one attacks a Gold Star family and survives politically, but Trump did. Right before the second debate in October, the infamous *Access Hollywood* video surfaced in which Trump boasted about his ability to commit sexual violence on women and get away with it because he

7   Mayer, 56.
8   Marc J. Hetherington, "The Election: The Allure of the Outsider," in *The Elections of 2016*, 63.
9   Hetherington, 64.

was a star. Traditionally, no politician who spoke this way—and few have, at least publicly—could continue to be a viable candidate, but Trump did. As Marc Hetherington writes, "One month later Trump was president-elect. Perhaps he was right when he said in January 2016, 'I could stand in the middle of 5th Avenue and shoot somebody and I wouldn't lose voters.'"[10]

Another factor in Trump's eventual win was that the Democrats had nominated a mostly unpopular candidate, former first lady, New York senator, and secretary of state Hillary Clinton. Clinton had a 43 percent favorable rating and a 55 percent unfavorable rating. Trump's numbers, as it happens, were even worse: 38 percent favorable and 60 percent unfavorable. Interestingly, Trump's numbers in 2016 were not very different from his numbers in 2020. The American people, by approximately a two-thirds margin, never liked or trusted him. Of course, there were times when the numbers were better, but in five years Trump never attained a 50 percent favorability rating, except for some weeks right before the general election in 2016. William Mayer explains that, on Election Day, while 94 percent of voters chose one of these two candidates, only 41 percent said that they strongly supported the candidate they voted for. 32 percent admitted that they had "reservations" about their choice, and 25 percent would only say that they voted for the person that they did because they disliked the other candidate more. A stronger Democratic candidate might have prevailed, but the two parties had offered the electorate a choice between two divisive and widely disliked figures in American public life.[11]

In the end the loser won the most votes by a margin of almost three million, and the winner won the decisive majority in the Electoral College on the basis of three razor-thin and questionable—given the unanimous view of the American intelligence community that there was substantial Russian manipulation of the 2016 election on behalf

10 Hetherington, 64.
11 Mayer, in *Elections*, 29.

of Trump—margins in three Midwest states that had rarely gone Republican in recent years: Wisconsin, Minnesota, and Michigan.[12] All in all, a deeply flawed election.

Has the Republican Party, particularly its conservative right-wing voters, given up all interest in truthful politicians and the rule of law? The events of the 2016 campaign would suggest that perhaps this is the case. Not every year does a real estate mogul whose business appears built on potentially faulty loans, who has filed for bankruptcy six times, and who has had a second career of reality TV, get elected president. Similarly, it is not every year that a candidate—in this case the one who prevailed—accepts the help of a hostile foreign power that intervenes massively in the campaign to his benefit (in the unanimous judgment of the American intelligence community, as noted above), and it is not every year that the partisans of the candidate receiving the assistance of a hostile foreign power seem unconcerned about it. As all know, such events had never happened before, and every American should hope to God that they never happen again.

Even in the face of damning evidence of Russian interference in the election—and Russian president Vladimir Putin's many other outrageous actions at home and around the world—many Republicans seemed to continually adjust their worldview to conform to Trump's own. A December 2016 poll showed that Republicans who had an unfavorable view of Putin exceeded those whose view was favorable by only 10 percent. At approximately the same time, the negatives in the Republican Party for former president Barack Obama exceeded the positives by 64 percentage points. "As Obama suggested, Ronald Reagan, Republicans' favorite Republican of the past hundred years, would be stunned by this development."[13] Has racism blotted out patriotism in the Republican Party?

Only by failing our obligations as citizens can an election outcome

---

12 Hetherington, in *Elections*, 84.
13 Hetherington, 84.

like that in 2016 happen. Many Americans, probably the majority, believed Trump unqualified to be president. Indeed, after talking with him during the transition process, President Barack Obama found him "uniquely unqualified." Paul J. Quirk, who holds the Phil Lind Chair in US Politics and Representation at the University of British Columbia, concurs. His widely admired writing on the presidency and US political issues includes a study of Trump's impotency in effectively carrying out the office of the presidency. He writes:

> Trump's negative traits were numerous and readily iden-tifiable. . . . Among reasonably rational or independent commentators, and many Republican leaders, it was widely accepted that Trump exhibited each of the following traits.

1. He made false statements with extreme frequency. [Experts believed] Trump's frequency of clearly false statements was "off the charts". . . . The falsehoods ranged from minor to important . . . and from plausible to bizarre. . . . They included denials of his own previous statements that were immediately available on video. Some observers wondered whether Trump lived in a fantasy world.

2. He issued a stream of coarse insults against his opponents and others who criticized or offended him . . . the *Economist*, in a cover story, charged Trump with the "debasing of American politics."

3. He ran his business and financial affairs in a way that en-couraged or allowed illegal and unethical conduct for his financial benefit.

4. He allegedly had a history of aggressive sexual conduct toward women, which in some cases had reached the level of criminal sexual assault.

5. He was prone to statements and practices that amounted to, or at least approached, racial and religious bigotry.

6. He entirely lacked experience in government, public service, the military, or public affairs. [Even when he was sitting in the Oval Office, he showed scant interest in the job.]

7. He was extremely uninformed about issues. . . . Relatedly, he had an extremely short attention span for receiving information.

8. His policy positions were casual, lacking serious deliberation, and often, by broad consensus among relevant experts, unworkable or dangerous. [Examples included cutting back on the US commitment to NATO, withdrawing military support from Japan and Korea, and building a wall on our southern border that he insisted Mexico would pay for.]

9. He made numerous promises and threats that indicated ignorance of, or lack of concern about, provisions of the Constitution. . . . In a more general way, Trump sometimes ignored, rejected, or did not understand fundamental values of the constitutional system. He publicly encouraged a foreign power, Russia, to interfere in the election . . .

10. He exhibited a consistent set of highly problematic personality traits, which fit broadly under the rubric of "narcissistic personality." [14]

And yet, as election results came in on the evening of November 8, 2016, the unthinkable became reality: Donald J. Trump would be the next president of the United States.

---

14 Paul J. Quirk, "The Presidency, Donald Trump and the Question of Fitness," in *The Elections of 2016*, ed. Michael Nelson (Thousand Oaks, CA: CQ Press, 2017), 200–203.

CHAPTER 8

THE BOTTOM

Trump was duly sworn in as president on January 20, 2017. After making a rather strange, dystopian inaugural speech, characterized by former president George W. Bush afterward as he strolled away with Hillary Clinton as "some weird shit," it wasn't long before he was questioning media estimates of the attending crowd's size.

Everyone knows that the crowd for Barack Obama's inauguration was probably the largest in American history, reaching even more than one million, because of the historic significance of Obama's election. Trump's crowd was, of course, smaller. But Trump and the White House insisted that he had attracted the largest crowd ever to witness a president's swearing-in. Photographs from the National Park Service contradicted Trump's boasts.[1] This silly dispute continued for several days.

It should be noted that Trump, after this dispute was forgotten by all except Trump, put himself forth as somewhat of an expert on estimating crowd size. Dickering about crowd size at his events became a hallmark of his presidency. His inflated numbers were usually seriously

---

1   Glenn Kessler, Salvador Rizzo, and Meg Kelly, *Donald Trump and His Assault on Truth: The President's Falsehoods, Misleading Claims and Flat-Out Lies* (New York: Scribner, 2020), 75.

at odds with those of local officials whose jobs included estimating crowd size for various events staged in their cities or counties. These officials refuted Trump's exaggerated numbers.

Just how good is Trump at estimating crowd size? The *Washington Post* Fact Checker team reported Trump's estimate of total attendance at nine rallies leading up to the 2018 midterms as 352,600 people. The Fact Checkers' review of news reports and local official counts led to an estimate of 101,000 people. Trump claimed a crowd of 50,000 at a rally in Houston; the local police chief said 3,000. On November 14, 2018, Trump asserted that he drew a crowd at an airport rally in Georgia large enough to fill a 747 hangar with 55,000 attendees and another with some 18,000. There was only one hangar. The sheriff's office estimated that there were 12,500 in that hangar and 6,000 outside. At an October 12, 2018, rally in Erie, Pennsylvania, Trump reported that there were 25,000 people outside the 12,000-seat arena. Police reported about 3,000 outside a 9,000-seat arena. When Donald Trump invited a friend at a November 15, 2018, Indiana rally to "take a look outside at the thousands of people that wanted to get inside. You were lucky," the friend likely had trouble seeing them.[2] Thus, with Trump's false claim about the numbers attending his inaugural being the greatest in history (despite the firm denial of this by the National Park Service), his administration continued to display the creative lying that would only accelerate as his presidency continued.

While we recognize—or should—that honesty and truth are the lifeblood of government and civilization, we wouldn't turn to Trump for those virtues. In fact, Trump makes false and misleading statements with great regularity. Donald Trump's relationship to the truth is a whole universe entire unto itself. As journalist Glenn Kessler puts it: About one-third of what he says can usually be believed and two-thirds of what he says is a lie.[3] How can anyone believe anything

---

2   Kessler, Rizzo, and Kelly, 75–77.
3   Kessler, Rizzo, and Kelly, xxix.

this man says? How can he be credited by other government officials, members of Congress, Americans, foreign governments, foreign diplomats, citizens of the world? As the Fact Checker team put it:

> And then there's Donald Trump, the most mendacious president in US history. He almost never expresses regret. He's not known for one big lie—just a constant stream of exaggerated, invented, boastful, purposefully outrageous, spiteful, inconsistent, dubious, and false claims.[4]

Here are a few examples from Trump's torrent of bedtime fairytales, hurricane of untruths, tsunami of lies, and volcano of misstatements:

> He repeatedly said that US Steel was building six to eight new steel plants, but that wasn't true. He said that as president, Obama gave citizenship to 2,500 Iranians during the nuclear-deal negotiations. It didn't happen. Over and over, Trump claimed that the Uzbekistan-born man who in 2001 was accused of killing eight people with a pickup truck in New York City had brought two dozen relatives to the United States through so-called chain migration. The actual number was zero.[5]

Trump's fairy tales would make for a very large volume. They are repeated by public speakers in the United States probably more often than those from Grimm or other such folk tales. Sadly, Trump's purpose is not to entertain little children with farcical stories; it's to do evil to grownups with them.

Trump's lack of reliability and truthfulness was well known in the business community. Of course, government agents overwhelmed by perjury, defrauded businesses, and banks misled by lying, would-be borrowers don't publish such behavior. Their usual response is to avoid

---

4   Kessler, Rizzo, and Kelly, x.
5   Kessler, Rizzo, and Kelly, xix.

doing business with such persons again. Kessler found a few records of Trump distorting the truth of his business activities. For example, after Trump sued a reporter for writing a biography that questioned his net worth, lawyers taking a deposition of Trump caught Trump 30 times making untrue statements about such things as condo sales, his debts, and his earnings. One article detailed Trump's claim that he had paid $10 million in cash for his luxury property Mar-a-Lago in Florida, while court records showed he had paid only $2,000. The balance of the payment had been a preposterous loan—so large that it was difficult for creditors to claim his property under the old principle "If you owe the bank $2 million, they own you, if you owe the bank $40 million, you own them."[6]

Kessler reports this interesting aspect of Trump's lying: he's apt to endlessly repeat the lie if he thinks it has been popular, even long after it has been proven false and its falsity is widely known. He just hammers away endlessly with his lies as though in an effort to replace *the* truth with *his own more favorable* "truth." Kessler and his team identified 14 "false" or "mostly false" claims that Trump had repeated more than 20 times by December 10, 2018. By January 20, 2020, the list of repeated falsehoods had grown to 32, by which time Trump had uttered a mind-boggling total of 16,241 lies.[7] At the end of his third year in office, Trump announced in a rally that he had "made a deal. I saved the country." He argued that he should be given the Nobel Peace Prize for achieving peace between Ethiopia and neighboring Eritrea. In fact, the horrible 20-year conflict between Ethiopia and Eritrea had been ended by Ethiopia's prime minister, who had received the Nobel Prize for the role he played in accomplishing this feat. Trump had nothing to do with these negotiations and appears to have confused them with other negotiations equally obscure to him.[8]

Given the gaffe, one wonders about Trump's level of knowledge.

---

6   Kessler, Rizzo, and Kelly, xxiii, xxiv.
7   Kessler, Rizzo, and Kelly, xvi.
8   Kessler, Rizzo, and Kelly, xi.

Can anyone imagine another prominent world leader making such a preposterous statement—Trudeau in Canada? Johnson in the United Kingdom? Macron in France? Even Putin in Russia or Xi in China? Beyond frivolous, such a puerile pronouncement might come from a precocious and fun-loving five-year old. Does Trump believe others as foolish as he is?

The amount and majesty of Trump's lying brings up the question of motivation for such behavior. A social scientist at the University of California has analyzed Trump's behavior in connection with truthfulness and done research on the subject generally over the years as well. She has found that the average person tells maybe one or two lies a day—usually for self-interest, sometimes to help others, and only very occasionally (1 or 2 percent of the time) to harm someone else. She estimated that 50 percent of Trump's lies fall in the third category.[9] Half of Trump's lies and false statements were designed to hurt or damage someone else! The following instances are illustrative.

> [Trump tweeted:] "Senator Bob Corker 'begged' me to endorse him for reelection in Tennessee. I said 'NO' and he dropped out (said he could not win without my endorsement)." Corker said he didn't do any begging; rather, Trump had called him to reconsider his decision not to seek reelection and offered his endorsement. More than 100 times . . . Trump has falsely claimed he passed into law the Veterans Choice Act. At one rally in 2018, Trump suggested the law was the result of a brilliant brainstorm. "I said, 'I have the greatest idea. We're going to do this. If a veteran has to wait, we're going to send them to a private doctor. We'll pay the bill.' What a genius—I said, I said, 'How good is that?' They said, 'Sir, we've been trying to get it passed for 44 years.'" Actually, Barack Obama signed into law the Veterans Choice Act in 2014.[10]

9   Kessler, Rizzo, and Kelly, xxviii–xxix.
10 Kessler, Rizzo, and Kelly, xxix.

The Fact Checker team estimated Trump's overall lack of truth-fulness. For two rallies in 2018 and 2019, the team cataloged and analyzed every factual assertion by Trump and found that "two-thirds to three-quarters of the claims were false, mostly false, or unsupported by evidence. . . . At a two-hour rally in Michigan in December 2019, Trump presented 179 statements as facts, more than one a minute, of which 67 percent were false or misleading."[11] Trump's statements are often preposterously separate from the facts. He said that he had witnessed thousands of Muslims in New Jersey cheering the fall of the World Trade Center, when no one ever identified anyone doing so. He said the wives of the 9/11 attackers had all been sent home before the attacks, when in reality only one of the attackers was married and his wife had never visited the United States.[12]

Why don't Trump's followers seem to mind his lies? To a certain extent, many people who watch and read media sources that are de-termined to back up Trump's lies simply don't know that they *are* lies. But there is another explanation. We are used to thinking that facts and figures are important to politicians. But just how much facts and figures still matter in the United States is debatable. Today, as Kessler points out, partisan identification seems to matter more—is the can-didate "red" or "blue"?

Republicans seem to care less about truth than they once did. In a 2007 Associated Press–Yahoo poll, 71 percent of Republicans said it was "extremely important" for presidential candidates to be honest; 70 percent of Democrats and 60 percent of Independents agreed. This finding is not surprising. As Founder Thomas Jefferson said, "The whole art of government consists in the art of being honest." Surprising, however, is the result of a 2018 *Washington Post* poll asking respondents the same question. Democrats and Independents gave honesty in presidential politics the same priority as in 2007. But the

---

11 Kessler, Rizzo, and Kelly, xxx.
12 Kessler, Rizzo, and Kelly, xxiv.

share of Republicans who said honesty was extremely important had fallen to 49 percent.[13] Just shy of half of the responding Republicans still thought honesty to be central to politics; a majority did not. Even when Trump's lies are detected, they are not problematic to the majority. Is it any wonder that so many Republican Party leaders have become slavish followers of a lying, fascistic president?

Before throwing up our hands in anxious trepidation for the future, let's remember these words, which while not actually original to Abraham Lincoln are often attributed to him and surely reflect his wisdom about human nature: "You can fool all of the people some of the time, you can fool some of the people all of the time, but you can't fool all of the people all of the time."

We have seen that Trump's statements are frequently untruthful. What of his actions? The stamp of a president is naturally revealed in his handling of the various issues his administration faces. What follows are some revealing episodes from Trump's four years.

IMMIGRATION BAN

On Monday, March 8, 2017, the Trump administration rolled out a "downscaled but still pernicious" version of its Muslim travel ban, restricting citizens from a list of majority-Muslim countries from traveling to the United States.[14] The initial version of this executive order, hastily introduced some days earlier, had caused great disorder and confusion, with many people being sequestered in airports both here and overseas. During the first four days of the ban, the American Civil Liberties Union did a yeoman's job of protecting people caught up in it—either locating lodging for them or finding relatives with whom they could stay. This was Trump's first unconstitutional attempt to discriminate against Muslims who, consistent

---

13 Kessler, Rizzo, and Kelly, xiii.
14 "President Trump's Muslim Ban Lite," editorial, *New York Times*, March 6, 2017, https://www.nytimes.com/2017/03/06/opinion/president-trumps-muslim-ban-lite.html.

with the law, were attempting to visit the United States for business or domestic reasons. It was promptly thrown out by the courts.

The court loss compelled the Trump administration to try again. The new executive order targeted refugees and travelers from six majority-Muslim countries. Banned were citizens from Syria, Iran, Libya, Sudan, Yemen, and Somalia. Iraq—not included in the first order—was added to the second even though the list in the first order was longer than the second. Though the new order perhaps disrupted fewer lives, it was justified by the same flawed rationale—religious discrimination in the name of heightened security. In an editorial, the *New York Times* dubbed it "The Muslim Ban Lite":

> Resorting to these bunker mentality tactics, which are being peddled with plenty of innuendo and little convincing evidence, will do lasting damage to America's standing in the world and erode its proud tradition of welcoming people fleeing strife. While these steps are being sold to make the nation safer, they stand to do the opposite.[15]

Some of the words from the poem by Emma Lazarus inscribed on the Statue of Liberty, which used to be taught in grade-school civics, apply to this situation:

> Give me your tired, your poor,
> Your huddled masses yearning to breathe free,
> The wretched refuse of your teeming shore.
> Send these, the homeless, tempest-tost to me,
> I lift my lamp beside the golden door![16]

---

15 "President Trump's Muslim Ban Lite," editorial, *New York Times*, March 6, 2017, https://www.nytimes.com/2017/03/06/opinion/president-trumps-muslim-ban-lite.html.

16 Emma Lazarus, "The New Colossus," National Park Service, https://www.nps.gov/stli/learn/historyculture/colossus.htm.

George Washington said this in a 1783 letter to an organization of Irish immigrants in New York:

> The bosom of America is open to receive not only the opulent & respectable Stranger, but the oppressed & persecuted of all Nations and Religions; whom we shall wellcome [*sic*] to a participation of all our rights & previleges [sic], if by decency & propriety of conduct they appear to merit the enjoyment.[17]

Muslim bans and other discriminatory tactics of the Republican Party don't partake of this welcoming spirit. Nor are they in harmony with our Founders' vision established in the Declaration of Independence:

> We hold these truths to be self-evident, that all men are created equal, that they are endowed by their Creator with certain unalienable Rights, that among these are Life, Liberty and the pursuit of Happiness.—That to secure these Rights, Governments are instituted among Men, deriving their just powers from the consent of the governed.[18]

Spurning these ideals is spurning America. A Muslim ban imperils America's standing in the world. It undercuts America's commitment to religious freedom, enshrined in the Bill of Rights. For these reasons Trump's second executive order was immediately challenged by Washington State, with other joining states. On March 16, 2017, federal courts in Hawaii and Maryland both issued orders temporarily blocking the implementation of the revised executive order that they correctly saw as another unconstitutional ban on Muslim immigration.

---

17 "From George Washington to Joshua Holmes, 2 December 1783," Founders Early Access, Rotunda, https://rotunda.upress.virginia.edu/founders/default. xqy?keys=FOEA-print-01-02-02-6127.

18 "The Declaration of Independence," National Archives, https://www.archives.gov/ founding-docs/declaration.

These challenges followed a harrowing report in the *New York Times* portraying the struggle of an immigrant family attempting to flee the United States near Champlain, New York, to seek asylum in Canada. Apparently, families—many of them with young children—traveled across the country to make such escapes, fearing that their legal status in the United States might change. Some were refugees from Yemen and Turkey who had fled their original countries in the hope of a better future and now believed they had become targets in their adopted country. A taxi driver who took many such refugees from the Plattsburg airport to a point near the Canadian border was quoted as saying, "People just want to live their life and not be scared."[19] America is supposed to be a country to which refugees flee, not a country from which they flee.

HEALTHCARE ROLLBACK

In February 2017, Rep. Mark Meadows, Republican of North Carolina, said, "Congress should repeal the Affordable Care Act right away. . . . We committed to the American people to repeal every tax, every mandate, the regulations . . ."[20] According to an earlier report in the *New York Times* on January 4, then vice president elect Mike Pence and the top Republicans in Congress made clear, more explicitly, that they were dead serious about repealing the Affordable Care Act.[21]

The *Guardian* newspaper in London, drawing on a US Congressional Budget Office report, said that "a Republican plan to repeal key provisions of the Affordable Care Act would leave 32 million people

---

19 Rick Rojas, "Since Trump, Quiet Upstate Road Becomes a Busy Exit from US," *New York Times*, March 7, 2017, https://www.nytimes.com/2017/03/07/nyregion/champlain-ny-canada-migrants.html.

20 Mark Barrett, "Repeal Affordable Care Act Right Away, Meadows Says," *Asheville (NC) Citizen-Times*, February 4, 2017, https://www.citizen-times.com/story/news/politics/elections/2017/02/04/repeal-affordable-care-act-right-away-meadows-says/97465490/.

21 Robert Pear, "Republicans' 4-Step Plan to Repeal the Affordable Care Act," *New York Times*, January 4, 2017, https://www.nytimes.com/2017/01/04/us/affordable-care-act-congress-repeal-plan.html.

without health coverage and double the cost of insurance premiums over the next decade . . ."[22] A repeal of the Affordable Care Act would thus likely cause many thousands of additional deaths each year. A *New England Journal of Medicine* study on death rates found that for every 455 people who gained coverage pursuant to an expansion of Medicaid, one life was saved per year.[23] In doing the math, we realize that 20 million people losing their health care insurance would result in a very large number of preventable deaths annually. A civilized society cannot enact policy that would cause an increase in preventable deaths—especially a society committed to the right of all human beings to "Life, Liberty and the pursuit of Happiness." Nor should we countenance a political party that advocates so appalling a policy.

Benjamin Franklin, one of the founders of the charity-supported Pennsylvania Hospital, saw the kind of health care that our republic needed. Franklin proposed that the Pennsylvania Hospital provide the finest healthcare available—free of charge—to all inhabitants of the province (this in 1755, before the revolution). Health care, he said, would be extended even to "poor, diseas'd Foreigners. . . . This Branch of *Charity* seems essential to the true Spirit of Christianity; and should be extended to all in general, whether Deserving or Undeserving, as far as our Power reaches."[24] About a system built on private donations, he said that it wouldn't work, because good health care cost a lot of money.[25] Government funding was requisite. The Republican

22 Lauren Gambino, "Repealing Obamacare Would Leave 32m Without Health Coverage, Analysis Finds," *The Guardian*, January 17, 2020, https://www.theguardian.com/us-news/2017/jan/17/obamacare-repeal-replace-health-insurance-costs.

23 David Himmelstein and Steffie Woolhandler, "Repealing the Affordable Care Act Will Kill More Than 43,000 People Annually," *Washington Post*, January 23, 2017, https://www.washingtonpost.com/posteverything/wp/2017/01/23/repealing-the-affordable-care-act-will-kill-more-than-43000-people-annually/.

24 Benjamin Franklin, "Appeal for the Hospital, 8 and 15 August 1751," Founders Online, National Archives, https://founders.archives.gov/documents/Franklin/01-04-02-0049. [Original source: *The Papers of Benjamin Franklin*, ed. Leonard W. Labaree, vol. 4, *July 1, 1750, through June 30, 1753* (New Haven: Yale University Press, 1961), 147–54.]

25 Svati Kirsten Narula, "What Does Benjamin Franklin Have to Do with Obamacare?"

attack on Obamacare runs afoul of this Founder's vision. Republicans propose the opposite of what Franklin said was right and necessary in keeping the country's founding vision.

EDUCATION

In September 2013, retired Supreme Court justice David Souter spoke in support of increased funding for the humanities at the State Museum in Albany, New York. In his speech he expressed concern about the level of civic ignorance in the United States. He noted that "less than a third of adult Americans in the United States understand that the basic constitutional structure of American government is one of power divided into three branches that they can name." These are, of course, the legislative, executive, and judicial branches—in other words, the president, the Congress, and the courts. "Two-thirds of the country doesn't have a clue about that," Souter said. The public and private secondary systems have failed to teach elemental civics to every student—a topic required until recently. And make no mistake about it, the public school system of the United States has been and will remain the bedrock of our democratic governance system. Private schools are fine, but it is the public schools that will make or break our way of life. Souter went on to say that he did not believe that constitutional government as we know it in the United States can ultimately survive in an atmosphere of pervasive civic ignorance and majority disassociation from the basic processes of American government.[26]

Donald J. Trump picked Betsy DeVos to head the Department of Education. After her confirmation, the *New York Times* commented on her selection in an editorial entitled "Betsy DeVos Teaches the Value of Ignorance." In it, the *Times* quoted from a 2015 speech by

---

The Atlantic, October 21, 2013, https://www.theatlantic.com/national/archive/2013/10/what-does-benjamin-franklin-have-to-do-with-obamacare/280735/.

26 Robert Gavin, "Souter's Lament: Civic Ignorance Hurts America," *Albany (NY) Times Union*, September 17, 2013, https://www.timesunion.com/local/article/Souter-s-lament-Civic-ignorance-hurts-America-4822882.php.

DeVos in which she said, "Government really sucks." The *Times* also noted that "[DeVos] has never run, taught in, attended, or sent a child to an American public school."[27] Little more need be said about where Trump and the Republican Party are on this one. Keeping citizens ignorant is an age-old practice of those who aspire to tyranny.

Our Founders recognized the indispensable role of education in a democracy. Jefferson wrote, "If a nation expects to be ignorant and free, in a state of civilization, it expects what never was and never will be." Madison likewise asserted, "It is universally admitted that a well-instructed people alone can be a free people . . ." And canny Samuel Adams warned, "It is in the interest of tyrants to reduce the people to ignorance and vice. For they cannot live in any country where virtue and knowledge prevail."

TRIMMING ENTITLEMENT PROGRAMS

In a radio interview after the passage of the Republican tax cut bill on December 6, 2017, Speaker of the House Paul Ryan was discussing what would happen when the tax cut legislation was signed by the president and became law. He said that the next year the target would be "entitlement reform, which is an important part of how you tackle the debt and the deficit"—including the huge additional debt of one trillion dollars caused by the tax cut legislation. He went on to say that, because Medicaid and Medicare programs "are the big drivers of debt, [Republicans] spend more time on the healthcare entitlements—because that's where the problem lies, fiscally speaking." But Republican Party objectives go beyond that. For many years privatizing Social Security and Medicare and destroying these central New Deal and Great Society programs have been primary Republican Party goals. Ryan added in his radio address that he believes that "the president understands that choice and competition works everywhere

---

27 "Betsy DeVos Teaches the Value of Ignorance," editorial, *New York Times*, February 7, 2017, https://www.nytimes.com/2017/02/07/opinion/betsy-devos-teaches-the-value-of-ignorance.html.

in healthcare, especially in Medicare"[28]—even though during the campaign Trump pledged to protect Social Security and Medicare from cuts.

There is more than one view on this bait-and-switch Republican position. The *New York Times* put it differently on December 3, 2017: "Republican leaders have been blunt about their motivation [for the tax cut bill]: to deliver on the promise to wealthy donors, and down the road, to use the leverage of huge deficits [created by the bill] to cut and privatize Medicare and Social Security."[29]

Noting that Republicans mention deficits when (1) Democrats are in power or when (2) social programs that help the needy can be cut, Paul Krugman says that the bait-and-switch tactic happened far faster than anyone imagined it would. He cites as an example the remarks of Orrin Hatch on the failure of Congress to continue the Children's Health Insurance Program—known as CHIP—which covers nine million US children. Senator Hatch asserted that he supported CHIP but insisted that "the reason CHIP is having trouble is because we don't have money anymore"[30]—just before voting for a trillion and a half tax cut that would deliver the bulk of its benefits to the richest few percent of the population.

Since the strength of a democracy is the strength of its middle class, the Republican Party is eroding democracy when it goes after fundamentally important social programs. Social Security has been an essential part of American life since the mid-1930s (nearly 90 years) and Medicare since the mid-1960s (nearly 60 years). The efforts of the

---

28 Jeff Stein, "Ryan Says Republicans to Target Welfare, Medicare, Medicaid Spending in 2018," *Washington Post,* December 6, 2017, https://www. washingtonpost.com/news/wonk/wp/2017/12/01/gop-eyes-post-tax-cut-changes-to-welfare-medicare-and-social-security/.

29 Thomas E. Mann and Norman J. Ornstein, "How the Republicans Broke Congress," *New York Times,* December 2, 2017, https://www.nytimes.com/2017/12/02/opinion/sunday/republicans-broke-congress-politics.html.

30 Paul Krugman, "Republicans Are Coming For Your Benefits," *New York Times,* December 4, 2017, https://www.nytimes.com/2017/12/04/opinion/republican-tax-bill-benefits.html.

Republican elitist cabal to weaken them would eventually eviscerate the middle class. It would push our vibrant republic status toward dictatorship. The moves to undercut Social Security and Medicare are unpatriotic and contrary to American democratic principles.

Moves to undercut entitlement programs are part of a larger long-term Republican Party strategy to take from the poor and middle class and give to the rich regardless of the impact on the economy and the welfare of citizens. From 1880 through 1920, Republican Party leadership—inspired by John C. Calhoun and the slaveholding South—neglected the country's sharp economic and social inequalities and led it straight into the Great Depression and the collapse of the American economy. If not for FDR, the country might have faced fascism or another civil war. The leadership of the Republican Party, inspired by the actions of Mussolini's Falange Party, turns its back on the promise of the American vision embedded in the Declaration of Independence that all have the unalienable right to liberty and the pursuit of happiness—a right that should never be abrogated, whether by the slaveholding South or by Gilded Age robber barons or by the country's deep structural inequalities.

Some comments by our Founders on this issue:

"As riches increase and accumulate in few hands . . . the tendency of things will be to depart from the republican standard."

—Alexander Hamilton, 1788

"Property monopolized or in the possession of a few is a curse to mankind."   —John Adams, 1765

FREEDOM OF THE PRESS AND DICTATOR ENVY

When President Trump (our newest Republican president) took office in 2017, he took an extremely combative position regarding our free press. In addition, he expressed admiration for such brutal dictators around the world as Duterte in the Philippines, Putin in Russia, and Xi in China. Not acknowledging the differences in the power of the press in China and the US, Trump continued to challenge the US press. While Xi has virtually suppressed the news media in China, Trump (despite his best efforts) has failed to discredit our press and has actually made it stronger. The rule of law has always been a weak restraint on rulers in China. Here, institutions that have been built up over the past two and a half centuries have continued to restrain Trump. But as Thomas Friedman warned in the *New York Times* on May 18, 2018:

> [These institutions] will have to hold for at least another two and a half years, and that will not be easy with a president like Trump, who was surely not 100 percent joking when he said in March of President Xi, "President for life . . . I think it's great. Maybe we will want to give that a shot someday."[31]

Trump clearly admired Xi's authoritarian state.

Donald Trump has been an admirer of Putin for many years. Since Putin's role in electing his friend and stooge Donald Trump president by means of the major intervention of the Russian government in the election of 2016, Trump has seemed desirous of carrying out Putin's every wish. In 2018, at a press conference he and Putin gave following the Helsinki summit meeting, Trump told the world community that, when he had asked Putin about US intelligence community claims of massive Russian intervention in his favor during the US election, Putin had said openly and directly that it wasn't true. Trump went on to say that he believed Putin and that there was nothing to the claim of Russian intervention. In front of the world press and with Putin sitting in a nearby chair with a slight smirk on his face, Trump overruled his own intelligence advisers in favor of Putin's account.

---

31 Thomas L. Friedman, "The US and China: More Alike Than We'd Like?" *New York Times*, May 9, 2018, https://www.nytimes.com/2018/05/08/opinion/us-china-more-alike.html.

President Trump's admiration of tyrants didn't stop with Putin and Xi. He bestowed lavish praise on Viktor Orbán, who appeared to be turning Hungary into a fascist state; Recep Erdoğan, who was well on his way to destroying Turkey's democracy; and Abdel Fattah al-Sisi, who was establishing a military dictatorship in Egypt. Sisi, in the process of seizing power, had ordered the massacre of thousands of people allegedly involved with drugs, both users and producers, without any sort of trial whatsoever. Then, in June 2018, Trump met for the first time with his true favorite, one of the most brutal tyrants of all, Kim Jong-Un of North Korea. Trump lavished on him sycophantic praise, announcing that he had forged an excellent relationship with Kim and that Kim was a "very talented man." [32]

On June 3, 2018, just before the anniversary of her father's death, Ronald Reagan's daughter Patti Davis published an article in the *Washington Post*. She commented that people often asked her what her father would say if he were here now. Among other things, she thought, he would remind us that

> America began as a dream in the minds of men who dared to envision a land that was free of tyranny, with a government designed and structured so that no branch could dominate the others. . . . Our democracy, because it is founded on the authority of "We the people," puts the burden of vigilance on all American citizens. Countries can be splintered from within, he would say. It's a sinister form of destruction that can happen gradually if people don't realize that our Constitution will protect us only if the principles of that document are adhered to and defended. He would be appalled and heartbroken at a Congress that refuses to stand up to a

---

32 Nicholas Kristof, "Trump Was Outfoxed in Singapore," *New York Times*, June 12, 2018, https://www.nytimes.com/2018/06/12/opinion/trump-kim-summit-north-korea.html?auth=login-email&login=email.

president who not only seems ignorant of the Constitution but who also attempts at every turn to dismantle and mock our system of checks and balances. . . . He would ask the people of this country to reflect on his own words from his most famous speech "A Time for Choosing," delivered in 1964. "You and I have a rendezvous with destiny. We'll preserve for our children this, the last best hope on earth, or we'll sentence them to take the last step into a thousand years of darkness." [33]

Picking up the theme of darkness, Sen. Kirsten Gillibrand asserted in a *Politico* interview that President Trump's policies "come from the darkness" and are "evil in the biblical sense." In another part of the interview, she referred to the Trump administration as pursuing "the devil's schemes." [34]

IMMIGRATION

Among the many policies of President Trump and his administration that deserve to be characterized as corrupt and catastrophically damaging to America was his "zero tolerance" policy of processing migrants at the southern border. These migrants—fleeing violent prosecution and death threats and, therefore, more refugee than migrant—come to our border as anticipated by George Washington in his letter to the Irish immigrants. Under Trump, migrants were being kept from legal entry, summarily thrown into jail, and their children—some of them toddlers—taken from them, in many cases literally ripped from their mothers' arms and placed in holding pens

---

33 Patti Davis, "Mourning America: What My Father, Ronald Reagan, Would Say Today," *Washington Post,* June 3, 2018, https://www.washingtonpost.com/opinions/mourning-america-what-my-father-ronald-reagan-would-say-today/2018/06/03/a0fe1cfe-65be-11e8-a69c-b944de66d9e7_story.html.

34 Edward-Isaac Dovere, "Trump's Policies 'Come from the Darkness,' Gillibrand Says," *Politico,* June 19, 2018, https://www.politico.com/magazine/story/2018/06/19/kirsten-gillibrand-interview-trump-religion-2020-218830.

all over the United States with few records kept as to who went where. Some of these children were too young to know the names of their parents, and Trump's subsequent executive order that parents and children could be detained together did little to reunite parents with children previously separated from them.

Attorney General Jeff Sessions sought to justify this policy by pointing to St. Paul's letter to the Romans, Chapter 13, in which the apostle urges everyone to be subject to the governing authorities—the same passage used by the Nazis to justify their actions. In discussing Sessions's rationalization, Michael Gerson noted Jesus's words in Matthew 19:14:

> Whosoever receives one such child in my name receives me; but whoever causes one of these little ones who believe in me to stumble, it would be better for him to have a heavy millstone hung around his neck, and to be drowned in the depths of the sea.

Gerson pointed out that the Bible, like a gun, is a dangerous thing in the hands of a bigot.[35]

Joe Scarborough, in his column of June 21, 2018, said that:

> [America's] president is a brutish political boss who has cheapened conversation, sullied the ethics of the presidency, and called into question the very character of the country once seen as the envy of the world. That so many Republicans still support this depraved man and his malignant movement could be the most alarming element of this tragic American tale.[36]

---

35 Michael Gerson, "This Is What Happens When You Put the Bible Into the Hands of a Bigot," *Harrisburg (PA) Patriot-News,* June 19, 2018, https://www.pennlive.com/opinion/2018/06/this_is_what_happens_when_you.html.

36 Joe Scarborough, "Trump Cheapens Conservatism, Sullies Office," *Hartford Courant,* June 22, 2018, https://www.courant.com/opinion/op-ed/hc-op-scarborough-trump-cheapens-conservatism-20180622-story.html.

Gillibrand declared that what we had with the Trump presidency was an issue of right versus wrong. She went on record as saying it was wrong for us to stand by silently, wrong to do nothing. "This is what darkness looks like. We have to stand against it," she urged.[37] Concurring, George Will urged Americans to vote against the GOP in November 2020, saying that "to vote against [Trump's] party's cowering congressional caucuses is to affirm the nation's honor while quarantining him."[38]

SUPREME COURT APPOINTMENT, 2018

Alexander Hamilton, arguing in 1788 in Federalist Paper Number 78 for the lifetime appointment of judges on good behavior, said the following:

> To avoid an arbitrary discretion in the courts, it is indispens-able that they [judges] should be bound down by strict rules and precedents, which serve to define and point out their duty in every particular case that comes before them . . . the records of those precedents must unavoidably swell to a very considerable bulk, and must demand long and laborious study to acquire a competent knowledge of them. Hence it is, that there can be but a few men in the society who will have sufficient skill in the laws to qualify them for the stations of judges. And making the proper deductions for the ordinary depravity of human nature, the number must be still smaller of those who unite the requisite integrity with the requisite knowledge.[39]

---

37 Dovere, "Trump's Policies 'Come from the Darkness.'"
38 George F. Will, "Vote Against the GOP This November," *Washington Post*, June 22, 2018, https://www.washingtonpost.com/opinions/vote-against-the-gop-this-november/2018/06/22/a6378306-7575-11e8-b4b7-308400242c2e_story.html.
39 Alexander Hamilton, "Federalist No. 78," Library of Congress, https://guides.loc.gov/federalist-papers/text-71-80#s-lg-box-wrapper-25493470.

It is clear from the above that our Founders required that the temperament and character of judges serving in the federal judiciary and on the Supreme Court include "an important integrity" (Hamilton) and "exemplary morals, great patience, calmness, coolness" (John Adams). Justice Kavanaugh, based on the spectacle of his confirmation hearing, would not appear to meet this standard articulated by our Founders. Indeed, Kavanaugh's appointment raises questions about whether other recent appointees by Republican presidents meet that standard. And if Hamilton's deference to precedence is used as a gauge, the other justices nominated by President Trump, Justices Gorsuch and Barrett, would not appear to have met this standard either.

Of Justice Kavanaugh's congressional hearing on his confirmation, journalist Dana Milbank reported that Kavanaugh cast aside all pretense of objectivity, judicial restraint, and even rational argument, succumbing to partisan fury while relying on ridicule and fantasy. Kavanaugh described the entire proceeding before the committee as a "national disgrace," "circus," "grotesque and orchestrated character assassination," and "search and destroy mission." Demonstrating the antithesis of "the great patience, calmness, coolness" that Founder John Adams required, Kavanaugh went on to personally insult the two senators who dared to question him about reports of excessive drinking.[40]

Justice Kavanaugh may be a good lawyer and a good family man, but he publicly demonstrated that he is not the kind of man our Founders expected to serve on the Supreme Court. He is not the kind of man we want if our system of government is to work as intended. Early in the confirmation proceedings, President Trump publicly mocked the conduct of the Senate in the confirmation hearing. But Trump's mockery did not make it acceptable for Supreme Court justices to behave the same way. Individuals do grow and mature on the

---

40 Dana Milbank, "Brett Kavanaugh, Disrobed," *Washington Post*, September 28, 2020, https://www.washingtonpost.com/opinions/brett-kavanaugh-disrobed/2018/09/28/0271a840-c2bf-11e8-a1f0-a4051b6ad114_story.html.

Supreme Court. Perhaps this will be true of Justice Kavanaugh and his Trump-appointed colleagues. Trump and the Republican leadership are beyond hope.

CLIMATE CHANGE

With the issue of climate change—an even more terrible threat than the pandemic—we know what's needed, and we often articulate the need. Taking action is another question. No countries are adequately facing up to the problem of climate change, and we are nearing a point where detrimental change will become irreversible. In not addressing the issue, Trump played his usual egocentric and catastrophically incompetent role. In an article entitled "Trump's Skepticism of Climate Science is Spread Across GOP," the *Washington Post* cited then representative (and soon to be senator) Marsha Blackburn of Tennessee as falsely asserting that the earth had started to cool and also (equally untruthfully) that scientists had not reached a consensus on climate change.[41]

Rick Scott, governor of Florida and also senator-elect, admitted that the seas are warmer, are rising, and will be harmful to his state but insisted that human activity had nothing to do with these changes. Sen. John Neely Kennedy, then a possible Republican candidate for governor of Louisiana, said he agreed that the earth was getting hotter but asserted that "I've seen many persuasive arguments that it's just a continuation of warming up from the Little Ice Age."[42]

At this point, as the *Post* noted, global carbon emissions were at a record high of 37.3 billion tons of carbon per year.[43] No nation was even close to meeting its voluntary carbon emission reductions level under

---

41 Matt Viser, "'Just a Lot of Alarmism': Trump's Skepticism of Climate Science Is Echoed across GOP," *Washington Post*, December 2, 2018, https://www.washingtonpost.com/politics/just-a-lot-of-alarmism-trumps-skepticism-of-climate-science-is-echoed-across-gop/2018/12/02/f6ee9ca6-f4de-11e8-bc79-68604ed88993_story.html.
42 Viser, "Alarmism."
43 Viser, "Alarmism."

the 2015 Paris Agreement. The United Nations secretary general said, "We are in trouble. We are in deep trouble with climate change."[44] And to top it off, the president announced the US withdrawal from the Paris Agreement—for personal political reasons—thereby perhaps dooming any effective response to climate change. Even though one of Biden's first acts as president in January 2021 was to restore the US to the Paris Agreement, Trump administration neglect had made the situation much worse. For example, research presented in mid-December 2021 at the "world's biggest earth science conference" showed that an enormous part of the Antarctic ice sheet could collapse in "three to five years, unleashing a river of ice that could dramatically raise sea levels."[45] This sort of change would not be reversible.

As President Trump became more and more isolated internationally and more and more irresponsible in denying climate change, he presided over a fundamental change in the Republican Party, making climate change denial a principle of its ideological mainstream. Republican politicians knew better; they knew that climate change was real. They knew that it was an existential threat to human civilization on the planet earth. The Trump administration even admitted this in arguing for a relaxation of the automobile efficiency rules instituted by the Obama administration, rules designed to prevent billions of tons of carbon from being ejected into the atmosphere. The Trump administration had the audacity to argue that, since the average temperature of the earth will reach four degrees Celsius above preindustrial norms (the point at which climate change will likely become irreversible) by the end of the century, what difference would a few billion tons of

44 Brady Dennis and Chris Mooney, "'We Are in Trouble.' Global Carbon Emissions Reached a Record High in 2018," *Washington Post*, December 5, 2020, https://www.washingtonpost.com/energy-environment/2018/12/05/we-are-trouble-global-carbon-emissions-reached-new-record-high/.
45 Sarah Kaplan, "Climate Change Has Destabilized the Earth's Poles, Putting the Rest of the Planet in Peril," *Washington Post*, December 14, 2021. https://www.washingtonpost.com/climate-environment/2021/12/14/climate-change-arctic-antarctic-poles/.

carbon make? They ignored completely the catastrophic effects on earth that likely could not be stopped before reaching plus-six Celsius above preindustrial norms—a level that could cause human extinction. Trump had more concern for the automotive gas guzzlers and short-term profits derived from them than for their drivers.

It has been argued that if the world average temperature reaches plus-3.7 Celsius, there is not enough wealth in the world to stop it. Temperatures will just keep rising until the world is too hot for human habitation. The point of no return is in sight, the time when—because of the buildup of carbon in the atmosphere—the world will continue to warm to human extinction levels no matter what we do. The great astrophysicist Stephen Hawking said, a year before he died in 2017, that in 100 years the earth would no longer be able to support human life and humanity would have to find another place to live. The children and grandchildren of these climate change deniers will curse those who made the world so difficult to live in or even uninhabitable. Is being remembered in this way what Republicans in Congress want to risk?

SUPREME COURT APPOINTMENT, 2020

In an October 2020 column, the *Washington Post*'s Michael Gerson proposed a parable: He described a magical garden, a rose garden, where a mad king gathers his most loyal supporters and sycophants and tells them that he will give each of them a golden apple, representing what they want most in life, if they will simply accept in their lives a harmless virus that will trouble few and then go away.[46] In Gerson's telling, the golden apple is then Supreme Court nominee Amy Coney Barrett.

---

46 Michael Gerson, "Confirming Barrett Is a Fairy-Tale Temptation Rife with Dark Trade-Offs," *Washington Post*, October 12, 2020, https://www.washingtonpost.com/opinions/confirming-barrett-is-a-fairy-tale-temptation-rife-with-dark-trade-offs/2020/10/12/7bc7694e-0cb6-11eb-b1e8-16b59b92b36d_story.html.

The king's most loyal and obedient subjects cannot decline such an offer. The golden apple, a devout believer in their brand of religious faith, will surely set things right for them in a world populated by so many nonbelievers. The golden apple will offer a generation-long domination of the Supreme Court for those subjects whose primary interest is a broadly conservative judiciary. Most importantly for many of the king's loyal subjects, the golden apple will be positioned to help overturn *Roe v. Wade*. All they need do to make this happen is to support the mad king—Trump, of course—whatever he does and says, ignoring the tens of thousands of deaths from the virus becoming hundreds of thousands of deaths. "But wouldn't we save many more lives by banning abortion?" his supporters reason, but the overturning of *Roe v. Wade* will not ban abortion; it will only return it to the maze of state regulation.

The king's golden apple is also a gift to subjects holding a certain conservative legal ideology—i.e., the Federalist Society—giving them a Supreme Court committed to judicial restraint (keeping the current legal structure in place despite changes in the country), contrary to the wishes of our Founders, who gave us a constitution that could move with the times. In return for the prize, the mad king simply asks that the federalists continue to support him, a king who has always despised any check on what he wants to do, a king who cares nothing for the rule of law. He continues targeting political enemies through false and fantastic changes, even threatening to jail his political opponents. This mad king will never agree to any peaceful transition from his royal palace. Thus his offer, for these subjects and others, is tainted: he will give them the power that they want only if they abandon all their principles and sense of honor.

In February 2016, Republicans had blocked the confirmation of a highly qualified candidate for the court, loudly declaiming that the nomination was much too close to the presidential election for the Senate to take a step with such long-term potential consequences.

Now, in 2020, Trump's nominee was duly considered and affirmed in October, while citizens *were already voting*. The nomination of Amy Coney Barrett—whose legal views were diametrically opposed to those of the much-beloved justice whose seat she would assume—underscored the hypocrisy of the Republican Senate minority. Such hasty action taken without any real justification beyond a corrupt grab for power invites retribution and will be long remembered—far longer than anyone's tenure in the Senate or on the Supreme Court.

Was the mad king's golden apple worth the price? Michael Gerson had this to say in closing:

> In the final, decadent days of the mad king's rule, all these groups within the Republican coalition are being made the same offer: power in exchange for the public disgracing of their ideals. The response was evident in the garden: the handshaking and air-kissing of the maskless, the faithless, and the doomed.[47]

In another article, Gerson further addressed the relationship of Trump, evangelicals, and the Republican Party:

> Trump evangelicals . . . sought to recover lost social influence through the cynical embrace of corrupt power. . . . "There has never been anyone," said Ralph Reed of the Faith and Freedom Coalition, "who has defended us and who has fought for us, who we have loved more than Donald J. Trump. No one!" . . . It is tempting to call unforgivable the equation of Christian truth with malice, cruelty, deception, bigotry, and sedition. But that statement is itself contradicted by Christian truth, which places no one beyond forgiveness and affirms that everyone needs grace in different ways."[48]

47 Gerson, "Confirming Barrett."
48 Michael Gerson, "Trump's Evangelicals Were Complicit in the Desecration of Our Democracy," *Washington Post*, January 7, 2021, https://www.washingtonpost.

In the wake of Trump's defeat, it may be that the complete and utter failure of one form of Christian engagement with the social order might provide an opportunity for the emergence of another, based on truth, morality, and compassion. Gerson suggests that a principled agenda could include:

- True concern for the weak and vulnerable, including the poor refugees who came (and come) to our shores; as Emma Lazarus put it in her poem on the Statue of Liberty, "Give me your tired, your poor, your huddled masses yearning to breathe free."
- A commitment to address and resolve the race question and improve our criminal justice system.
- A total commitment to public health here and abroad.
- An emphasis on political civility.
- A recognition of other religions also committed to love and grace for humanity.
- "An insistence on public honesty and a belief in the transforming power of unarmed truth." [49]

Gerson puts a question to us: "What would America be like if these had been the priorities of evangelical Christians over the past four years—or over the past four decades? It would mean something very different, in that world, to raise the banner 'Jesus Saves.'" [50]

com/opinions/trumps-evangelicals-were-complicit-in-the-desecration-of-our-democracy/2021/01/07/69a51402-5110-11eb-83e3-322644d82356_story.html.
49 Gerson, "Trump's Evangelicals."
50 Gerson, "Trump's Evangelicals."

CHAPTER 9

THE PANDEMIC

IN LATE DECEMBER 2019, it became clear that the coronavirus could be a threat. Already in November the US intelligence community had notified the president that the outbreak beginning in China could be dangerous. The Trump administration received formal notification of the epidemic in the first week of January 2020. The first confirmed case in the US was diagnosed in mid-January, and the first fatality from COVID-19 took place on February 29. The financial markets had already begun to crash. The 100th victim of the pandemic in the US died on March 17, and on March 20 there were 5,800 confirmed cases. Only on March 21 did the Department of Health and Human Services place its first large order for N-95 masks.

The president was briefed on the dangers of a pandemic around the time he entered the office of the presidency. As the Washington Post reported, "The warnings from US intelligence agencies increased in volume toward the end of January and into early February, said officials familiar with the reports. . . . Inside the White House, Trump's advisers struggled to get him to take the virus seriously, according to multiple officials with knowledge of meetings among those advisers and with the president."[1]

The first three months of 2020 and—most importantly—the period between January 3 and March 21 were entirely wasted; nothing was done to prepare the United States in any way for a pandemic threat. The travel ban placed on China in late January was of very little significance: it applied only to those who were not US citizens. At least 40,000 people traveled from China to the United States in the next two months.

That the pandemic occurred is not President Trump's fault, of course. But as David Frum makes clear in his article "This Is Trump's Fault," the "utter unpreparedness of the United States for a pandemic is Trump's fault."[2] Trump is culpable for the federal government's allowing maintenance contracts to lapse in 2018. The failure to store sufficient protective gear is his fault. And beyond Trump's failure to prepare, there was his failure to warn Americans of the dangers during the critical period from January 3 to March 21 and later.

When the first confirmed case of COVID-19 in the US was diagnosed in mid-January, the president, as reported by David Leonhardt in a *New York Times* article, was asked in an interview on CNBC whether he was worried about a pandemic. He replied, "No, not at all. We have it totally under control."[3] But the seriousness of the

1   Shane Harris, Greg Miller, Josh Dawsey, and Ellen Nakashima, "US Intelligence Reports from January and February Warned about a Likely Pandemic, *Washington Post*, March 20, 2020, https://www.washingtonpost.com/national-security/us-intelligence-reports-from-january-and-february-warned-about-a-likely-pandemic/2020/03/20/299d8cda-6ad5-11ea-b5f1-a5a804158597_story.html.

2   David Frum, "This Is Trump's Fault," *The Atlantic*, April 7, 2020, https://www.theatlantic.com/ideas/archive/2020/04/americans-are-paying-the-price-for-trumps-failures/609532/.

3   David Leonhardt, "A Complete List of Trump's Attempts to Play Down Coronavirus," *New York Times*, March 15, 2020, https://www.nytimes.com/2020/03/15/opinion/trump-coronavirus.html. Other direct quotations from Trump in these paragraphs are documented in this article unless otherwise indicated.

epidemic was becoming clearer; there were many warnings of the danger of the virus by prominent experts in January, as Frum reported. Trump ignored these and other warnings. On January 24, he tweeted, "It will all work out well." On January 30, he said in a speech in Michigan, "We have it very well under control. We have a little problem in this country at this moment—five—and those people are all recuperating successfully." That same day the World Health Organization declared the coronavirus "a public health emergency of international concern."

In early February, when the president was asked by Sean Hannity on Fox News about the virus, he replied, "Well, we pretty much shot it down coming from China [referring to the previous ban on travel from China to the US by non–US citizens]. We have a tremendous relationship with China, which is a very positive thing." By this time there were nearly 15,000 cases worldwide, a doubling over the previous three days. On February 5 the CDC began shipping test kits to laboratories—kits that had a technical flaw. The Trump administration did little. To be sure, creating a new virus test is not easy, although other countries were working hard to develop effective test equipment. The World Health Organization offered the US test equipment that was functional, but the administration turned it down. As a result, the United States fell behind South Korea, Singapore, and China in fighting the epidemic. A Harvard epidemiologist put it this way: "We just twiddled our thumbs as the coronavirus waltzed in."[4]

The president kept telling the American people that the virus would go away, that warm weather would stop it. He told a campaign rally on February 10, "Looks like by April, you know, in theory when it gets a little warmer, it miraculously goes away." On February 19 he told a Phoenix television station, "I think the numbers are going to get progressively better as we go along." A few days later he said the virus

---

4   Leonhardt, "A Complete List."

was "very much under control . . . we had 12 at one point. And now they've gotten very much better. Many of them are fully recovered." The message from the president to the American people was clear: the coronavirus is a small problem getting better. The truth was that the US didn't know how bad the problem had become; we had done very little testing. But many scientists had data suggesting it was getting worse rapidly.

The president seemed uninterested in the pandemic until the stock market began to crash. He did care about that. He began blaming others. He criticized the media, particularly CNN and MSNBC, for "panicking markets." He said at one of his rallies, falsely, that "the Democrat policy of open borders" had brought the virus into the country. The virus turned out to have come not from China and not from Mexico, but from Europe.

He lashed out at "do-nothing Democrat comrades." He tweeted about "Cryin' Chuck Schumer" mocking him for arguing that the president should be more aggressive in fighting the virus. At a rally on February 28 in South Carolina, the president denounced the Democrats by politicizing the coronavirus pandemic, calling it "their new hoax."[5]

On multiple occasions, the president claimed that the coronavirus was less serious than the flu. "We're talking about a much smaller range of deaths than the flu." He said on March 2, "It's very mild."[6] He told Fox News on March 4, "Compared to some countries, we're talking about very small numbers in this—in our country, very, very small because of what I did with the borders."[7] On March 7, "I'm not concerned at all." On March 10, "It will go away, just stay calm. It will

5   Donald Trump, "Charleston, South Carolina, Rally Transcript—February 28, 2020," *Rev*, February 28, 2020, https://www.rev.com/blog/transcripts/donald-trump-charleston-south-carolina-rally-transcript-february-28-2020.

6   Leonhardt, "A Complete List."

7   "Sean Hannity Interviews Donald Trump via Telephone," Factbase, March 4, 2020, https://factba.se/transcript/donald-trump-interview-sean-hannity-fox-telephone-march-4-2020.

go away."[8] At this time, in the first half of March, the public began to understand. Secretary of Health and Human Services Alex Azar told ABC, "There is no testing kit shortage, nor has there ever been." While touring the CDC, the president said on TV news channels, "Anybody that wants a test can get a test." On the same newscast he commented extraneously about his impeachment and his having as much knowledge as any scientist. On March 16, the president finally called for social distancing orders to be issued in the United States.

At the beginning of the pandemic, the United States and South Korea experienced a similar impact. Trump squandered nearly two months belittling the significance of the crisis. He failed to put the government to work assembling personal protective equipment for hospital workers; failed to arrange for the manufacture of more ventilators; and failed to roll out a mass testing program—something that only the federal government can do. Hence, just a few weeks later, the United States was in a much worse place than South Korea. The president took his first real action in calling for social distancing guidelines on March 16 and in making the first equipment purchase on March 21. By contrast, former vice president and now president Joe Biden, on January 29 in an op-ed article, had sounded the alarm about a coming dangerous coronavirus pandemic and called for strong responsive measures.

The United States soon fell far behind South Korea in its response to the pandemic. The per capita death rate from COVID-19 in early April was 12 or 13 times higher in the US than in South Korea, whereas the rates had been roughly the same in early March 2020. After a series of administrative failures and the president's essentially ignoring and substantially playing down the danger of the pandemic to focus on his own personal political interests, there were 22,000 deaths in the US from COVID-19 by April 12, far more than there might have been had the administration responded in a timely fashion.

---

8   Leonhardt, "A Complete List."

A few days later, there were more than 30,000 fatalities. Now, of course, there are hundreds of thousands more deaths than if the US had gotten this right in 2020. As of this writing, in May of 2022, COVID-19 deaths in the US have reached one million.[9]

In September 2019, the World Health Organization Global Preparedness Monitoring Board had issued a warning of the lack of preparedness worldwide should there be a lethal respiratory virus pandemic, as follows:

> A rapidly spreading pandemic due to a lethal respiratory pathogen (whether naturally emergent or accidentally or deliberately released) poses additional preparedness requirements. Donors and multilateral institutions must ensure adequate investment in developing innovative vaccines and therapeutics, surge manufacturing capacity, broad spectrum antivirals, and appropriate non-pharmaceutical interventions.[10]

Three months later, on January 3, the United States received formal notification of the coronavirus epidemic. As said, Trump took his first real action on March 16. At a White House press briefing on March 13, the president had said about the chaos descending on the United States because of the coronavirus threat, "I don't take responsibility at all." This after misleading Americans about the severity of the virus and confusing the public about a federal response for months.

Scientific experts in the field and Democratic Party leaders who addressed the subject publicly called for immediate strong actions in response to so large a threat. In contrast, the president dismissed the danger, asserting that the epidemic would "disappear like magic."

---

9   Sergio Peçanha and Yan Wu, "One Million of Us," *Washington Post*, May 18, 2022, https://www.washingtonpost.com/opinions/interactive/2022/how-many-people-died-covid-united-states-1-million-graphic/.

10 "A World at Risk: Annual Report on Global Preparedness for Health Emergencies," Global Preparedness Monitoring Board, World Health Organization, September 2020, https://apps.who.int/gpmb/assets/annual_report/GPMB_annualreport_2019.pdf.

Weeks before the president took action, it was clear that the United States was seriously threatened by a deadly pathogen that would, if not properly checked, destroy the health, economy, and lives of Americans. For the historical record, journalists Frum and Leonhardt have documented most of the sad story of how Trump drove America into a dark hole from which, in subsequent months, he was unwilling and ultimately unable to extricate the country. All he seemed able and willing to do was to lie.

The president pressed for an early end to the quarantine against the coronavirus, demanding a prompt reopening of the economy of the United States after a shutdown of a few weeks to try to slow down the pandemic. Against all scientific advice, he first advocated for an Easter opening but then settled for a May 1 reopening. The medical community and its scientists urged a delayed reopening—the end of May or perhaps even the middle of June. Quarantining and social distancing were the best weapons then available against the virus. (Somewhat later, masks became seen as the most important weapon, and finally, at the end of the year, vaccines.) But in the spring of 2020, it was quarantining and social distancing—separations to inhibit spread were the best weapons. The president asserted he wanted to reopen to save the economy, but many believed it was his reelection in November that he wanted to save. Nevertheless, his science advisers agreed to a strict set of procedures that, if followed by a state, would help to avoid a second wave of the pandemic should that state reopen its economy around May 1.

As soon as reopening procedures were announced, the president took to his favorite means of communication—Twitter—to encourage states to throw caution to the winds. He tweeted, "LIBERATE MINNESOTA, LIBERATE MICHIGAN, LIBERATE VIRGINIA!"[11] The tweets targeted Democratic states, but the real targets were states with Republican Trump-leaning politicians in the

---

11 Donald Trump (@realDonaldTrump), Twitter, April 17, 2020.

governor's office. This misguided bravado in flaunting CDC guidance was acted on by some state legislatures. The Tea Party and other right-wing allies of the president were led to equate medical protective measures such as social distancing and quarantining with tyranny. Their doing so was dangerous foolishness, and as the president's tweets had urged, some states began to open, dismissing scientific advice. In a few weeks, as expected, there was a devastating rise in the number of COVID-19 cases, reversing a promising slowdown.

In the wake of a politicized response to the pandemic before many of the actual reopenings, Michael Gerson assessed these events in this way:

> The Trump captivity of the GOP has reached its sad, inevitable destination: a failed presidency defended by a cowed party. As President Trump's malignant narcissism and incompetence have been fully revealed—and can be effectively measured by the level of needless death from COVID-19— his approval among Republicans has remained strong. Across a continent filled with elected Republicans, only a few have taken a stand for sanity and effective governance.[12]

What is said by the president on his bully pulpit in the White House is always taken seriously by a sizable portion of the American people, no matter how confused and irrational and self-serving it might be. For weeks President Trump had touted the use of the antimalarial drugs chloroquine and hydroxychloroquine as "game changers" for promptly curing COVID-19.[13] Their efficacy had been under consideration in some laboratories until the Food and Drug Administration,

---

12 Michael Gerson, "The GOP Has Reached Its Sad, Inevitable Destination," *Washington Post*, April 23, 2020, https://www.washingtonpost.com/opinions/reforming-the-gop-begins-by-voting-democratic-in-november/2020/04/23/24d47534-8582-11ea-878a-86477a724bdb_story.html.

13 Ellen Gabler and Michael H. Keller, "Prescriptions Surged as Trump Praised Drugs in Coronavirus Fight," *New York Times*, April 25, 2020, https://www.nytimes.com/2020/04/25/us/coronavirus-trump-chloroquine-hydroxychloroquine.html.

in late April, published the results of a study indicating that the use of these drugs could promote dangerous, irregular heart rhythms and possible death. Cases of serious poisoning and death from using these drugs had been reported. To promote the use of the two antimalarial drugs to treat COVID-19, President Trump said, "I think that it could be something incredible," adding that the two drugs had shown "very, very encouraging results." [14]

There had been little study of these drugs being used for this purpose, but even so, first-time prescriptions for them poured into retail pharmacies around the country at 45 times the usual rate per average weekday, according to an analysis by the *New York Times*.[15] Even after the FDA report on these drugs showing they had no effect on reducing the impact of COVID-19 on patients but instead created very serious risks for COVID-19 patients who took them, the drugs were being prescribed and purchased at pharmacies at more than six times the normal rate. With leadership like this, was there any doubt why the United States' efforts against the coronavirus were among the world's least effective? The US had 4 percent of the world's population and 32 percent of its COVID-19 cases.

Perhaps President Trump's most dangerous idea for dealing with the coronavirus was offered on April 24, when the president promoted the use of disinfectants internally in the human body to cure the virus-caused disease. He recommended that disinfectants like Lysol, Clorox, or isopropyl alcohol (rubbing alcohol) be injected like a tonic into the human body—maybe this would do the trick. As reported in the *New York Times*, the president said, "I see the disinfectant where it knocks it out in a minute" [on a tabletop-like surface]. "One minute—and is there a way we can do something like that by injection inside, or almost a cleaning? Because, you see, it gets in the lungs, so it would be interesting to check that." [16]

---

14 Gabler and Keller, "Prescriptions Surged."
15 Gabler and Keller, "Prescriptions Surged."
16 William J. Broad and Dan Levin, "Trump Muses about Light as Remedy, but Also

Immediately there was an outcry in medical and (some) political communities, affirming what every ten-year-old child knows—that injecting such products as Lysol, Clorox, or isopropyl alcohol into the human body would cause an immediate severe reaction and possible death. An FDA commissioner said, "I certainly wouldn't recommend the internal ingestion of a disinfectant."[17] The Environmental Protection Agency advised people never to "ingest disinfectant products."[18] Companies that make such disinfectants publicly pleaded with Americans to never ingest or inject their products.

Again from the *New York Times* report: "In Maryland, so many calls flooded a health hotline with questions that the state's Emergency Management Agency had to issue a warning that 'under no circumstances' should any disinfectant be taken to treat the coronavirus." The alarm was sounded by officials everywhere across the country. The *Times* quoted the medical director of the New Jersey Poison Information and Education System in an interview, writing, "Injecting bleach or highly concentrated rubbing alcohol 'causes massive organ damage and the blood cells in the body to basically burst. It can definitely be a fatal event.'"[19] If it wasn't clear before, this incident should have convinced everyone in the country of the positive danger of Trump's guidance regarding staying healthy during the pandemic. Instead of offering effective leadership, the president was only making the crisis worse.

Disinfectant, Which is Dangerous," *New York Times,* April 24, 2020, https://www.nytimes.com/2020/04/24/health/sunlight-coronavirus-trump.html.

17 Anderson Cooper (@AC360), Twitter, April 23, 2020, https://twitter.com/ac360/status/1253498117057634304?lang=en.

18 "EPA Provides Critical Information to the American Public about Safe Disinfectant Use," Environmental Protection Agency, April 23, 2020, https://www.epa.gov/newsreleases/epa-provides-critical-information-american-public-about-safe-disinfectant-use#:~:text=Do%.

19 Katie Rogers, Christine Hauser, Alan Yuhas, and Maggie Haberman, "Trump's Suggestion That Disinfectants Could Be Used to Treat Coronavirus Prompts Aggressive Pushback," *New York Times,* April 24, 2020, https://www.nytimes.com/2020/04/24/us/politics/trump-inject-disinfectant-bleach-coronavirus.html.

The evening White House briefing on the pandemic had been originally established by the White House Coronavirus Task Force to communicate facts about the virus to the American people. The speakers were to include world-renowned scientists like Anthony Fauci. But when President Trump saw how popular these briefings were with the public, he rudely pushed the scientists aside and conducted the briefings himself. He converted what were to have been scientific briefings, designed to educate the public about the virus, into Trump political rallies disguised as briefings. In this way, the president promoted his foolish and dangerous ideas as advice to Americans seeking to protect themselves during the pandemic. Doubtless thousands of deaths have taken place that wouldn't have if the White House leadership had been in sound hands.

Michelle Goldberg, in her *New York Times* reporting, wrote:

> Over the last three and a half years, Americans have had to accustom themselves to a relentless, numbing barrage of lies from the federal government. In one sector after another, we've seen experts systematically purged and replaced with toadying apparatchiks. The few professionals who've kept their jobs have often had to engage in degrading acts of public obeisance more common to autocracies. Public policy has zigzagged to presidential whim. Empirical reality has been subsumed to Trump's cult of personality. America was once the technological envy of the world. Now doctors have to warn the public that, contrary to the president's musing in the briefing room, it is neither safe nor effective to inject disinfectant."[20]

In his *New Yorker* article "The Plague Year," Lawrence Wright wrote much about US leadership, noting that one of the critical elements in

---

20 Michelle Goldberg, "Coronavirus and the Price of Trump's Delusions," *New York Times*, April 25, 2020, https://www.nytimes.com/2020/04/25/opinion/sunday/trump-coronavirus.html?searchResultPosition=1.

dealing with a pandemic is good leadership. He wrote, "Nations and states that have done relatively well during this crisis have been led by strong, compassionate, decisive leaders who speak candidly with their constituents."[21] In the US, on a fateful day in March 2020, President Trump explicitly abandoned any effort to adopt a rational response to the pandemic. As Wright concludes:

> Trump, by his words and his example, became not a leader but a saboteur. He subverted his health agencies by installing political operatives who meddled with the science and suppressed the truth. His crowded, unmasked political rallies were reckless acts of effrontery. In his Tulsa speech, he said that he'd asked his health officials to "slow the testing down"—impeding data collection just to make his administration look better.[22]

That series of decisions ended any possibility of an effective or rational policy on the pandemic in the remaining months of the Trump administration. It was deeply contrary to the interests of the American people and represented a violation of the essential meaning of the presidential oath of office.

---

21 Lawrence Wright, "The Plague Year," *New Yorker*, January 4, 2021, https://www. newyorker.com/magazine/2021/01/04/the-plague-year.
22 Wright, "The Plague Year."

CHAPTER 10

OWNING THE BOTTOM

ON NOVEMBER 3, 2020, Joe Biden, the nominee of the Democratic Party, decisively won the election for president of the United States, along with his running mate for vice president, Kamala Harris. Biden won the popular vote by more than seven million votes and the Electoral College by a vote of 306 to 232. There is no doubt about the result of this election. It was more conclusive than the presidential election in 2016. Biden was indisputably the choice of the American people.

Yet Trump contested the election. During the campaign he had always declined to agree to the peaceful transfer of power should he lose the election, although peaceful transfer of power is essential to democracy. He defined a fair election as an election in which he was the winner. Any other result would be fraudulent, he said. During the early hours of the vote counting he tweeted to "Stop the counting! Stop the counting!" in states where he was leading and to "Keep counting!" in Arizona, where he was behind.

The result? Biden's clear victory in a free and fair election as envisaged by the framers of the Constitution. On November 11, the Department of Homeland Security, charged with protecting the integrity of the election, released the following statement:

The November 3 election was the most secure in American history. Right now, across the country, election officials are reviewing and double-checking the entire election process prior to finalizing the result. When states have close elections, many will recount ballots. All of the states with close results in the 2020 presidential race have paper records of each vote, allowing the ability to go back and count each ballot if necessary. This is an added benefit for security and resilience. This process allows for the identification and correction of any mistakes or errors. There is no evidence that any voting system deleted or lost votes, changed votes, or was in any way compromised.[1]

It didn't take long for many Americans to understand that Trump was trying to engineer a coup to illegally overturn his loss. The *Washington Post* said so on November 13:

President Trump is attempting to overturn the lawful results of a free election by spreading lies and suborning local officials to abet the conspiracy.[2]

Michael Gerson agreed, calling Republican leaders' muted or nonexistent protests to Trump's actions "a massive failure of character—a nationwide blackout of integrity—among elected Republicans."[3]

1 "Joint Statement from Elections Infrastructure Government Coordinating Council & the Election Infrastructure Sector Coordinating Executive Committees," Cybersecurity & Infrastructure Security Agency (CISA), November 12, 2020, https://www.cisa.gov/news/2020/11/12/joint-statement-elections-infrastructure-government-coordinating-council-election.

2 "Some Local Officials Are Resisting Trump's Big Lie. Sadly, GOP Senators Aren't as Principled," editorial, *Washington Post*, November 12, 2020, https://www.washingtonpost.com/opinions/some-local-officials-are-resisting-trumps-big-lie-sadly-gop-senators-arent-as-principled/2020/11/12/a229df7e-2532-11eb-a688-5298ad5d580a_story.html.

3 Michael Gerson, "This Is a Massive Failure of Character among Republicans— with Evangelicals Out in Front," *Washington Post*, November 12, 2020, https://www.washingtonpost.com/opinions/this-is-a-massive-failure-of-character-among-

As noted above, Joe Biden and Kamala Harris decisively won the US presidential and vice presidential election on November 3, 2020. Having forewarned us that he would not accept any election of which he was not the winner, Trump contested the results, even in the face of his own Department of Homeland Security declaring the election to have been "the most secure in American history." Despite the overwhelming evidence supporting Biden's victory, and without producing any evidence himself, Trump continued to insist that he had won the election and that the Democrats had stolen it from him.

A year and a half later, he continues to reach out to his committed followers, largely through the extremist TV channel Newsmax and social media, with his most ardent supporters increasingly using the Parler social media platform to spew a cascade of fantastical lies and conspiracy theories, reminiscent of lies propounded by the far right in Germany after its defeat in World War I. Through promotion of the so-called "stab in the back" theory that Germany had been winning the war until traitorous "communists and Jews" in the government surrendered to the other side, a permanent and violent opposition to the government was established and subsequently exploited by Hitler to support his Third Reich. Given his current TV campaign of lies, Trump could create something similar in America, setting up a potential for the destruction of democracy in 2024.

After the election, Trump abandoned governing, choosing instead to spend his time agitating for the overturning of the election results. Trump carried on in this way while the American people—whose president he still was until January 20, 2021—were suffering severely from the escalating pandemic. While millions became sick and thousands died, Trump paid no attention to this crisis and his government did nothing to ameliorate it. In normal times this neglect alone would be grounds for impeachment.

republicans--with-evangelicals-out-in-front/2020/11/12/c7a05396-251e-11eb-8672-c281c7a2c96e_story.html.

Trump's repetitive insistence that the election had been stolen also amounted to incitement to violence. Long ago, Justice Oliver Wendell Holmes of the Supreme Court said in a famous opinion that the protection of free speech found in the First Amendment to the Constitution did not extend to shouting "Fire!" in a crowded theater. Trump was shouting "Fire!"—and the theater was very crowded.

Does such behavior make Trump a modern-day Don Quixote, the Man of La Mancha, causing chaos and tilting at windmills to cover what he sees as an ignominious and embarrassing exit from the government? Or is he the Manchurian candidate, aiming at the destruction of American life and democracy while establishing himself as dictator in alliance with Vladimir Putin of Russia? A quixotic fantasy or a coup plot? *Newsweek* correspondent Masha Gessen, in David Rohde's *New Yorker* article published in the second week of November 2020, weighed in on the question:

> Trump is trying to achieve an "autocratic breakthrough" and to discredit the election results that would end his rule. His chances of succeeding appear low, but it is important to state that the president of the United States is attempting to carry out a coup.[4]

Gessen, a journalist in Russia for many years and once an acquaintance of Putin, would know.

What might Trump's chances be in 2024, after four years of inciting his base? Rohde reported that "a new Politico/Morning Consult survey finds [that] 70 percent of Republicans do not think that the 2020 election was 'free and fair.'" He added that false voter-fraud claims were gaining enormous audiences on Facebook, energizing and enraging the president's supporters.[5]

---

4   David Rohde, "William Barr Can Stop Trump's Attempted Coup," *New Yorker*, November 11, 2020, https://www.newyorker.com/news/daily-comment/william-barr-can-stop-donald-trumps-attempted-coup.
5   Rohde, "Trump's Attempted Coup."

The president refused to allow Biden's presidential transition team to begin working with the incumbent government. He fired his defense secretary—the official who oversees the nuclear arsenal—and replaced much of the top echelon at Defense, all of whom were succeeded by apparent sycophants. The directors of the CIA and FBI appeared to be next on the to-be-fired list. Trump moved to give himself a large degree of control over the important national security part of the government, filling it largely with likely incompetent stooges.

Rohde also commented that Senate Majority Leader Mitch McConnell "in a speech on the Senate floor defended the president's right to challenge the election results."[6] Several prominent Republicans also said that the president was within his rights to do so. A week and a half after the election, only four Senate Republicans had called Biden to congratulate him as president-elect, and only four or five others had called for Trump to at least allow the transition process to begin so that Biden could receive necessary intelligence information. Statements by senators in response to the question, "Have you congratulated Mr. Biden?" suggested either that "maybe Biden didn't really win" or that "maybe there is nothing to congratulate him for." These answers were of a sort one would expect in Hungary or Turkey but not in America. The remaining more than 40 Republican senators had not publicly recognized Biden as the president-elect. They were joined by Vladimir Putin. As Susan Glasser noted in the *New Yorker,* "When Gov. Mike DeWine, Republican of Ohio, said on CNN, 'Joe Biden is the president-elect,' it was treated as breaking news. Merely acknowledging basic math, it seems, is now considered an act of political courage."[7] Thus, Republican leaders responded to Trump's trashing this most sacred rite of democracy, the peaceful passage of

---

6   Rohde, "Trump's Attempted Coup."
7   Susan B. Glasser, "Is This a Coup, or Just Another Trump Con?" *New Yorker,* November 13, 2020, https://www.newyorker.com/news/letter-from-trumps-washington/is-this-a-coup-or-just-another-trump-con/.

power, just as they have "to virtually all of Trump's norm-shattering behavior for the last four years: by enabling it."[8]

When Rohde concluded near the end of his article that "there is no excuse for allowing a sitting president to flirt with authoritarianism,"[9] he illuminated the problem with the Republican Party itself. It appears to have become an anti-democratic party interested only in power, with a minority that is pro-democracy—a minority in every situation like this one. In the interest of democracy and as a better reflection of political reality, would it be better to split the party in two—one authoritarian, the other conservative democratic?

Continuing further with the question of whether Trump would seek a coup in 2024, Fareed Zakaria, in the November 12 *Washington Post*, after referring to the so-called "stab in the back" myth in Germany in 1920, quoted Newt Gingrich as follows: "I think [Biden] would have to do a lot to convince Republicans that this is anything except a left-wing power grab financed by people like George Soros. . . . It's very hard to understand how we're going to work together."

Zakaria further noted:

> A political system is not simply a collection of laws and rules. It is also an accumulation of norms and behavior. When Senate Majority Leader Mitch McConnell (R-KY) says Trump is "100 percent within his rights" to behave as he is, he is missing this crucial distinction. . . . Democracy is above all about the peaceful transfer of power. Trump is shredding those norms for his own egotistical needs. But his actions today will have a large and lasting effect on this country's politics for decades, creating a cancer that will metastasize in gruesome ways.[10]

---

8   Glasser, "Is This a Coup?"
9   Rohde, "Trump's Attempted Coup."
10 Fareed Zakaria, "Trump's Contempt for Democratic Norms Could Haunt Us for Years," *Washington Post*, November 12, 2020, https://www.washingtonpost.com/opinions/trumps-contempt-for-democratic-norms-could-haunt-us-for-years/2020/11/12/0d65b0ba-252e-11eb-8672-c281c7a2c96e_story.html.

Michael Gerson concurred and elaborated on the harmful role of the Republican Party in its reaction to Trump's norm-shattering and norm-shaping response to the election.

> What America is experiencing is a massive failure of character—a nationwide blackout of integrity—among elected Republicans. From the president, a graceless and deceptive insistence on victory after a loss that was not even close. From congressional Republicans, a broad willingness to conspire in President Trump's lies and to slander the electoral system without consideration of the public good. Only a few have stood up against Republican peer pressure of contempt for the constitutional order.[11]

The threat to democracy was discussed by the *Washington Post* in its lead editorial on November 13. The editors wrote:

> President Trump is attempting to overturn the lawful results of a free election by spreading lies and suborning local officials to abet the conspiracy. He is not likely to succeed, but the toxic effect on US democracy will not soon dissipate. Republicans such as Senate Majority Leader Mitch McConnell (KY) who think they can pander to Mr. Trump's lies with no harmful effect are complicit in the damage.[12]

On the assumption that Trump was attempting a coup, there were three possible routes that attempt might have taken. The first would have been to persuade Republican-dominated state legislatures to override the results of their state elections and introduce Republican slates of electors to send to Congress when the voters of each state cast their ballots for certification by the election commission. Few if any state legislatures were likely to do this, as it would be a blatantly illegal

---

11 Michael Gerson, "This Is a Massive Failure."
12 "Some Local Officials," *Washington Post*.

act, frustrating the will of the people. State courts, federal courts, and—should it come to that—ultimately the Supreme Court would not have allowed it.

Second, there could have been a direct appeal to the US Supreme Court alleging fraud, which could have been said to justify disallowing the entire election. Such a legal appeal appeared to be a nonstarter.

Third, with his decimation of top defense and intelligence officials and installation of presidential stooges, Trump could have ordered the army to occupy the cities and declare the election disallowed because of some fabricated domestic emergency. Or he could have ordered the military to do something like invade Iran with special forces to destroy its nuclear installations, claiming there was a clear and present danger to the national security, possibly sparking a war in the process. The response of our military almost certainly would have been, "We were trained and educated not to obey illegal orders. Our loyalty is to the Constitution, not to Donald Trump."

Thus, whereas Trump may have desired to be a Manchurian candidate desirous of carrying out a coup and abolishing our freedoms and democratic way of life, his chances of success were small in 2020. 2024 could be a different matter. Quite possibly Trump will try over the coming years to follow Hitler's game plan and influence his base to reelect him and then support him in establishing some sort of neo-fascist dictatorship. Of course, Trump must first somehow get past two significant criminal actions pending against him in New York State as well as handling his hundreds of millions of dollars in debt. If Senate Republicans prevent the Biden administration from accomplishing anything that would make things better for our country, congressional stagnation could set the stage. Such concerns are a subject that media and analysts must follow closely in the run-up to 2024. Sunshine is the cure for evil and corruption.

A closer look at Trump's post-election actions can inform our continued vigilance going forward. As soon as Joe Biden's decisive victory was called by the networks and recognized by most Americans,

defeated candidate Donald Trump began an all-out attempt to discredit and illegally reverse the decision the American people had made
through their democratic election. He said repeatedly that the election had been rigged against him. He filled the TV airways with lies
and conspiracy theories. Of the first 40 lawsuits he filed to disqualify
large numbers of Biden votes based on claims of fraud or other irregularities (for which he offered no evidence), 39 were peremptorily,
and sometimes angrily, thrown out by the courts. Ultimately, it was
in the range of 50, all with this outcome. A sample fake claim of
voter fraud, wrapped tight in a loony conspiracy theory, was his charge
that the company that serviced most of the voting machines around
the country had used software developed for the former dictator of
Venezuela, Hugo Chávez, who had died nearly a decade earlier.

As these suits failed, Trump resorted to pressuring Republican-
controlled state legislatures in states won by Biden to overthrow the
voice of the people by declaring the states for Trump—in other words,
he attempted a coup d'état in each state. Meanwhile, with a few exceptions, Republican members of the House and Senate were either
supporting these efforts or remaining silent and not opposing them. A
president who had been decisively defeated in his attempt for reelection was attempting to overturn the votes of 81 million Americans, the
largest total for any candidate in history. While Republican claims of
Democrat voter fraud, as we have seen, go back many decades, Trump's
efforts amount to the most serious attack on America's democratic
principles ever attempted by a sitting president. Such actions—potentially beneficial to our enemies, like Russia—set a troubling precedent.
As reported in the *Washington Post*:

> For the past three weeks [since the November 2020 election],
> as the president refused to concede the election, the federal
> government, the Trump campaign legal team, and whole
> swaths of the Republican Party have worked in tandem to
> interfere with the peaceful transfer of power. . . . By lodging

baseless claims of voter fraud and embracing—or declining to reject—outlandish conspiracy theories about the process, Trump and his allies have normalized the kind of post-election assault on institutions typically seen in less-developed democracies, according to historians, former administration officials, and lawmakers and diplomats across the political spectrum. Lingering damage to the US electoral system could be among the most consequential legacies of the Trump presidency.[13]

Given the complicity of Republicans in the House and Senate, it is difficult to see why no ethics violations were levied.

Perhaps a few of the appalling statements made by Republican quislings with respect to this attack on American democracy are worth including here. On November 10, after Trump's tactic of undermining the election through baseless charges of fraud became clear, Senate Majority Leader Mitch McConnell said there was "no reason for alarm,"[14] and the newly elected chairman of the Republican Senate Policy Committee, Sen. Roy Blunt (R-MO), said, "You know the president wasn't defeated by huge numbers; in fact, he may not have been defeated at all."[15] "There's nothing to congratulate him about," Republican senator Ron Johnson of Wisconsin told reporters a week after the election, when asked if he had congratulated Biden on his

---

13 Toluse Olorunnipa, Michelle Ye Hee Lee, and Rosalind S. Helderman, "Trump's Assault on the Election Could Leave a Lasting Mark on American Democracy," *Washington Post*, November 24, 2020, https://www.washingtonpost.com/politics/trump-election-democracy/2020/11/24/e78b8194-2e6a-11eb-bae0-50bb17126614_story.html.

14 Lisa Mascaro, "McConnell Says Electoral College Will Determine President," *Boston Globe*, November 10, 2020, https://www.bostonglobe.com/2020/11/10/nation/mcconnell-says-electoral-college-will-determine-president.

15 Lisa Mascaro, "Sen. Roy Blunt: Trump 'May Not Have Been Defeated' in Election," KMOV4, November 11, 2020, https://www.kmov.com/news/sen-roy-blunt-trump-may-not-have-been-defeated-in-election/article_e57d4691-2dc9-55f0-8e3e-e3b22e074ea4.html.

win.[16] Yet "Biden won the popular vote by six million votes [eventually seven million votes] and the Electoral College by 306–232, the same margin Trump won in 2016, which he described as a 'landslide.'"[17]

US House Minority Leader Kevin McCarthy said, "President Trump won this election. . . . So everyone who's listening, do not be quiet about this. We cannot let this happen before our very eyes."[18] McCarthy subsequently suggested that it doesn't matter what is true, only what Republicans can make Republicans believe is true. When he was asked by Jonathan Martin of the *New York Times* as to Biden's prospects of bringing the country together, McCarthy said, "It depends how it turns out. If you have 70 percent of Republicans who thought he cheated, he's still going to have a hard time."[19]

Only four or five Republicans openly opposed President Trump's antics. Sen. Lisa Murkowski (R-AL) said in part,

> President Trump has had the opportunity to litigate his claims, and the courts thus far have found them without merit. A pressure campaign on state legislators to influence the electoral outcome is not only unprecedented but inconsistent with our democratic process.[20]

16 Ariana Figueroa, "Wisconsin Republicans in Congress Chime In on Trump Claims of a Stolen Election," *Wisconsin Examiner,* November 12, 2020, https://wisconsinexaminer.com/2020/11/12/wisconsin-republicans-in-congress-chime-in-on-trump-claims-of-a-stolen-election/.

17 Kate Sullivan, "Biden's Margin of Victory over Trump Surpasses 6 Million Votes," CNN, November 21, 2020, https://www.cnn.com/2020/11/20/politics/biden-6-million-votes/index.html; Mike Dennison, "Daines, Gianforte Still Not Acknowledging Biden's Sweeping Victory," *Missoula (MT) Current,* December 2, 2020, https://missoulacurrent.com/government/2020/12/daines-gianforte-biden/.

18 Karen Tumulty, "Republican Leaders Swore an Oath to Defend the Constitution. That Means Telling Trump It's Over," *Washington Post,* November 20, 2020, https://www.washingtonpost.com/opinions/2020/11/20/republicans-must-tell-trump-its-over/.

19 Jonathan Martin, "Kevin McCarthy, the House Minority Leader, Doesn't Think Trump Is Going Away," *New York Times,* November 18, 2020, https://www.nytimes.com/2020/11/18/us/politics/kevin-mccarthy-trump.html.

20 Tess Williams, "Murkowski Calls for Presidential Transition to Begin, Saying Trump's Attempts to Influence Electoral Results Are 'Unprecedented,'" *Anchorage (AK) Daily News,* November 22, 2020, https://www.adn.com/politics/2020/11/22/

And on November 19, Senator Romney called Trump's pressure campaign an attempt to

> subvert the will of the people. Having failed to make even a plausible case of widespread fraud or conspiracy before any court of law, the president has now resorted to overt pressure on state and local officials to subvert the will of the people and overturn the election. It is difficult to imagine a worse, more undemocratic action by a sitting American president.[21]

There were strong words from the United States Congress on Trump's efforts to overthrow the people's electoral decision. House Majority Leader Steny Hoyer said, "I think this borders on treason. He is undermining the very essence of democracy, which is: you go to the poll, you vote, and the people decide. There is no doubt that the people decided."[22] The *Washington Post* lamented:

> Day by day, President Trump's efforts to overturn the results of a free and fair election grow more brazen. Day by day, Senate Majority Leader Mitch McConnell (R-KY) and other so-called leaders of the Republican Party grow more complicit in this banana-republic-style assault on democracy.[23]

---

murkowski-calls-for-presidential-transition-to-begin-saying-trumps-attempts-to-influence-electoral-results-are-unprecedented/.

21 Burgess Everett, "Sasse, Romney Pan Trump Campaign's Tactics in Contesting Election," *Politico*, November 19, 2020, https://www.politico.com/news/2020/11/19/ben-sasse-trump-fraud-allegations-438574.

22 Philip Rucker, Amy Gardner, and Josh Dawsey, "Trump Uses Power of Presidency to Try to Overturn the Election and Stay in Office," *Washington Post*, November 19, 2020, https://www.washingtonpost.com/politics/trump-uses-power-of-presidency-to-try-to-overturn-the-election-and-stay-in-office/2020/11/19/bc89caa6-2a9f-11eb-8fa2-06e7cbb145c0_story.html.

23 "Trump Is Past Exploring Legal Options. He's Using Lies and Chicanery to Try to Undo His Defeat," editorial, *Washington Post*, November 19, 2020, https://www.washingtonpost.com/opinions/trump-is-past-exploring-legal-options-hes-using-lies-and-chicanery-to-try-to-undo-his-defeat/2020/11/19/3199e8ec-2aa7-11eb-9b14-ad872157ebc9_story.html.

The coup attempt and subsequent denial of what was a direct, un-principled attack on the Constitution and the American democratic system would seem fantastical, even comical, were it not so serious. Fortunately, the American people have stood firm, as did some of their (mostly Democratic) representatives in Congress and both Republican and Democratic representatives at the state and local levels. These principled men and women helped to save our democracy from the worst threat it has ever faced. Their acts of civic heroism did not extend to the Republican leadership in the US House and Senate, with a few highly important exceptions, including Senators Romney, Collins, Murkowski, and Sasse. The majority of Senate and House Republicans were either a vocal or silent part of the Trump coup conspiracy.

During the extended Thanksgiving holiday of 2020, many Americans began to realize the severity of the threat and acted on that realization. What follows is a partial account of some who, in carrying out their duties, played a direct role in democracy's salvation, as reported in the *New York Times* and the *Washington Post*:

- FBI director Christopher Wray defied Trump and said that in the past there had been no "coordinated national voter fraud effort in a major election" resulting from mail-in voting.[24]
- Chris Krebs, director of the Cybersecurity and Infrastructure Security Agency, refused to back up Trump's claims of election fraud. Furthermore, his agency issued a statement calling the 2020 election "the most secure in American history," adding in bold type, "There is no evidence that any voting system deleted or lost votes or was in any other way compromised."[25]

---

24 Thomas L. Friedman, "Happy Thanksgiving to All Those Who Told the Truth in This Election," *New York Times*, November 24, 2020, https://www.nytimes.com/2020/11/24/opinion/trump-election-democracy.html.

25 "Joint Statement from Elections Infrastructure Government Coordinating Council & the Election Infrastructure Sector Coordinating Executive Committees," Cybersecurity & Infrastructure Security Agency (CISA), November 12, 2020,

- The Republican-led Board of Supervisors (composed of four Republicans and one Democrat) in Maricopa County, the most populous county in Arizona, according to the *Washington Post*, "voted unanimously Friday to certify the county's election results, with the board chairman declaring there was no evidence of fraud or misconduct 'and that is with a big zero.'"[26]
- Georgia's Republican secretary of state, Brad Raffensperger, made a patriotic contribution by running a superb, by-the-book election in that state. Two Republican US Senate candidates demanded his resignation "while offering absolutely no evidence of misconduct." Trump called him a RINO because he competently and honestly oversaw the election that Trump lost. Raffensperger said, in response to objections from some Republicans that Biden had carried the state, "People are just going to have to accept the results. . . . I am a Republican and I believe in fair and secure elections."[27]
- Ohio governor Mike DeWine agreed that "Joe Biden is the president-elect," drawing down upon himself Trump's threat to block his 2022 reelection.[28]

As Thomas Friedman pointed out in his Thanksgiving 2020 column, all Americans should be grateful to "the critical mass of civil servants, elected officials and judges" all over the country (though most at the state level) "who did their jobs, always opting for 'the harder right' that justice demanded, not 'the easier wrong' that Trump and his allies were pressing for. It was their collective integrity, their willingness to stand with 'Team America,' not either party, that pro-

https://www.cisa.gov/news/2020/11/12/joint-statement-elections-infrastructure-government-coordinating-council-election.

26 Friedman, "Happy Thanksgiving."

27 "The Longer Republicans Cower to Trump, the More Damage They Do to Democracy," editorial, *Washington Post*, November 16, 2020, https://www.washingtonpost.com/opinions/the-longer-republicans-cower-to-trump-the-more-damage-they-do-to-democracy/2020/11/16/2ac4e96c-282d-11eb-9b14-ad872157ebc9_story.html.

28 "Republicans Cower," *Washington Post*.

tected our democracy when it was facing one of its greatest threats from within. History will remember them fondly."[29]

Several state officials demonstrated such integrity when Republicans saw an opening to advance Trump's game plan in the composition of Michigan's county- and statewide canvassing boards, which certify the vote. Each board has two Democrats and two Republicans. If the Republicans of one or more of these boards were to block certification, Trump-supporting Republican leaders thought that the legislature might step in, override the state election results (which showed Biden as the victor by a margin of more than 150,000 votes), and send a Republican slate of electors to the Electoral College. Further, they reasoned, if such a step could be repeated in other states, Trump could overthrow the election.

The Republicans, after a direct intervention by Trump, tried to block certification in Wayne County, where Detroit is located. On November 13, a state judge there dismissed the Republican suit, saying he saw "no convincing evidence of election fraud." Trump then summoned both the Republican majority leader of the Michigan Senate, Mike Shirkey, and the Republican speaker of the Michigan House of Representatives, Lee Chatfield, to the White House to pressure them. The legislators came to Washington, as Trump had requested, and after meeting with him issued a joint statement in which they said:

> We have not yet been made aware of any information that would change the outcome of the election in Michigan and, as legislative leaders, we will follow the law and follow the normal process regarding Michigan's elections, just as we have said throughout this election.[30]

29 Friedman, "Happy Thanksgiving."
30 Craig Mauger and Melissa Nann Burke, "Michigan GOP Leaders after White House Meeting: 'We Will Follow the Law,'" *Detroit News*, November 20, 2020, https://www.detroitnews.com/story/news/politics/2020/11/20/biden-adviser-michigan-lawmakers-cant-intervene-election-result/6355274002/.

So the results in Michigan came down to a vote of the statewide Board of State Canvassers on November 23. All the county boards had certified. The state board had to certify the statewide vote—otherwise, chaos. There were two Democrat and two Republican members on this board, as on the others. One Republican announced in advance that he would vote for a delay. The two Democrats would vote to certify. The other Republican did not say in advance what he would do. Suddenly the eyes of the world were on this one Michigander. After three hours—with people screaming just outside the closed doors—the meeting ended with the other Republican, Aaron Van Langevelde, having voted with the two Democrats. The Michigan votes were certified.

In explaining his vote, Langevelde said, "We have a clear legal duty to certify the results of the election. . . . We cannot and should not go beyond that. As John Adams once said, 'We are a government of laws, not men.'" [31] Langevelde is a true patriot if ever there were one. The Michigan vote was probably a turning point in Trump's long struggle to reverse the outcome of the election. Trump allowed the transition process to begin the next day, having blocked it until then.

With the defeat in Michigan, the Trump campaign escalated its efforts in Pennsylvania. It sued Secretary of State Kathy Boockvar, alleging that, under her guidance (to all counties), those voters who had mailed in ballots with errors could be notified and allowed to make minor "fixes" to correct those errors. The Democrat-majority counties largely implemented her guidance, and the Republican-majority counties did not. This was a violation of the equal protection clause of the Constitution, it was argued. Both the *New York Times* and the *Washington Post* documented the responses of US District Judge Matthew W. Brann:

---

31 Craig Mauger and Melissa Nann Burke, "Michigan Board Certifies Nov. 3 Election, Cementing Biden Victory," *Detroit News*, November 23, 2020, htps://www.detroitnews.com/story/news/politics/2020/11/23/michigan-election-state-canvassers-certification/6390475002/.

"That some counties may have chosen to implement" Ms. Boockvar's suggestions, but others did not, "does not constitute an equal-protection violation," Judge Brann wrote. . . . President Trump's campaign, which had asked him to effectively disenfranchise nearly seven million voters, should have come to court "armed with compelling legal arguments and factual proof of rampant corruption" in its efforts to essentially nullify the results of Pennsylvania's election. But instead, Judge Brann complained, the Trump campaign provided only "strained legal arguments without merit and speculative accusations" that were "unsupported by evidence. . . . In the United States of America, this [argument] cannot justify the disenfranchisement of a single voter, let alone all the voters of its sixth most populated state . . . our people, laws and institutions demand more." [32]

Judge Brann heard the case on November 21, and it was promptly appealed to the Third Circuit. The Third Circuit found that the Trump campaign appeal had "no merit." At the appellate level the case was heard by a three-judge panel of the court, all Republicans. Judge Stephanos Bibas (a Trump appointee), writing for all three judges, stated, "Charges of unfairness are serious. But calling an election unfair does not make it so. Charges require specific allegations and then proof. We have neither of these here." Judge Bibas also wrote, "Voters, not lawyers, choose the President. Ballots, not briefs, decide elections." [33] The Third Circuit rejected the Trump case and, although one of the Trump lawyers said the case would be appealed to the Supreme Court, it was not, perhaps having nothing of legal merit

32 Alan Feuer, "Judge Dismisses Trump Lawsuit Seeking to Delay Certification in Pennsylvania," *New York Times,* November 21, 2020, https://www.nytimes.com/2020/11/21/us/politics/pennsylvania-trump-court-ballots.html.

33 Maryclaire Dale, "Appeals Court Rejects Trump Challenge of Pennsylvania Race," PBS, November 27, 2020, https://www.pbs.org/newshour/politics/appeals-court-rejects-trump-challenge-of-pennsylvania-race.

for the Supreme Court to pursue. Another Pennsylvania case brought soon afterward did make it to the Supreme Court and was rejected 9–0. After these legal decisions, "President Trump said that he would leave the White House if the Electoral College voted for president-elect Joe Biden next month, though he vowed to keep fighting to overturn the election he lost and said he may never concede."[34]

His earlier legal challenges having failed, Trump continued to directly pressure state officials and legislatures to corrupt the process for electoral vote certification, ignore the will of the people, and flip the election to him, the loser. When Trump flew to Georgia to campaign for the two Republican Senate candidates, he phoned Governor Kemp, a former ally. Although Georgia election officials had conducted three electoral recounts, including one by hand, Trump directed the governor to call a special session of the state legislature to discuss the replacement of Georgia electors pledged under the certified popular vote with a slate selected by the Republican-dominated state legislature. Governor Kemp refused, saying that he was not permitted to do so under either state or federal law.

Republican Georgia lieutenant governor Geoff Duncan gave an interview on CNN's *State of the Union* during which he said that he "'absolutely' thought that Kemp would not accede to Trump's demand that he persuade the state legislature to appoint electors who would override the popular vote and nullify Biden's victory in the state."[35] Later that evening Kemp and Duncan issued a joint statement in response to Trump's call for a special session of the legislature to override Biden's victory, saying that "doing this in order to select a

34 Josh Dawsey, "Trump Commits to Stepping Down if Electoral College Votes for Biden," *Washington Post*, November 26, 2020, https://www.washingtonpost.com/politics/trump-says-he-will-leave-if-electoral-college-votes-for-biden/2020/11/26/7883351c-303b-11eb-96c2-aac3f162215d_story.html.

35 Felicia Sonmez, "Georgia Leaders Rebuff Trump's Call for Special Session to Overturn Election Results," *Washington Post*, December 6, 2020, https://www.washingtonpost.com/politics/brian-kemp-trump-election-results/2020/12/06/4c5db908-37d4-11eb-9276-ae0ca72729be_story.html.

separate slate of presidential electors is not an option that is allowed under state or federal law." [36] Kemp went from ally to whipping boy as far as his relations with Trump were concerned.

The *Washington Post* reported on Trump's hour-long call a month later with Republican Georgia secretary of state Brad Raffensperger. Also on the call were several Trump lawyers, White House chief of staff Mark Meadows (muttering about conspiracy theories), and Raffensperger's general counsel, Ryan Germany. Alternately pleading, demanding, threatening, and begging, Trump insisted that Raffensperger recalibrate the Georgia vote count and show him as the victor. Trump threw an endless cascade of false claims, unsubstantiated charges, and strange conspiracy theories at the two Georgia officials. Either the secretary of state or his general counsel batted down each one. Reporting on the meeting for the *Washington Post*, Amy Gardner wrote that Trump—sounding more and more unhinged—told the secretary of state that he would be subject to criminal action if he didn't fix the vote. Finally, Raffensperger politely ended the call. Looking at possible legal ramifications of such a call, Gardner reported:

> Prosecutors would likely exercise discretion in considering a case against an outgoing president, experts said. Edward B. Foley, a law professor at Ohio State University, said the legal questions are murky, and it could be difficult to prove that Trump knew he was encouraging illegal behavior. But Foley also emphasized that the call was "inappropriate and contemptible" and should prompt outrage. . . . [However, other legal scholars pointed out that] by exhorting the secretary of state to "find" votes and to deploy investigators who "want to find answers," the president appeared to be encouraging him to doctor the election outcome in Georgia, which could violate both state and federal law. . . . [They went on to note

---

36 Sonmez, "Georgia Leaders Rebuff."

that] Trump's apparent threat of criminal consequences if Raffensperger failed to act could be seen as an attempt at extortion and a suggestion that he might deploy the Justice Department to launch an investigation.[37]

In Michigan, Pennsylvania, and Georgia, we saw efforts to undermine our free democratic elections thwarted by state officials—not by elected federal representatives or leaders in the GOP. Wrote the *Washington Post*:

> It is a pathetic spectacle when the burden of defending democracy is falling on such state leaders, as well as principled secretaries of state such as Georgia Republican Brad Raffensperger, while the likes of Mr. McConnell and Sen. Lindsey O. Graham (R-SC)—who, having both just won reelection, have no conceivable excuse for such spinelessness—hide behind platitudes about allowing Mr. Trump to play out his legal options. Mr. Trump is not playing out legitimate legal options. He is maneuvering to undo his defeat through lies and chicanery. Let us all remember who abetted this disgrace and who stood up to it.[38]

---

37 Amy Gardner, "'I Just Want to Find 11,780 Votes': In Extraordinary Hour-Long Call, Trump Pressures Georgia Secretary of State to Recalculate the Vote in His Favor," *Washington Post*, January 3, 2021, https://www.washingtonpost.com/politics/trump-raffensperger-call-georgia-vote/2021/01/03/d45acb92-4dc4-11eb-bda4-615aaefd0555_story.html.

38 "Trump Is Past Exploring Legal Options," *Washington Post*.

CHAPTER 11

TEXAS V. PENNSYLVANIA

WHILE STATE OFFICIALS held the line in preserving the integrity of the November election, some states did file legal challenges to establish Trump's lie of a stolen election. On December 8, 2020, the attorney general of the State of Texas filed a lawsuit in the US Supreme Court that, if successful, would have upended the electoral will of the American people and democracy in the process. Attorney General Ken Paxton, who was under indictment for bribery (a federal crime) and likely looking for a pardon from Trump, put forward the claim that "the election in four swing states—Georgia, Michigan, Pennsylvania, and Wisconsin—suffered from 'unconstitutional irregularities.'"[1]

This suit was based on the unfounded voter fraud claims rooted in Trump's incessant lying—recognized by officials in both parties as mendacious. The untruths behind the case were widely understood.

---

1   David Leonhardt, "The US Gets Closer to Vaccines. And Dozens of Republicans Join the Campaign to Overturn the Election," *New York Times*, December 11, 2020, https://www.nytimes.com/2020/12/11/briefing/pfizer-trump-lawsuit-star-wars-your-morning-briefing.html.

Even former US attorney general Bill Barr has publicly concluded that no significant fraud took place in the election. Just claiming there is fraud doesn't establish its presence. Just believing fraud took place isn't proof it took place. Evidence constituting proof is required. Nevertheless, "the attorneys general of 17 states—including Florida, South Carolina, Tennessee, Indiana, Utah, Arizona, and the Dakotas" also signed on to this bizarre legal action.[2]

On December 9, Trump increased pressure on the Supreme Court to give him a favorable ruling by persuading 126 members of the 196-member Republican caucus in the House of Representatives, including House Minority Leader Kevin McCarthy, to sign an amicus brief in his favor. The suit asked the court to essentially nullify the 10.4 million votes for Biden in the four swing states charged in the suit—two of which were led by Republican governors—as remedy for the claims made in the complaint. The suit asked that the electors from these states be blocked from voting and that the state legislatures support alternate electors.

In response, 20 states, along with the US territories of Guam and the Virgin Islands, filed counter amicus briefs urging the court to reject the Texas suit. The four states targeted by the Texas suit excoriated it in their submissions to the Supreme Court. "Texas's effort to get the court to pick the next president has no basis in law and fact," Pennsylvania attorney general Josh Shapiro said in a court filing that labeled the case a bid to construct "a surreal alternate reality." He added that the court "should not abide this seditious abuse of the judicial process and should send a clear and unmistakable signal that such abuse must never be replicated."[3] In his December 11 *New York*

---

2   Leonhardt, "Dozens of Republicans Join."
3   Will Smith, "Pennsylvania, Georgia, Michigan and Wisconsin Strongly Condemned the Texas Case to Overturn the Election Results," *Press Stories*, December 11, 2020, https://presstories.com/2020/12/11/pennsylvania-georgia-michigan-and-wisconsin-strongly-condemned-the-texas-case-to-overturn-the-election-results/.

Times column, David Leonhardt cited David French of *The Dispatch*, a conservative publication: "'If [the plaintiffs] get their way in court, they would break the country.'" "They won't," commented Leonhardt.[4] The *Washington Post* made the same prediction, summarizing its legal argument in this way:

> Latching on to *Texas v. Pennsylvania*, the last-ditch lawsuit from Republican state attorneys general, the Trump team admitted that it cannot show fraud but argued that the Supreme Court should block the Electoral College from finalizing its votes anyway. Judges will reject this wild argument too.[5]

The Supreme Court delivered its formal opinion in the case of *Texas v. Pennsylvania* on December 11, 2020:

> The State of Texas's motion for leave to file a bill of complaint is denied for lack of standing under Article III of the Constitution. Texas has not demonstrated a judicially cognizable interest in the manner in which another state conducts its election. All other pending motions are dismissed as moot.
>
> Statement of Justice Alito with which Justice Thomas joins: In my view, we do not have discretion to deny the filing of a bill of complaint in a case that falls within our original jurisdiction. See *Arizona v. California* 589 US—February 24, 2020. (Thomas, J., dissenting). I would therefore grant the motion to file a bill of complaint, but would not grant other relief, and I express no view on any other issue.[6]

---

4   Leonhardt, "Dozens of Republicans Join."
5   "Trump and His GOP Enablers Are Slandering American Democracy," editorial, *Washington Post*, December 11, 2020, https://www.washingtonpost.com/opinions/trump-and-his-gop-enablers-are-slandering-american-democracy/2020/12/10/f8466170-3b30-11eb-bc68-96af0daae728_story.html.
6   Texas v. Pennsylvania et al., 592 US (2020), https://www.supremecourt.gov/orders/

The dissent by Alito and Thomas was procedural in nature. On the substance they made clear that they stood with the majority. So, on the substance of the case, the vote was 9–0 here as well. President Nixon had been rejected once by a 9–0 vote of the Supreme Court; President Trump had accomplished it twice—a new record—in one week.

The plaintiffs in *Texas v. Pennsylvania* included 18 of the 26 sitting Republican state attorneys general, and the associated amicus brief was signed by 126 of the 196 Republican House members, including House Minority Leader Kevin McCarthy. This legal action, correctly described by the Pennsylvania attorney general, is indeed a seditious abuse of the legal process. There is no evidence of any significant fraud or impropriety associated with this election, as some 80 judges (Republican and Democrat), the Supreme Court justices (twice), and then attorney general Bill Barr have affirmed. Biden was elected in a free and fair election. Trump's baseless claims of fraud and impropriety are establishing the principle that it's acceptable to try to overturn an election result with lies and conspiracy theories by legal or even extra-legal means. Anyone in office who contributes to a direct assault on American democracy in support of a corrupt and malicious would-be dictator is in violation of his or her constitutional oath and, therefore, should be banned from public positions that require an oath to the Constitution to assume office.

Some Republicans have been rightly appalled by such actions.

- "The act itself by the 126 members of the House of Representatives is an affront to our country," said Michael Steele, the former chairman of the Republican National Committee. "It's an offense to the Constitution and it leaves an indelible stain that will be hard for those 126 members to wipe off their skin for a long time to come."[7]

---

courtorders/121120zr_p860.pdf.
7 Jim Rutenberg and Nick Corasaniti, "In Rejecting Texas Lawsuit, Supreme Court

- The president of Freedom House, Michael Abramowitz, stated, "From a global perspective this certainly looks like many of the cases we've seen around the world where an incumbent tries to hold on to power . . . there's no question that people around the world are now looking to America and it's really important for Americans of all parties to stand up for the rule of law and democracy."[8]
- Former New Jersey governor Christine Todd Whitman, long an important figure in the Republican Party, said, "I have been comparing it to Jonestown. They've all drunk the Kool-Aid. It just hasn't killed them yet."[9]
- Sen. Ben Sasse (R-NE) released this statement: "Since election night, a lot of people have been confusing voters by spinning Kenyan birther type, 'Chávez rigged the election from the grave' conspiracy theories, but every American who cares about the rule of law should take comfort that the Supreme Court—including all three of President Trump's picks—closed the book on this nonsense."[10]
- The editorial board of the *Washington Post* put it this way: "House Republicans have faced what amounts to a choice for or against democracy: whether to sign on to Texas Attorney General Ken Paxton's delusional lawsuit to overturn the presidential election. A large majority failed that test."[11]

Delivers a Rebuke to GOP," *New York Times*, December 13, 2020, https://www.nytimes.com/2020/12/13/us/politics/in-rejecting-texas-lawsuit-supreme-court-delivers-a-rebuke-to-gop.html.

8 Jim Rutenberg and Nick Corasaniti, "'An Indelible Stain': How the GOP Tried to Topple a Pillar of Democracy," *New York Times,* December 12, 2020, https://www.nytimes.com/2020/12/12/us/politics/trump-lawsuits-electoral-college.html.

9 Rutenberg and Corasaniti, "An Indelible Stain."

10 Mili Godio, "GOP Senator Reacts to SCOTUS Decision on 'Nonsense' Election Reversal Bid," *Newsweek*, December 12, 2020, https://www.newsweek.com/gop-senator-sasse-reacts-scotus-decision-nonsense-election-reversal-bid-1554333.

11 "Republicans Faced a Simple Choice: For or Against Democracy," editorial, *Washington Post*, December 13, 2020, https://www.washingtonpost.com/opinions/republicans-faced-a-simple-choice-for-or-against-democracy/2020/12/11/e2e9a610-3bef-11eb-98c4-25dc9f4987e8_story.html.

- Sen. Mitt Romney's comment was, "The idea of supplanting the vote of the people with partisan legislators . . . is so completely out of our national character that it's simply mad."[12]

The Texas suit was a wrongful, unpatriotic action that seriously damaged the standing of the United States in the world community. It was deeply contrary to the best interests of America's people. Amidst many bad things and no good things, as David Leonhardt points out, it encouraged violence, of which the following are a few of the more immediate instances:

- Dozens of Trump supporters, some armed, went to the home of Jocelyn Benson, Michigan's Democratic secretary of state, and began shouting obscenities.
- On Twitter, Trump supporters posted photographs of the home of Ann Jacobs, a Wisconsin official, and mentioned her children.
- In Phoenix, about 100 Trump supporters, some armed, protested at the building where officials were counting votes.
- In Vermont, officials received a voice message threatening them with "execution by firing squad."
- Seth Bluestein, a Philadelphia official, received anti-Semitic and violent threats after Pam Bondi, a Trump ally, publicly mentioned him.
- A Georgia poll worker went into hiding after a viral video falsely claimed he had discarded ballots.
- Brad Raffensperger, Georgia's Republican secretary of state, and his wife received death threats, including by text message, and caravans circled their house.
- Gabriel Sterling, another Georgia official, received a message wishing him a happy birthday and saying it would be his last.[13] Despite this type of intimidation, Sterling held firm, not only

---

12 "Republicans Faced a Simple Choice," *Washington Post*.
13 Leonhardt, "Dozens of Republicans Join."

refusing to play along with Trump's lies but holding two press conferences to decry the tactics of Trump and his minions. "Stop inspiring people to commit potential acts of violence," Sterling demanded.[14]

Such threats of danger call to mind the planned abduction and killing of Michigan's governor a few months back—a plan that appeared to amuse Trump.

Journalist Max Boot reported that on December 18, 2020, Trump moved into uncharted territory in an effort to hang on to power:

> Trump met at the White House with retired Lt. Gen. Michael Flynn, a pardoned felon, and attorney Sidney Powell, who was fired from the Trump legal team after promoting conspiracy theories about the late Venezuelan president Hugo Chávez's programming US voting machines too wacky even for Trump. Trump reportedly discussed with the duo Flynn's idea of declaring martial law and having the military 'rerun' the election—or, failing that, appointing Powell as a special counsel to probe (nonexistent) election fraud. . . . Never before in US history has there been a record of a president discussing a military coup to stay in office.[15]

Promptly, on December 22, Trump received a response to this suggestion from the US military. Army chief of staff Gen. James C. McConville and army secretary Ryan D. McCarthy declared that "there is no role for the US military in determining the outcome of an American election."[16] Then Bill Barr, before leaving the office

---

14 Graham Kates, "Gabriel Sterling, Georgia Elections Official Who Harshly Criticized Trump, to Testify Before Grand Jury," CBS News, June 7, 2022, https://www.cbsnews.com/news/gabriel-sterling-georgia-election-testify-trump-grand-jury/.

15 Max Boot, "Trump Saved the Worst for Last," *Washington Post*, December 20, 2020, https://www.washingtonpost.com/opinions/2020/12/20/trump-saved-worst-last/.

16 "Trump's Final Month Might Make the Past Four Years Seem Calm," editorial, *Washington Post*, December 22, 2020, https://www.washingtonpost.com/

of attorney general on December 23, defied Trump—who had been pressuring him to take legal action to overturn the election—by saying, in the *Washington Post*'s account, that "he saw no evidence of 'systematic or broad-based' election fraud and no basis for seizing election machines, appointing a special counsel to investigate voting irregularities, or tapping a special counsel to examine president-elect Joe Biden's son Hunter."[17]

Judging by past comments, Donald Trump has long dreamed of becoming president for life, like his former friend President Xi of China. As president for life, he could indulge to the fullest his obsessive narcissism, his penchant for corruption, and his indifference to the hundreds of thousands of Americans—now more than a million—who have died from the coronavirus. The one thing he didn't want—his greatest fear—was to be a loser. But that is what he is. He was decisively beaten by Joe Biden with a seven-million-vote margin and 306 Electoral College votes, 36 more than necessary to win the presidency. Both he and his visions of becoming dictator for life were roundly defeated. So was his effort to destroy our democracy, crush liberty, and abolish the rule of law.

Trump is not worth having as chief federal dogcatcher. During the greatest public health crisis in the history of our republic, a crisis that should have been Job One for the chief executive, our president was consumed only by his own electoral prospects. After the abject failure of 40-plus legal challenges directed at overthrowing election results,[18] he continued to insist on the Big Lie of a stolen election, supporting the possibility of directly overturning the election by vio-

---

opinions/trumps-final-month-might-make-the-past-four-years-seem-calm/2020/12/22/792db7ac-449b-11eb-a277-49a6d1f9dff1_story.html.

17 "Trump's Final Month," *Washington Post*.

18 Jacob Shamsian and Sonam Sheth, "Trump and His Allies Filed More than 40 Lawsuits Challenging the 2020 Election Results. All of Them Failed." *Business Insider*, February 22, 2021, https://www.businessinsider.com/trump-campaign-lawsuits-election-results-2020-11.

lence—ignoring the suffering of Americans as the pandemic surged toward a new peak.

Over the years certain policies of delegitimization have moved to the fore. President Clinton was accused of murder by prominent evangelicals, for example. Donald J. Trump, by his endless lies about what his own administration declared to have been the "most secure election in American history,"[19] has become the greatest practitioner of delegitimization. Trump converted his actual defeat into victory in the minds of some followers through his claims of vast nationwide fraud and supposed manipulations of US voting machines by a dead Venezuelan dictator. Trump made these baseless assertions cardinal principles of GOP loyalty. With the extremist cult QAnon becoming more mainstream politically, fanatics repeated its irrational claims that Democratic leaders are pedophiles, Vladimir Putin is a better friend to the US government than our own intelligence agencies, Mexican immigrants are rapists, White fascists are "good people," and on and on.

Thus, by means of the Big Lie, Trump attempted to systematically deconstruct the institutions of our democracy and make the population a servile mass. Trump humiliated the United States and trampled on and made a mockery of the Constitution he was sworn to defend—all the while enriching himself. Though technically, under the Constitution, the crime of treason can only be committed during wartime, that term seems the best way to describe Trump's actions. And despite the constitutional definition, in 1807, Aaron Burr was charged with treason during peacetime and only escaped conviction on a technicality.

While acknowledging the many specific acts of patriotic heroism on behalf of constitutional democracy that pushed against the Big Lie, we should also be wary about precedents being set. Such challenges

---

19 Scott Pelley, "Fired Director of US Cyber Agency Chris Krebs Explains Why President Trump's Claims of Election Interference Are False," *60 Minutes*, https://www.cbs news.com/news/election-results-security-chris-krebs-60-minutes-2020-11-29/.

may recur. "What Trump is doing is creating a road map to destabilization and chaos in future years," predicted Trevor Potter, a Republican who served as chairman of the Federal Election Commission in the 1990s. "What he is saying, explicitly, is that if a party doesn't like the election result, they have the right to change it by gaming the system."[20] Liberty is precious and also fragile; Americans must be forever vigilant. This time, a majority of Americans kept their sacred trust with the Founders. Aaron Van Langevelde of the Michigan statewide Board of State Canvassers, quoting John Adams, heroically affirmed, "We are a government of laws, not of men."[21]

In 2020, Thomas Friedman weighed in on what is certainly a continuing question. Noting Republican support for Trump's efforts to overturn the election and destroy our democracy, he asked, "How do you trust this version of the Republican Party to ever hold the White House again?" In its leadership and through its representatives in Washington, it is no longer the party of Lincoln or even a party of principles. It has become a party that loves power for its own sake. As Friedman said of the party:

> Its members sat mute while Trump, rather than using the federal bureaucracy to launch a war against our surging pandemic, has launched a war against his perceived enemies inside that federal bureaucracy. . . . A political party that will not speak up against such a reckless leader is not a party any longer. It is some kind of populist cult of personality. That's been obvious ever since this GOP was the first party to conclude its presidential nominating convention without offering any platform. It declared that its platform was whatever its

---

20 Jim Rutenberg and Kathleen Gray, "Duty or Party? For Republicans, a Test of Whether to Enable Trump," *New York Times*, November 22, 2020, https://www.nytimes.com/2020/11/21/us/politics/trump-vote.html.

21 Tim Alberta, "The Michigan Republican Who Stopped Trump," *Politico*, November 24, 2020, https://www.politico.com/newsletters/politico-nightly/2020/11/24/the-michigan-republican-who-stopped-trump-490984.

Dear Leader said it was. . . . That is why Biden's mission—and the mission of all decent conservatives—is not just to repair America. It is to marginalize this Trumpian version of the GOP and help to nurture a healthy conservative party—one that brings conservative approaches to economic growth, infrastructure, social policy, education, regulation, and climate change, but also cares about governing and therefore accepts compromise.[22]

So there you have it—a criminal president, a largely supine party enabling him in any way they can, and a neo-fascist attack on our liberty, our values, our democracy, and our country. Trump seems to be hoping for the destruction of our democracy and, with that, America's conversion to a northern version of Venezuela's banana republic, and the majority of Republicans in both houses of Congress are either supporting the coup attempt openly or are complicit by their silence, like the "good Germans" of the Third Reich. The Republican Party continues to act as though it no longer cares about America but only power. It has tried to sell us out to Russia to enrich its senior members. One of its prominent Senate members is reported to have urged voter tampering in Georgia during the recount—thus engaging in a criminal act.

Senate Minority Leader Mitch McConnell (R-KY) is in many ways indistinguishable from Trump. He said, "What we all say about [the election] is frankly irrelevant. [The transition] will happen right on time, and we will swear in the next administration on January 20."[23] This intimated that it was okay to tell outlandish and malicious lies about our election process and about the president-elect since Biden would be sworn in on schedule. In taking this position, McConnell

22 Thomas L. Friedman, "How Can We Trust This GOP in Power Again?" *New York Times*, November 17, 2020, https://www.nytimes.com/2020/11/17/opinion/trump-democracy-republican-party.html.
23 Tumulty, "Republican Leaders Swore."

ignored the huge damage done to confidence in our democracy. The GOP is heading for a split, with one part—a minority—evolving into a party of principled, pragmatic, and patriotic conservatives and the larger part left to sink further into its morass of neo-fascism, fake conspiracy narratives, and limitless lies. Our current president, Joe Biden, needs the support of the Democratic Party and of the principled conservatives who remain in the Republican Party.

CHAPTER 12

ESCALATION

ON DECEMBER 28, then president-elect Joe Biden complained that the White House was trying to make things more difficult for his transition team. He cited the Office of Management and Budget and the Department of Defense particularly, where "roadblocks" had been placed in front of his transition team. In this regard, he mentioned the national security sector more broadly:

> Right now, we just aren't getting all the information that we need from the outgoing administration in key national security areas. It's nothing short, in my view, of irresponsibility. . . . As our nation is in a period of transition, we need to make sure that nothing is lost in the handoff between administrations. My team needs a clear picture of our force posture around the world and our operations to deter our enemies.[1]

Now, why would President Trump have obstructed the transition? To force important civilian elements of the national security sector to

---

1 Amy B. Wang, Jenna Johnson, and Dan Lamothe, "Biden Accuses Trump Appointees of Obstructing Transition on National Security Issues," *Washington Post*, December 28, 2020, https://www.washingtonpost.com/politics/biden-trump-obstruction/2020/12/28/d4dd6e7e-4925-11eb-839a-cf4ba7b7c48c_story.html.

support his coup d'état effort to overturn the election and help him achieve his dream of being dictator for life? Or to "salt the earth" and "poison the well" so that Biden would have a difficult time doing anything in his first few months and, thereby, be open to blame for the inevitable catastrophes resulting from Trump administration obstruction? Or to provoke a war with Iran in a wag-the-dog effort? Trump could then have argued that no matter what the Constitution says, he needed to stay in office because of a national emergency.

Trump's attention had already turned to the January 6 joint session at which the Electoral College votes cast to elect Joe Biden as president would formally be certified and Biden declared the next president. Trump expressed a desire to use this pro forma session as one more opportunity to overturn the election and take the voting franchise away from the American people. He returned from Mar-a-Lago on December 31, cutting his stay in Florida short by a day, to plan with Senator Hawley and others how to enhance efforts to overturn the election.

The January 6 meeting, provided for by the Constitution and more fully defined by the Electoral Count Act of 1887, is intended as the final procedural step before the inauguration of the president two weeks later. For electoral votes gained pursuant to state law "regularly given," the decision of the Electoral College is final. "Regularly given" includes meeting such procedural steps as certification by the state in accordance with state law, the placing of the state seal on the document by the governor, and completing these steps in a timely fashion—in 2020, by the "safe harbor" December 8 date. The role of the Congress is to verify that it has the valid electoral state certificates and then to have the president of the Senate count them and declare the winner. In summary:

> The 1887 act obligates Congress to consider "conclusive" a state's own "final determination" of litigation over a state's appointment of electors when two conditions are met. The

"final determination" must occur by a certain date, December 8 [in 2020], and must be based on state laws existing before Election Day. . . . Congress instructs governors to provide verification of these two conditions in their certifications.[2]

The congressional session on January 6 is intended to be simply a procedural ratification of the states' decisions on the election of president by means of the Electoral College. Under the Constitution, as further elaborated in the Electoral Count Act of 1887, the electoral vote, cast the month before congressional certification, is final. If the two legal conditions detailed above have been met, Congress cannot change anything. This was the case in 2020: all the electoral vote certificates had their respective governors' signatures on them, certifying that the two conditions were met. Thus there was nothing for Congress to do except count and announce the winner. Substantive debate about something like fraud has no place at the January 6 joint session.

Under the 1887 law, a member of Congress can raise an objection to a particular state's slate of electors, but the objection must be signed by at least one member of the House and one member of the Senate. If this happens, the houses of Congress go into separate rooms, debate the issue for two hours, and then vote. Only if both houses agree to accept the objection does anything further happen. Shortly before the January 6 date, a right-wing House member said he was willing to enter an objection, and then Sen. Josh Hawley of Missouri said he would do so as well—in spite of the fact that the Senate Majority Leader and head of the Senate Republican caucus, Mitch McConnell, had strongly urged that no member of his caucus do this. Michael Gerson commented on Senator Hawley's decision for the *Washington Post*:

---

2   Edward B. Foley, "Sorry, President Trump. January 6 Is Not an Election Do-Over," *Washington Post*, December 29, 2020, https://www.washingtonpost.com/opinions/2020/12/29/sorry-president-trump-january-6-is-not-an-election-do-over/.

The announced intention of Sen. Josh Hawley (R-MO) to object to certification of Joe Biden's Electoral College victory is a particularly bad omen for the GOP's future. . . . In the cause of his own advancement, the senator from Missouri is willing to endorse the disenfranchisement of millions of Americans—particularly voters of color—and justify the attempted theft of an election. He is willing to credit malicious lies that will poison our democracy for generations. The fulfillment of Hawley's intention—the ultimate overturning of the election—would be the collapse of US self-government. The attempt should be a source of shame.[3]

Senator Hawley is known as a man who strongly opposes authoritarianism in China, but he appeared to like it here—if he could be something like deputy dictator for life under Trump. Indeed, Hawley is a younger, smarter, and perhaps more dangerous would-be Trump. What is America to do? Will there be an endless parade of smarter and more capable Trumps? Gerson saw it this way:

We can praise and support Republican politicians such as Sens. Mitt Romney (R-UT) and Ben Sasse (R-NE) and Govs. Larry Hogan (Maryland) and Brian Kemp (Georgia) who are standing in the gap. And we must ensure that the aspirations of people such as Hawley—who has made the madness more mainstream—come to nothing. This begins with a simple and sad recognition: The ambitions of this knowledgeable and talented young man are now a threat to the republic.[4]

---

3   Michael Gerson, "Josh Hawley's Heedless Ambition Is a Threat to the Republic," *Washington Post*, December 31, 2020, https://www.washingtonpost.com/opinions/ josh-hawleys-heedless-ambition-is-a-threat-to-the-republic/2020/12/31/ 1d3f8260-4b9c-11eb-a9f4-0e668b9772ba_story.html.

4   Gerson, "Josh Hawley's Heedless Ambition."

Hawley's Senate colleague Ben Sasse (R-NE) called the effort to use the forthcoming January 6 joint session as a vehicle to overturn the election a "dangerous ploy."[5]

> In an open letter to his constituents, Sasse wrote that there is no evidence of fraud so widespread that it could change the results and said he has urged his colleagues to reject "a project to overturn the election. . . . All the clever arguments and rhetorical gymnastics in the world won't change the fact that this January 6 effort is designed to disenfranchise millions of Americans simply because they voted for someone in a different party." Sasse wrote on Facebook shortly before midnight Wednesday [December 30], "We ought to be better than that."[6]

Additionally, former House speaker Paul Ryan (R-WI), on January 3, said that "the efforts to upend the Electoral College results 'strike at the foundation of our republic,' adding that he could not think of 'a more anti-democratic and anti-conservative act than a federal intervention to overturn the results of state-certified elections and disenfranchise millions of Americans.'"[7]

Rep. Louie Gohmert (R-TX) and a group of Arizona Republicans filed a suit in a federal district court in Texas, arguing that the 1887 act was unconstitutional and that the court should rule that the Constitution gives the vice president sole discretion as president of the Senate to determine whether electors approved by the states are

---

5   Rosalind S. Helderman and John Wagner, "Pence Seeks Rejection of Lawsuit That Aimed to Expand His Power to Overturn the Election," *Washington Post*, December 31, 2020, https://www.washingtonpost.com/politics/sasse-letter-electoral-college-ploy/2020/12/31/44da8dba-4b65-11eb-a9d9-1e3ec4a928b9_story.html.

6   Helderman and Wagner, "Pence Seeks Rejection."

7   Dan Balz, "Trump Knows No Limits as He Tries to Overturn the Election," *Washington Post*, January 3, 2021, https://www.washingtonpost.com/politics/trump-knows-no-limits-as-he-tries-to-overturn-the-election/2021/01/03/e192bf90-4e05-11eb-83e3-322644d82356_story.html.

valid. Vice President Pence disavowed the suit and promptly had a Justice Department lawyer oppose it in court. Lawyers representing the House of Representatives also asked the court to reject the suit.

There is no provision in the Constitution to justify such an absurd theory. Such a view of Senate certification would have meant that Al Gore could have simply ruled unilaterally in his own favor in *Bush v. Gore*. Vice President Pence clearly wanted none of this. The judge asked for pleadings by Friday, December 31, initially saying nothing about the suit. However, within 12 hours of the filing of the pleadings, on January 1, 2021, the judge rejected the case on the grounds that the plaintiffs did not have standing.

Why was this case brought? Hawley, Gohmert, and others in the House were trying to persuade Congress to do what it cannot legally do—overturn the election in the joint session. As noted above, the Electoral College result is final. Minor objections can be debated for two hours in separate sessions in each house, but nothing can happen unless both houses vote to do something. The Democrats held a majority in the House, and many Republicans in the Senate had declared against Hawley.

Trump himself, not caring about the Constitution or the law, still wanted to overthrow the election. He didn't realize this aim, though some 100-plus House members signaled that they would support an objection, likely to curry favor with Trump's base and thereby ease their reelections two years later. Perhaps Hawley also had a goal in mind, hoping to run for president in 2024. If so, he took the republic to the brink of calamity to further his own ambitions. Not to be outdone, a group of 11 senators and senators-elect led by Sen. Ted Cruz (R-TX) announced their intent to join Hawley in calling for an "emergency ten-day audit" to investigate nonexistent irregularities in certain states based on Trump's unfounded claims.[8]

---

8   Philip Rucker and Josh Dawsey, "Growing Number of Trump Loyalists in the Senate Vow to Challenge Biden's Victory," *Washington Post*, January 2, 2021, https://www. washingtonpost.com/politics/senators-challenge-election/2021/01/02/81a4e5c4-

What had been happening beyond Capitol Hill? The *Washington Post* published a comprehensive answer to this question on October 31, 2021. They noted that, before the January 6 attack, Donell Harvin, the head of intelligence at the District of Columbia Homeland Security Office, had spotted increasing signs indicating planned violence against the government to take place on January 6, the day of the joint session. With consternation, before dawn on January 2, Harvin called his counterpart in San Francisco, Mike Sena:

> Sena listened with alarm. The Northern California intelligence office he commanded had also been inundated with political threats flagged by social media companies, several involving plans to disrupt the joint session or hurt lawmakers on January 6.
>
> He organized an unusual call for all the nation's regional Homeland Security offices—known as fusion centers—to find out what others were seeing. Sena expected a couple dozen people to get on the line that Monday. But then the numbers of callers hit 100. Then 200. Then nearly 300. Officials from nearly all 80 regions, from New York to Guam, logged on.
>
> In the 20 years since the country had created fusion centers in response to the attacks of September 11, 2001, Sena couldn't remember a moment like this. For the first time, from coast to coast, the centers were blinking red. The hour, date, and location of concern was the same: 1 p.m., the US Capitol, January 6.[9]

Once counterparts and colleagues were asked to share what they had, alerts came from many sources all over America outside the

---

4c7d-11eb-a9d9-1e3ec4a928b9_story.html.

9   Aaron C. Davis, "The Attack (Before): Red Flags. The Jan. 6 Siege of the US Capitol Was Neither a Spontaneous Act Nor an Isolated Event," *Washington Post*, October 31, 2021, https://www.washingtonpost.com/politics/interactive/2021/warnings-jan-6-insurrection/.

fusion centers. Within minutes an avalanche of information surged in: Extremists were circulating radio frequencies to communicate with one another. People with criminal records and weapons were exchanging plans to be in Washington on January 6. Dangerous extremist groups such as the Proud Boys and the Oath Keepers—along with adherents of QAnon, the spreader of conspiracy stories—were planning to be there in force.

Two days before the attack, Harvin offered to share his information with everyone he could in the federal government—the FBI, the Department of Homeland Security, military intelligence services, and other agencies. He offered to make available, in real time, overwhelming evidence that a huge and violent attack was about to happen in Washington in 48 hours. The *Washington Post*, in its later investigation, found an enormous number of previously undisclosed warnings that had been made available to government agencies prior to the attack. These warnings were made by local officials, FBI informants, social media companies, German national security officials, researchers, lawmakers, and tipsters. As the *Post* reported: "While the public [and apparently much of the federal government] may have been surprised by what happened on January 6, the makings of the insurrection had been spotted at every level from one side of the country to the other. The red flags were everywhere."[10]

One particularly interesting report that came to the FBI from an online tipster described how to smuggle guns into Washington. Extremists planned to

> "overrun" police and arrest members of Congress. . . . Those planning violence believed they had "orders from the president," used code words such as "pickaxe" to describe guns, and posted the times and locations of four spots around the country for caravans to meet the day before the joint session.

10 Davis, "The Attack (Before): Red Flags."

On one site, a poster specifically mentioned Sen. Mitt Romney. An FBI official who assessed the tip noted that its criminal division had received a "significant number" of alerts about threats to Congress and other governmental officials . . . but did not pursue the matter.[11]

The FBI and other intelligence and enforcement agencies were, for the most part, not particularly interested in this information coming from all over America and painting a picture of what was likely going to happen in Washington. Why didn't state and federal officials act on the information? Had some been told by Trump to stand back, and they obeyed? Were others simply afraid of the politics? Were they concerned about being called "suppressors of free speech"? Did they lack confidence in the men and women in the field? The *Post* analysis points to a structural failure:

> The paralysis that led to one of the biggest security failures in the nation's history was driven by unique breakdowns inside each law enforcement agency and was exacerbated by the patchwork nature of security across a country where responsibilities are split between local and federal authorities. . . . [Federal] agencies failed to effectively harness the security and intelligence infrastructure built in the wake of [the] assault by Islamic extremists to look inward at domestic threats. . . .
>
> Yet Trump was the driving force at every turn as he orchestrated what would become an attempted political coup in the months leading up to January 6, calling his supporters to Washington, encouraging the mob to march on the Capitol, and freezing in place federal agencies whose job it was to investigate and stop threats to national security.[12]

---

11 Davis, "The Attack (Before): Red Flags."
12 Davis, "The Attack (Before): Red Flags."

Politics also played a role. President Trump had often threatened to fire FBI director Christopher Wray. Senior officials at the FBI worried that one of the director's public statements would lead to the president firing him. The military was worried too:

> At the Pentagon, leaders had acute fears about widespread violence, and some feared Trump could misuse the National Guard to remain in power. . . . Military officials took fateful steps to avoid being entangled in domestic unrest. . . . Gen. Mark A. Milley, the chairman of the Joint Chiefs of Staff, and then army secretary Ryan McCarthy sought to require that only senior Pentagon leaders could approve changes to missions for National Guard soldiers. In the end, that posture contributed to the hours-long delay in getting the Guard to the Capitol to help restore order.[13]

After the additional 11 Republican senators announced that they would join Senator Hawley in challenging the electoral tally, other Republican colleagues pushed back:

> Sen. Patrick J. Toomey (R-PA) responded in a blistering statement that the effort "directly undermines" Americans' right to choose their leaders, and Sen. Mitt Romney (R-UT) called it an "egregious ploy." Hawley shot back that Toomey and others were engaging in "shameless personal attacks." . . . Sen. Shelley Moore Capito (R-WV) said lawmakers had "a solemn responsibility to accept these Electoral College votes that have been certified" by state officials. Sen. Roger Wicker (R-MS) added, "I think the overwhelming weight of the evidence is that Joe Biden defeated my candidate, Donald Trump, and I have to live with it." Late Sunday Sen. Tom Cotton (R-AR) issued a statement saying that he shares the

---

13 Davis, "The Attack (Before): Red Flags."

"concerns of many Arkansans about irregularities in the presidential election," but that the Founders "entrusted our elections chiefly to the states—not Congress," and that he therefore will not oppose the counting of certified electoral votes.[14]

The dissension within the Republican Party on Capitol Hill reached into the House as well. Rep. Liz Cheney (R-WY), number three in the House leadership, broke with Minority Leader Kevin McCarthy and the Trumpists around him.

> On December 12 . . . thousands of pro-Trump supporters and protesters converged on DC, . . . including about 700 Proud Boys. . . . Watching the rally on a computer popped open in her kitchen in the Washington area, Rep. Liz Cheney (R-WY) couldn't believe what she was seeing. Her thoughts flashed forward to January 6, and she started to fear just how far Trump's most avid supporters might go. Cheney imagined a bomb threat halting the count to certify the election. "We have to count the votes that day," she said to herself. Cheney soon began a shadow effort to block Trump. She recruited ten former secretaries of defense, from Republican and Democratic administrations, to sign an op-ed published in the *Post* that warned military officials to steer clear of any effort to use soldiers to thwart the peaceful transfer of power.[15]

The op-ed signed by the former secretaries of defense was entitled "Involving the Military in Election Disputes Would Cross into Dangerous Territory." It read, in part:

---

14 Mike DeBonis and Paul Kane, "Bitter GOP Split Upends the Pomp as a New Congress Takes Over," *Washington Post*, January 3, 2021, https://www.washington post.com/politics/senate-republicans-fight-new-congress/2021/01/03/27eff4d0-4dd4-11eb-bda4-615aaefd0555_story.html.
15 Davis, "The Attack (Before): Red Flags."

As senior Defense Department leaders have noted, "there's no role for the US military in determining the outcome of a US election." Efforts to involve the US armed forces in resolving election disputes would take us into dangerous, unlawful, and unconstitutional territory. . . . Transitions, which all of us have experienced, are a crucial part of the successful transfer of power. . . . American elections and the peaceful transfers of power that result are hallmarks of our democracy. . . . [Transitions] often occur at times of international uncertainty about US national security policy and posture. They can be a moment when the nation is vulnerable to actions by adversaries seeking to take advantage of the situation. Given these factors, particularly at a time when US forces are engaged in active operations around the world, it is all the more imperative that the transition at the Defense Department be carried out fully, cooperatively and transparently.[16]

The ten former secretaries of defense then called on the current acting defense secretary, Christopher C. Miller, and his staff to ensure that such a transition happened.

Cheney also circulated a 21-page memo rebutting the case made by the dissenting senators. She urged members not to go down the path of questioning states' voting tallies. Such objections "set an exceptionally dangerous precedent," threatening to steal states' explicit constitutional responsibility for choosing the president and bestowing it instead

---

16 Ashton Carter, Dick Cheney, William Cohen, Mark Esper, Robert Gates, Chuck Hagel, James Mattis, Leon Panetta, William Perry, and Donald Rumsfeld, "All 10 Living Former Defense Secretaries: Involving the Military in Election Disputes Would Cross into Dangerous Territory," *Washington Post*, January 3, 2021, https://www.washingtonpost.com/opinions/10-former-defense-secretaries-military-peaceful-transfer-of-power/2021/01/03/2a23d52e-4c4d-11eb-a9f4-0e668b9772ba_story.html.

on Congress. Cheney wrote that this was "directly at odds with the Constitution's clear text and our core beliefs as Republicans."[17]

Cheney later commented that Trump's phone call with the Georgia officials was "deeply troubling."[18] Additionally, "Sen. Rob Portman (R-OH), who was up for reelection in 2022, but subsequently decided not to seek reelection, said he would vote to affirm the duly chosen electors from any contested state. He said that he 'cannot support allowing Congress to thwart the will of the voters.'"[19] Josh Holmes, an outside adviser to Senator McConnell, said:

> I think it is revealing that there is not a single senator who is arguing that the election was stolen from President Trump. The divide in the party is whether it's appropriate to pull the pin on an Electoral College grenade, hoping that there are enough responsible people standing around who can shove it back in before they detonate American democracy.[20]

Except for a few billionaires, why would anyone have wanted to keep Trump in office? He was soundly rejected by 81 million Americans—a solid majority. If he were to have returned as president by subterfuge, for which substantial elements of the Republican Party were arguing, the American people would have revolted. There could have been civil war. And what might we have gotten? An incompetent, unhinged, neo-fascist racist ready to sell the United States out to Russia at the drop of a hat? Trump had mishandled the pandemic. Indeed, his simple, arrogant cluelessness that later morphed into malevolent action makes him personally responsible for some significant

---

17 Philip Rucker, Ashley Parker, Josh Dawsey, and Seung Min Kim, "Trump Sabotaging GOP on His Way Out of Office with Push to Overturn Election," *Washington Post*, January 4, 2021, https://www.washingtonpost.com/politics/trump-sabotage-republicans/2021/01/04/df5d301e-4eb1-11eb-83e3-322644d82356_story.html.
18 Rucker et al., "Trump Sabotaging GOP."
19 Rucker et al., "Trump Sabotaging GOP."
20 Rucker et al., "Trump Sabotaging GOP."

portion of the more than one million American deaths from coronavirus that had occurred by May 2022. Would any want him in a position to cause more unnecessary deaths? Were a second presidential vote to have been cast a few days later, Biden's majority would probably have been considerably greater.

This book has discussed the options Trump had to carry out his coup, including pressuring legislators and election officials, filing lawsuits, and declaring martial law. When those seemed to be failing, Trump turned to Mike Pence. As Aaron Davis reported in the *Washington Post*:

> As Jan. 6 neared, Trump ratcheted up the calls for action on that day—and the pressure on Vice President Mike Pence, whose role was to preside over the joint session. The president embraced a cast of renegade lawyers who argued that Pence could reject electors from a handful of states and, ultimately, nullify Biden's victory. The plan was far-fetched and, according to legal experts, unconstitutional. . . . Trump primed his base to view Pence as either a would-be hero or villain, depending on the path the vice president took. "I hope Mike Pence comes through for us," he declared at a rally in Georgia two days before the joint session, adding: "If he doesn't come through, I won't like him as much." [21]

This, of course, made Pence an assassination target.

While Pence likely understood his jeopardy, Trump's tweet at 2:24 p.m. on January 6, asserting that Pence did not have the courage to do what needed to be done, likely confirmed the danger of his situation. Trump's tweet was the equivalent of pulling a trigger. After the tweet, the mob surged and elements began chanting "Hang Mike Pence! Hang Mike Pence!" A model gallows was set up in front of the Capitol. The *New York Times* reported that "a confidential witness

---

21 Davis, "The Attack (Before): Red Flags."

who traveled to Washington with the Proud Boys . . . later told investigators the group would have killed Mr. Pence—and Speaker Nancy Pelosi—if they got the chance."[22] Similarly, an article in the *Washington Post* reported that the committee also "cited an affidavit from an FBI informant who told authorities that rioters would have killed Pence had they found him that day."[23]

But Pence informed Trump on the night of January 5 and the morning of January 6 that the Constitution left him no other choice than to formally count the vote and declare Biden the winner, and that was what he would do. It was an extraordinary act of patriotic heroism for Vice President Pence to carry out his constitutional duties in the face of assassins believing they were following Trump's will. Pence carried on, never wavering, until the job was done.

Pence also had his office issue a public statement announcing his intention to count the electoral votes and declare Joe Biden the winner. It said, in part:

> As a student of history who loves the Constitution and reveres its framers, I do not believe that the Founders of our country intended to invest the vice president with unilateral authority to decide which electoral votes should be counted during the joint session of Congress, and no vice president in American history has ever asserted such authority.[24]

Coincidentally, on January 5, Georgia held two runoff elections

22 Annie Karni and Maggie Haberman, "For Mike Pence, Jan. 6 Began Like Many Days. It Ended Like No Other," *New York Times*, June 16, 2022, https://www.nytimes.com/2022/06/16/us/politics/pence-trump-jan-6.html?searchResultPosition=1.

23 Rosalind S. Helderman and Josh Dawsey, "Jan. 6 Committee Reveals New Details of Pence's Terrifying Day," *Washington Post*, June 16, 2022, https://www.washingtonpost.com/politics/2022/06/16/jan-6-committee-reveals-new-details-about-pences-terrifying-day/.

24 Annie Karni, "Pence Rejects Trump's Pressure to Block Certification Saying He 'Loves the Constitution,'" *New York Times,* January 6, 2021, https://www.nytimes.com/2021/01/06/us/politics/pence-rejects-trumps-pressure-to-block-certification-saying-he-loves-the-constitution.html.

for the Senate, as required by state law. One of the two senators was running for election to a full term; the other incumbent, who had been appointed to fill an open seat, was seeking confirmation to complete the expired term of the seat. Neither of the two incumbent Republicans had garnered more than 50 percent of votes cast in the November 3 election. The Democratic candidates won both seats, both coming from behind. The Georgia secretary of state's office credited Trump with causing the Republican defeat with his attacks on Georgia state officials for not supporting his baseless claims of widespread voter fraud. Indeed, so fixated was Trump on his own fate that he rarely spoke about the candidates while in Georgia.

President-elect Biden had won Georgia in the November 3 election. Georgia's senatorial elections brought the number of Democrats in the US Senate up to 50, meaning that, when the Biden administration took office, Vice President Kamala Harris would be the tiebreaking presiding officer, thereby giving Democrats control of the Senate. The Democratic leader would become the majority leader. All this would give Democrats the presidency as well as House and Senate majorities. As the vote counts came in on January 5 and 6 and these results became clear, it was yet another blow for Trump and the Republicans who followed him.

CHAPTER 13

COUP

AND SO, AS JANUARY 6 ARRIVED, Trump, frustrated and angry, apparently decided to further weaponize his followers. Whether he knew it or not, they were well on their way to violent action already, many of them having arrived in Washington armed and in full tactical combat gear despite the fact that for this rally, as for most rallies, everyone attending was supposed to be unarmed. They knew where they were supposed to gather, what they were supposed to do, and whom they were supposed to target. On January 6, 2021, the serving president of the United States, Donald J. Trump, stood in front of the White House and incited an insurrectionary mob of thugs and domestic terrorists to march on the US Capitol.

They obeyed. They marched, broke in, halted the formal certification of the duly elected next president of the United States, Joe Biden, and wrecked the Capitol Building—the citadel of our democracy. Mayhem and violence followed President Trump's words. Possibly some in the mob intended to kill whatever senior government officials they could find. Perhaps some thought that, if a few senators and members of Congress were killed as a side benefit, all the better.

The scene at the Capitol was terrible. Thousands of insurrection-ists and terrorists pushed, shoved, and beat their way into the Capitol Building. Many offices were trashed. One man allegedly held an au-tomatic rifle. Another had ten Molotov cocktails at the ready.

Writing for the *Washington Post* in a series about the attack, Philip Rucker described the terrible scenes of that day:

> President Donald Trump had just returned to the White House from his rally at the Ellipse on January 6 when he retired to his private dining room just off the Oval Office. . . . At the other end of Pennsylvania Avenue, thousands of his supporters were wearing his red caps, waving his blue flags, and chanting his name. Live television news coverage showed the horror accelerating minute by minute after 1:10 p.m., when Trump had called upon his followers to march on the US Capitol. The pro-Trump rioters toppled security barri-cades. They bludgeoned police. They scaled granite walls. And then they smashed windows and doors to breach the hallowed building that has stood for more than two centuries as the seat of American democracy.
>
> The Capitol was under siege—and the president, glued to the television, did nothing. For 187 minutes, Trump resisted entreaties to intervene from advisers, allies, and his elder daughter, as well as lawmakers [including the Republican House leader] under attack. Even as the violence at the Capitol intensified, even after Vice President Mike Pence, his family, and hundreds of Congress members and their staffers hid to protect themselves, even after the first two people died and scores of others were assaulted, Trump declined for more than three hours to tell the renegades rioting in his name to stand down and go home. During the 187 minutes that Trump stood by, harrowing scenes of violence played out in and around the Capitol:

- Twenty-five minutes into Trump's silence, a news photographer was dragged down a flight of stairs and thrown over a wall.
- Seventy-three minutes in, another police officer was sprayed in the face with chemicals. Seventy-eight minutes in, yet another police officer was assaulted with a flagpole.
- Eighty-three minutes in, rioters broke into and began looting the House speaker's office.
- Ninety-four minutes in, a rioter was shot and killed.
- One hundred and two minutes in, rioters stormed the Senate chambers, stealing papers.
- One hundred and sixteen minutes in, a fourth police officer was crushed in a doorway and beaten with his own baton.[1]

Many tried to influence the president to stop the violence.

> House Minority Leader Kevin McCarthy (R-CA), a Trump booster, called him and said, "You have to denounce this." Trump falsely claimed to McCarthy that the rioters were members of Antifa, but McCarthy corrected him and said they were in fact Trump supporters. "You know what I see, Kevin? I see people who are more upset about the election than you are. They like Trump more than you do," the president replied. "You've got to hold them," McCarthy said. "You need to get on TV right now, you need to get on Twitter, you need to call these people off." Trump responded, "Kevin, they're not my people." McCarthy told the president, "Yes they are, they just came through my windows and my staff is running for cover. Yeah, they're your people. Call them off."

---

1   Philip Rucker, "The Attack (During): Bloodshed. The Jan. 6 Siege of the US Capitol Was Neither a Spontaneous Act Nor an Isolated Event," *Washington Post*, October 31, 2021, https://www.washingtonpost.com/politics/interactive/2021/what-happened-trump-jan-6-insurrection/.

The *Post*'s investigation also found that signs of escalating danger were in full view hours before the Capitol attack. . . . The mounting red flags did not trigger stepped-up security responses that morning, underscoring how unprepared law enforcement authorities were for the violence that transpired. Yet some officials knew what to expect; Liz Cheney (R-WY) had hired a personal security detail for her own safety.[2]

She and her father, former vice president Dick Cheney, had had an important telephone discussion while Trump was still speaking in front of the White House. The elder Cheney had called his daughter after watching Trump denounce her by name. He feared for her safety. While the situation was deteriorating around the Capitol,

they discussed whether she should tone down the remarks she planned to deliver in support of Biden's victory. "Should it affect what you're going to do?" her father asked. After some discussion, they agreed she should press on. "You can't let that sort of threat stop you from doing what is right."

At 12:30 p.m., Pence arrived at the Capitol. As the motorcade drew near, one of his staffers was struck by the scale of the crowd. Pence's team did not imagine the scene would turn violent; none of the relevant agencies had briefed the vice president or his team about what to expect. Pence brought his wife, Karen, and daughter Charlotte along with him to the Capitol, where they were joined by his brother, Greg, a Republican congressman from Indiana. The vice president didn't have them accompany him to enjoy a historic day. He knew he might need them by his side for emotional support.[3]

Pence and his family, along with many others, were endangered that day by Trump's actions. Some at the Capitol were injured or even

---

2 Rucker, "The Attack (During): Bloodshed."
3 Rucker, "The Attack (During): Bloodshed."

killed. Trump watched the carnage on television, but he would only agree to stop the attack after many urged him to do so—and, perhaps more importantly, after he began to see that it might lead to even more negative consequences for him.

This coup attempt was perhaps the most anti-American and unconstitutional act that Trump contemplated during his four years in office. Had Pence, at Trump's bidding, tried to change votes to declare Trump reelected and Biden defeated, the result could have been a revolution, a civil war, a secession—or maybe all three. In the process, President Trump committed high crimes and misdemeanors far exceeding those of the previous presidents who had been impeached, Andrew Johnson and Bill Clinton. Trump's crimes also far exceeded those of Richard Nixon, who resigned in disgrace before he could be impeached.

At last, after over three hours of violent insurrection, a pleading phone call from DC mayor Muriel Bowser to chief of staff Mark Meadows, and an intervention by Mike Pence, the Defense Department released National Guard troops that began to add their efforts to protect the Capitol. Also, after the many, many requests from Trump's aides, supporters, and allies, including Meadows and Trump's daughter Ivanka, he agreed to consider telling the rioters to go home.

> Ivanka Trump shuttled between her second-floor West Wing office, where she watched the riot unfold on television, and the president's dining room, where he was watching television, trying to persuade her dad to use stronger language to bring an end to the insurrection. But just when she thought she had gotten him into the right headspace, Meadows would call her because the president was still unconvinced.

Finally, Trump agreed and recorded a message in the Rose Garden between 4:00 and 4:30 p.m. "Trump's message was ambiguous. He opened his speech by repeating the lie that the election was rigged.

He told his supporters to 'go home,' but immediately added: 'We love you. You're very special.'"[4]

Gradually the mob began to disperse. Later Trump excused the riot, tweeting that "these are the things and events that happen when a sacred landslide election victory is so unceremoniously & viciously stripped away."[5]

Afterward, as details of the day were reported in the press, it became clear how frightening the objectives behind the attack had been. According to the *Post* account, there were some whose mission appeared to be to kill Nancy Pelosi and Vice President Pence. Luke Mogelson of the *New Yorker* reported one man taunting "Nancy, I'm ho-ome!" and others yelling, "Where's Pence?" and "Hang Mike Pence!" A gallows had been set up on the Mall.[6] Pence was definitely target number one, designated so by Trump himself because he refused to obey Trump's demand that he simply gavel Trump back into office while doing the Electoral College vote count. The mob missed Pence by the narrowest of margins.

On Saturday, January 9, CNN's Wolf Blitzer interviewed Rep. Abigail Spanberger (D-VA). When the January 6 attack came, she had been in the gallery of the House chamber, as had many members, in an effort to maintain social distancing during the House proceeding. One of the Capitol policemen placed benches against the door. She could hear considerable noise on the other side of the door—shouts and epithets. There was heavy banging on the door. The members on the floor were evacuated first to a secure location. Those in the gallery had to crawl to a door on their hands and knees—for fear of gunfire—so that they could be evacuated as well. Spanberger was a CIA veteran,

4   Rucker, "The Attack (During): Bloodshed."

5   "Trump Caused the Assault on the Capitol. He Must Be Removed," editorial, *Washington Post*, January 6, 2021, https://www.washingtonpost.com/opinions/remove-trump-incitement-sedition-25th-amendment/2021/01/06/b22c6ad4-506d-11eb-b96e-0e54447b23a1_story.html.

6   Luke Mogelson, "Among the Insurrectionists," *New Yorker*, January 25, 2021, https://www.newyorker.com/magazine/2021/01/25/among-the-insurrectionists.

but she had never experienced anything like this. Throughout the short interview with Blitzer, she had a very sober look.

The prime objective of the attack—halting the vote count—succeeded for perhaps six hours, as the Capitol was temporarily filled with dangerous barbarians. Senators and representatives who had fled for their lives, however, bravely returned after the crisis had passed. They persisted until, with Vice President Pence presiding, Joe Biden was confirmed as president in the wee hours of the next morning.

In its January 6 editorial "Trump Caused the Assault," the *Post* wrote of the attack on the Capitol:

> Responsibility for this act of sedition lies squarely with the president, who has shown that his continued tenure in office poses a grave threat to US democracy. He should be removed. Mr. Trump encouraged the mob to gather on Wednesday, as Congress was set to convene [to confirm the Electoral College vote count], and to "be wild." After repeating a panoply of absurd conspiracy theories about the election, he urged the crowd to march on the Capitol. "We're going to walk down, and I'll be there with you," he said. "You'll never take back our country with weakness. You have to show strength, and you have to be strong."[7]

The *Post* concluded,

> The president is unfit to remain in office for the next 14 days. Every second he retains the vast powers of the presidency is a threat to public order and national security. . . . The highest voice in the land incited people to break that faith, not just in tweets, but by inciting them to action. Mr. Trump is a menace, and as long as he remains in the White House, the country will be in danger.[8]

7   "Trump Caused the Assault," *Washington Post.*
8   "Trump Caused the Assault," *Washington Post.*

In supporting Trump's illegal attack on our Constitution, Senators Cruz and Hawley were not patriots. George Will concurred in blaming Cruz and Hawley along with Trump:

> The three repulsive architects of Wednesday's heartbreaking spectacle—mobs desecrating the republic's noblest building and preventing the completion of a constitutional process— must be named and forevermore shunned. They are Donald Trump and Sens. Josh Hawley and Ted Cruz. Trump lit the fuse for the riot in the weeks before the election, with his successful effort to delegitimize the election in the eyes of his supporters. But Wednesday's explosion required the help of Hawley (R-MO) and Cruz (R-TX). . . . The Trump-Hawley-Cruz insurrection against constitutional government will be an indelible stain on the nation. They, however, will not be so permanent. In 14 days, one of them will be removed from office by the constitutional processes he neither fathoms nor favors. It will take longer to scrub the other two from public life. Until that hygienic outcome is accomplished, from this day forward, everything they say or do or advocate should be disregarded as patent attempts to distract attention from the lurid fact of what they have become. Each will wear a scarlet 'S' as a seditionist.[9]

The *Post* editors reported Biden's response to the insurrection and commented:

> "I call on this mob, now, to pull back and allow the work of democracy to go forward. It's not protest. It's insurrection. Today is a reminder, a painful one, that democracy is fragile."

---

9   George F. Will, "Trump, Hawley and Cruz Will Each Wear the Scarlet 'S' of a Seditionist," *Washington Post*, January 6, 2021, https://www.washingtonpost.com/ opinions/trump-hawley-and-cruz-will-each-wear-the-scarlet-s-of-a-seditionist/ 2021/01/06/65b0ad1a-506c-11eb-bda4-615aaefd0555_story.html.

Mr. Biden is right. Rules, norms, laws, even the Constitution itself are worth something only if people believe in them. [Americans carry out all their civic duties] because of faith in a system—and that faith makes it work.[10]

Michael Gerson, in one of the most important articles of the past few years, raised the question of the longer-term impact of the January 6 insurrection. He wrote:

The practical effects of the fascist occupation of the US Capitol Building were quickly undone. The symbols it left behind are indelible. A Confederate flag waved in triumph in the halls of a building never taken by Jefferson Davis. Guns drawn to protect the floor of the House of Representatives from violent attack. A cloddish barbarian in the presiding officer's chair. The desecration of democracy under the banner "Jesus Saves." This postapocalyptic vision of chaos and national humiliation was the direct and intended consequence of a president's incitement. It was made possible by quislings such as Sens. Josh Hawley (R-MO) and Ted Cruz (R-TX), who turned a ceremony of continuity into a rallying cry for hatred and treason. In the aftermath, Republican legislators who still don't support President Trump's immediate removal from office by constitutional means are guilty of continuing complicity.[11]

Trump had stood before thousands in front of the White House and called Joe Biden "an illegitimate president." Subsequent events soon demonstrated that Trump himself was the one who was trying to become an illegitimate president. Ivanka Trump tweeted that the crowd were "American patriots."[12] Trump's attorney Rudy Giuliani

---

10 "Trump Caused the Assault," *Washington Post*.
11 Gerson, "Trump's Evangelicals."
12 Sara Nathan, "Ivanka Trump 'Surprised and Hurt' by Karlie Kloss' Tweets after

suggested on stage before Trump appeared that "trial by combat" decide the election.[13] And Trump himself told the crowd that they should march to the Capitol "to try and give [Republicans] the kind of pride and boldness that they need to take back our country."[14]

Former president George W. Bush posted a statement that said, in part:

> It is a sickening and heartbreaking sight. This is how election results are disputed in a banana republic—not our democratic republic. I am appalled by the reckless behavior of some political leaders since the election and by the lack of respect shown today for our institutions, our traditions, and our law enforcement.[15]

Sen. Mitt Romney asserted, "What happened here today was an insurrection, incited by the president of the United States."[16]

After the coup had failed and the crowd had dissipated, the way Republicans and Democrats discovered their common bonds and spoke to one another—not as fractious party members but as patriots and Americans—was inspiring. Hours after Sen. James Lankford's speech challenging Arizona's Electoral College vote was interrupted by the barbaric mob that invaded our Capitol, he resumed his speech but with a different message. As described in a *Washington Post* editorial:

Capitol Siege," *Page Six*, January 8, 2021, https://pagesix.com/2021/01/08/ivanka-surprised-and-hurt-by-karlie-kloss-tweets/.

13 Aaron Blake, "What Trump Said Before His Supporters Stormed the Capitol, Annotated," *Washington Post*, January 11, 2021, https://www.washingtonpost.com/politics/interactive/2021/annotated-trump-speech-jan-6-capitol/.

14 Blake, "What Trump Said."

15 George W. Bush, "Statement by President George W. Bush on Insurrection at the Capitol," George W. Bush Presidential Center, https://www.bushcenter.org/about-the-center/newsroom/press-releases/2021/statement-by-president-george-w-bush-on-insurrection-at-the-capitol.html.

16 Philip Rucker, "Trump's Presidency Finishes in 'American Carnage' as Rioters Storm the Capitol," *Washington Post*, January 6, 2021, https://www.washingtonpost.com/politics/trump-rioters-incite/2021/01/06/0acfc778-5035-11eb-bda4-615aaefd0555_story.html.

"We're the United States of America," he said. "We disagree on a lot of things, and we have a lot of spirited debate in this room. But we talk it out, and we honor each other—even in our disagreement. That person, that person, that person"—here the senator gestured to other senators, presumably of the other party—"is not my enemy. That's my fellow American."[17]

Senator Romney was also quoted in the *Post* editorial:

"I was shaken to the core as I thought about the people I met in China and Russia and Afghanistan and Iraq and other places who yearn for freedom, and who look to this building and these shores as a place of hope. And I saw the images being broadcast around the world, and it breaks my heart."[18]

Unfortunately, this atmosphere of cooperation was too soon gone. In the wake of all this, House Speaker Nancy Pelosi and Senate Minority (soon to be Majority) Leader Chuck Schumer both called for Trump's removal from office. A growing number of Republicans were coming to the same conclusion, including Trump's former chief of staff, John Kelly, and Rep. Adam Kinzinger (R-IL), who supported the idea of action to remove Trump as unfit for office pursuant to the 25th Amendment to the Constitution. Sen. Lindsay Graham (R-SC), a close confidant of Trump, said that "the president needs to understand that his actions were the problem."[19] Graham also urged

---

17 "To Heal America, We Must Repudiate Not Just Trump but Also His Politics of Demonization," editorial, *Washington Post*, January 7, 2021, https://www.washington post.com/opinions/to-heal-america-we-must-repudiate-not-just-trump-but-also-his-politics-of-demonization/2021/01/07/8f6a7388-5117-11eb-b96e-0e54447b23a1_story.html.

18 "To Heal America," *Washington Post*.

19 Josh Dawsey, Michael Scherer, and Matt Viser, "Trump's Failures This Week Open Rifts in a Republican Party He Has Controlled," *Washington Post*, January 7, 2021, https://www.washingtonpost.com/politics/trump-republicans-capitol-mob/2021/01/07/f56300ac-5111-11eb-b96e-0e54447b23a1_story.html.

the prosecution and imprisonment of all those who had forced their way onto the grounds of the US Capitol. The attackers were people with whom Trump sympathized and whom, after the situation was completely out of control and had been for a while, he directed only reluctantly to call off their attack on the Capitol and go home, adding that he loved them. Graham dismissed them as "domestic terrorists." He pointed out that some of the terrorists on the Hill had been specifically seeking the vice president, adding, "In this debacle of the last week or so, there's one person who stands out above all others. That is Vice President Pence. . . . The things he was asked to do in the name of loyalty were over the top, unconstitutional, illegal, and would have been wrong for the country."[20]

Never before had American democracy been threatened in quite this way—by a president who wished to make himself dictator and who did not shy from destroying American institutions. He was abetted by organizations on the conservative side of the spectrum and by people who knew better. They helped Trump corrupt a large group of voters with real or perceived grievances—voters who perhaps did not know better, their gullibility pointing to the failure of American education. Trump banked on endless lies and conspiracy theories that those supporting him did not rebut.

The Trump insurrection had been, in fact, the work of four or more years, years during which he had painted himself as the hero in many conspiracy theories. These theories, encouraged by such groups as QAnon, convinced many people that the nation and the world were in terrible danger from shady liberal cabals and that Americans must be prepared to fight these evildoers. To people with this mindset—and there were more and more of them as Trump's presidency continued— Trump was not just a politician, nor even just a president, but a savior.

Trump had begun his career of political lies and deception as a prominent mouthpiece for the so-called birther movement during the

---

20 Dawsey, Scherer, and Viser, "Trump's Failures This Week."

Obama administration. Soon he began spouting other conspiracy theories. During the 2016 campaign, Trump appeared on Alex Jones's *InfoWars*—a show constantly warning, according to Luke Mogelson, "that the *deep state*—a nefarious shadow authority manipulating US policy for the profit of elites—opposed Trump because he threatened its power. Jones has asserted that the Bush administration was responsible for 9/11 and that the Sandy Hook Elementary School massacre never happened."[21] In 2018, when Jones accused the bereaved parents of the children murdered at Sandy Hook of being paid actors, he was promptly expelled by Facebook, Twitter, Apple, Spotify, and YouTube. For a time his presence faded, but the pandemic brought him back on proprietary websites. Roger Stone, a Trump aide later convicted of seven felonies in connection with the Mueller investigation of Trump's links to Russia, had arranged for Trump's appearance on the show, during which Trump had promised Jones, "I will not let you down."[22] Jones continued to give Trump fawning coverage, and Trump's supposedly stolen election fit right in with his rants on the "deep state," the "evil elite world order," and "tyrannical COVID-19 restrictions."

Thus there was a compact with the conspiracists early on that strengthened over the next four years. From Trump during that time came perhaps upward of 30,000 lies to the public, of which 16,000-plus have been verified from his first three years, with the number escalating in 2020.[23] As Mogelson writes, "The claim of a plot to steal the election makes sense to people who see Trump as a warrior against deep-state chicanery."[24] These are people who, having been taken in by Trump's vision of an alternate universe, found it strengthened by thousands of Trump lies alleging fake news, fraud, and malevolent conspiracy, to the point that they were conditioned to believe whatever Trump said.

---

21 Mogelson, "Among the Insurrectionists."
22 Mogelson, "Among the Insurrectionists."
23 Kessler, Rizzo, and Kelly, "Trump Assault on Truth," x, xi.
24 Mogelson, "Among the Insurrectionists."

Notably, Robert O'Harrow, writing for the *Washington Post*, revealed the extent to which the insurrection was rooted in broad-based conservative activism:

> The fiery rallies that preceded the deadly riot at the US Capitol on January 6 were organized and promoted by an array of established conservative insiders and activists. . . . The Republican Attorneys General Association was involved, as were the activist groups Turning Point Action and Tea Party Patriots. At least six current or former members of the Council for National Policy (CNP), an influential group that for decades has served as a hub for conservative and Christian activists, also played roles in promoting the rallies. The two days of rallies were staged not by white nationalists and other extremists, but by well-funded nonprofit groups and individuals that figure prominently in the machinery of conservative activism in Washington.[25]

O'Harrow cites Ali Alexander as an example of those who mobilized extremists to attack the Capitol. According to O'Harrow, Alexander, a former CNP fellow who organized the "Stop the Steal" movement, on January 5 led protesters at Freedom Plaza in DC in a chant of "Victory or death!" Earlier he had tweeted that unless Congress responded to the protests, "Everyone can guess what me and 500,000 others will do to that building . . . 1776 is *always* an option."[26]

Another January 6 recruiter O'Harrow mentioned was

> the attorneys general group [that] used an affiliated nonprofit called the Rule of Law Defense Fund to pay for a robocall that urged supporters to march on the Capitol at 1 p.m. on

25 Robert O'Harrow Jr., "Rallies Ahead of Capitol Riot Were Planned by Established Washington Insiders," *Washington Post*, January 17, 2021, https://www.washingtonpost.com/investigations/capitol-rally-organizers-before-riots/2021/01/16/c5b40250-552d-11eb-a931-5b162d0d033d_story.html.

26 O'Harrow, "Rallies Ahead of Capitol Riot."

January 6 to "call on Congress to stop the steal." [The rob-ocall recording said,] "We are hoping patriots like you will join us to continue the fight."[27]

In addition, the FBI continues to look closely at three extremist groups: the Proud Boys, Oath Keepers, and Three Percenters. These organizations were among the earliest of the coup planners, active weeks before January 6. Many of their members are White suprem-acists, to whom Trump, a racist of long standing, has continued to appeal; some whom the FBI had already been following were present at the assault on the Capitol. Several have since been arrested by the FBI.

Domestic terrorism and White supremist organizations antedated Trump and will continue after he has left the scene. Before he was elected, he promised to make them more powerful. And he did so, giving them opportunities. Although he thought that they would help him stay in office, they did not manage that. But these movements and organizations grew far stronger under Trump. They represent a threat to the nation, and likely we will have to deal with them for many years.

From the beginning, Trump had never intended to be the president of all the people. After the 2020 election, he created an opening for the extremist right by his attack on the validity of the election, creating a cause that could fuel them for years. The violence of January 6, 2021, was not a chance insurrection; it was carefully planned.

The attack on the Capitol was the predictable apotheosis of a months-long ferment. Throughout the pandemic, aided and abetted by Trump, right-wing protesters had been gathering at statehouses, demanding entry. In April, an armed mob had filled the Michigan state capitol, chanting "Treason!" and "Let us in!" In December, con-servatives had broken the glass doors of the Oregon State Capitol, overrunning officers and spraying them with chemical agents.[28]

---

27 O'Harrow, "Rallies Ahead of Capitol Riot."
28 Mogelson, "Among the Insurrectionists."

Two weeks before the Michigan event, Trump had tweeted, "LIBERATE MICHIGAN!"

The attack on the Capitol appeared far more sinister. But what was the point? Once Pence had refused to accede to Trump's urging, all hope for overturning the election had disappeared. It is therefore difficult to understand the goals of those who fomented, planned, and executed the attack. A display of apparent power? A signal that Trump would continue to contend until the date when he would, somehow, return? Whatever its fuzzy objectives, the siege was a direct assault on democracy and constitutional order. As former New Jersey governor Chris Christie said, "If inciting to insurrection isn't [an impeachable offense], then I don't really know what is." [29]

The day after the attack, the National Association of Manufacturers called for Trump's immediate removal. Some called for Trump to resign, which he said he would never do. Some called for Vice President Pence to lead the effort to remove him under the 25th Amendment to the Constitution, which addresses the need to remove a president when he can no longer carry out the duties of president. Pence, who would have had to lead a 25th Amendment process, indicated he would not support such an action; perhaps the possibility of his being shot on Capitol Hill was too great. Two cabinet officers—Elaine Chao at Transportation and Betsy DeVos at Education—resigned, ostensibly because they rejected the January 6 violence but possibly because they didn't want to become targets by signing a 25th Amendment petition. No one believed there was any chance that Trump would resign; Pence would certainly not have pardoned him had he done so.

That left impeachment, for which support had been growing since the attack. Speaker Nancy Pelosi (D-CA) had said for the first time

---

29 Felicia Sonmez, Mike DeBonis, and Juliet Eilperin, "Pelosi Moves Ahead with Efforts for Trump's Removal as Democrats Split on How Hard to Push for Impeachment," *Washington Post*, January 10, 2021, https://www.washingtonpost.com/politics/clybrn-impeachment-trump/2021/01/10/fd10fa88-5356-11eb-a08b-f1381ef3d207_story.html.

on Sunday, January 10, that the House would proceed with bringing impeachment legislation to the floor if Vice President Pence declined to proceed under the 25th Amendment. She said, "As the days go by, the horror of the ongoing assault on our democracy perpetrated by this president is intensified and so is the immediate need for action."[30] Rep. Dean Phillips (D-MN) noted, "There has to be consequences."[31]

When Pence refused to invoke the 25th Amendment, support for impeachment increased in the House; all the Democrats favored it, together with a small number of Republicans. Some additional Republican members also wished to vote for impeachment but were deterred from doing so by death threats. Other Republicans who opposed impeachment and who spoke on the floor against it sounded, for the most part, like mini-Trumps. House Minority Leader Kevin McCarthy—a strong supporter of the stolen-election lies but also an opponent of the attack on the Capitol—refused to support impeachment, saying that it would divide the country even more, but he said he would support censure. In his article on sedition the day before the impeachment vote, Michael Gerson noted that McCarthy had "a vested interest in ignoring sedition. So he is not, perhaps, the best source of advice on events moving forward."[32]

Gerson also referenced the rallying cry of Rep. Lauren Boebert, who in the past had praised QAnon and promised to bring her Glock automatic pistol to the Capitol:[33]

> The problem with McCarthy's approach is that it assumes the threat has passed. On the morning of the Capitol attack, newly seated Rep. Lauren Boebert (R-CO) tweeted, "Today

---

30 Sonmez, DeBonis, and Eilperin, "Pelosi Moves Ahead."
31 Sonmez, DeBonis, and Eilperin, "Pelosi Moves Ahead."
32 Michael Gerson, "The US Must Punish Sedition—or Risk More of It," *Washington Post*, January 11, 2021, https://www.washingtonpost.com/opinions/the-us-must-punish-sedition--or-risk-more-of-it/2021/01/11/97907746-5438-11eb-a931-5b162d0d033d_story.html.
33 Mogelson, "Among the Insurrectionists."

is 1776"—comparing a revolt of treasonous misfits and conspiracy theorists to the conduct of a justified revolution. . . . Violent insurrectionists are still being fed the lie that their cause is equivalent to the American founding. . . . This conspiracy against the constitutional order has grown strong in an atmosphere of Republican appeasement. Those who want to continue that appeasement are inviting further disorder and violence. Stopping this rot in the political order will require accountability. That begins with the president, who deserves every legal and constitutional consequence our system offers. He should be impeached for sedition. He should be prevented from holding any further elective office. He should be stripped of all the perks of the post-presidency. He should be prosecuted for insurrection against the US government.[34]

Some Republicans were open about their support for impeachment—notably Liz Cheney, then the third highest ranking Republican in the House, a position from which she was (not unexpectedly) soon removed. Cheney said:

The president of the United States summoned this mob, assembled the mob, and lit the flame of this attack. . . . There has never been a greater betrayal by a president of the United States of his office and his oath to the Constitution.[35]

Rep. John Katko (R-NY), the ranking Republican on the Homeland Security Committee, Rep. Adam Kinzinger (R-IL), and Rep. Fred Upton (R-MI) also announced their support for impeachment. Katko said, "To allow the president of the United States to incite this attack

---

34 Michael Gerson, "The US Must Punish Sedition."

35 Mike DeBonis, Josh Dawsey, and Seung Min Kim, "Several Senior Republicans Join Impeachment Push," *Washington Post*, January 13, 2021, https://www. washingtonpost.com/politics/house-trump-impeach/2021/01/12/5e873dd0-54ed-11eb-a08b-f1381ef3d207_story.html.

without consequences is a direct threat to the future of our democracy. If these actions . . . are not worthy of impeachment, then what is an impeachable offense?"[36]

According to Michael Kranish, "Rep. Liz Cheney's historic decision Tuesday [January 12, 2021] to vote to impeach President Trump had its roots in a dramatic phone call from her father, former vice president Richard B. Cheney." Kranish reported that Dick Cheney had warned her in his call on the morning of January 6 that she was being attacked by the president in his speech to the crowd that would soon become rioters and terrorists. Trump had told them, "We got to get rid of the weak congresspeople, the ones that aren't any good, the Liz Cheneys of the world." After the call from her father, she had walked back onto the House floor to continue her efforts to stop the House from questioning the Electoral College vote. Then she heard banging on the chamber's door by an angry mob and a shot fired. She then realized that an attempted coup or insurrection was underway. "The president could have immediately and forcefully intervened to stop the violence. . . . He did not," she said in her statement. Her conclusion: "I will vote to impeach the president."[37]

On the day of the impeachment vote in the House, the *Post* editorialized:

> [Some Republicans and] right-wing commentators have argued that there is little difference between what the Republicans have done since last November and what Democrats did following Mr. Trump's 2016 victory. . . . This is unhinged. Democrats immediately acknowledged Mr. Trump's win."[38]

---

36 DeBonis, Dawsey, and Kim, "Several Senior Republicans."

37 Michael Kranish, "Before Riot, Trump Said 'We Got to Get Rid' of Rep. Liz Cheney. Now She Supports Impeaching Him," *Washington Post*, January 12, 2021, https://www.washingtonpost.com/politics/cheney-trump-house-impeach/2021/01/12/648c677a-54d2-11eb-a08b-f1381ef3d207_story.html.

38 "Republicans Want Reconciliation. Here's What They Need to Do First," editorial,

On Wednesday, January 13, the bill of impeachment—the second one for Trump—was placed before the House. It passed by a vote of 232 to 197, with 222 Democrats and 10 Republicans voting in favor. The Senate was informed on Friday, January 15, that the bill of impeachment would be sent over to the Senate early in the next week. Majority Leader McConnell made clear that he would not call the Senate back before January 19, to attend President Biden's inauguration the following day. The *Washington Post* editorialized on January 13:

> If Mr. McConnell refuses to convene the Senate this week, senators must move with dispatch once they have convened, and split their time between trying Mr. Trump and enabling the launch of the Biden administration. But the nation would be better served by a prompt trial ending in the guilty verdict Mr. Trump deserves.[39]

The Senate did not act upon the articles of impeachment by January 20; they would not do so until February, when they would vote to acquit.

Trump walked away from the presidency with a $200,000 annual pension, $1 million a year for travel, Secret Service protection for life, and the freedom to run for president again in 2024. Trump ending his term without sanctions seemed almost like a reward, rather than a punishment, for attempting to overthrow the government and destroy our democracy.

In response to the violence of January 6, US industry opted to largely silence Mr. Trump in a display of patriotism widely noticed

Washington Post, January 12, 2021, https://www.washingtonpost.com/opinions/republicans-want-reconciliation-heres-what-they-need-to-do-first/2021/01/12/a0db0dfa-5520-11eb-a817-e5e7f8a406d6_story.html.

39 "President Trump Deserved Impeachment. The Senate Must Convict Him Quickly," editorial, *Washington Post*, January 13, 2021, https://www.washingtonpost.com/opinions/president-trump-deserved-impeachment-the-senate-must-convict-him-quickly/2021/01/13/746e3b2c-55cd-11eb-a931-5b162d0d033d_story.html.

and appreciated. Twitter and Facebook banned Trump from using
their platforms. According to an opinion piece in the *New York Times*:

> Twitter's decision to permanently suspend Mr. Trump's
> account on Friday [January 8] "due to the risk of further in-
> citement of violence," after a decision a day earlier by Facebook
> to ban the president at least through the end of his term, was
> a watershed moment in the history of social media.[40]

And then, as mentioned above, there are the many would-be
Trumps and mini-Trumps. Their roles in the insurrection must be addressed, however difficult it is to do so. Those most responsible for the
post-election, traitorous behavior by some leaders of the Republican
Party—actions stoking insurrection or refusing to recognize it—
must be called to account. According to Gerson, that means—as a
beginning—"ethics investigations of people such as Sen. Josh Hawley
(R-MO), Sen. Ted Cruz (R-TX), and McCarthy, leading to their possible expulsion" from Congress. "These legislators urged surrender to
the pernicious lies and seditious demands of violent insurrectionists
who had just left the building. That is the betrayal of the oath they
took to defend the Constitution."[41]

This is good advice. It would be supported by the American people,
and it would be the beginning of our country's return to a place where
all people are truly understood to be created equal and to have an
inherent right to life, liberty, and the pursuit of happiness.

There are three other individuals from the House of Representatives
who should be included on Gerson's list. They are Reps. Andy Biggs
(R-AZ), Mo Brooks (R-AL), and Paul A. Gosar (R-AZ). These three
representatives, according to Alexander, worked with him on a plan
to disrupt the electoral count at the Capitol. "We four schemed up

---

40 Kevin Roose, "In Pulling Trump's Megaphone, Twitter Shows Where Power Now
    Lies," *New York Times*, January 9, 2021, https://www.nytimes.com/2021/01/09/
    technology/trump-twitter-ban.html.
41 Gerson, "The US Must Punish Sedition."

of putting maximum pressure on Congress while they were voting," Alexander said in a video.[42] In a podcast interview last month, Brooks said:

> The question is really simple. Are you as an American citizen going to surrender in the face of unparalleled, massive voter fraud and election theft? . . . Or are you going to do what your ancestors did and fight for your country, your republic?[43]

Additionally, speaking shortly before Trump to the crowd of domestic terrorists and enablers on January 6, Brooks had said to "stop at the Capitol" and "begin kicking ass."[44]

What course of action should we follow? There are perhaps two broad approaches open. One is that of Ulysses S. Grant in 1861: "There are but two parties now, traitors and patriots."[45] The other is that of Abraham Lincoln, who wrote in his second inaugural address in 1865, as the nation was emerging from a bitterly fought war, words not of revenge but of unity:

> With malice toward none; with charity for all; with firmness in the right, as God gives us to see the right, let us strive on to finish the work we are in; to bind up the nation's wounds; to care for him who shall have borne the battle, and for his widow, and his orphan—to do all which may achieve and cherish a just, and a lasting peace, among ourselves, and with all nations.[46]

---

42 O'Harrow, "Rallies Ahead of Capitol Riot."

43 O'Harrow, "Rallies Ahead of Capitol Riot."

44 Amy Davidson Sorkin, "Why Trump Must Go On Trial," *New Yorker,* January 17, 2021, https://www.newyorker.com/magazine/2021/01/25/why-trump-must-go-on-trial; Teri Kanefield and Mark Reichel, "'Trump Said I Could': One Possible Legal Defense for Accused Rioters," *Washington Post,* January 11, 2021, https://www.washingtonpost.com/outlook/2021/01/11/public-authority-trump-mob-capitol/.

45 Ulysses S. Grant, *Letters of Ulysses S. Grant to His Father and His Youngest Sister,* accessed on Bookrags, http://www.bookrags.com/ebooks/13471/11.html#gsc.tab=0.

46 "Abraham Lincoln's Second Inaugural Address," Library of Congress, https://www.

Which road is chosen will depend to a degree on how the two parties—Democrat and Republican—respond, like McCarthy or like Lankford. Perhaps the appalling siege of the Capitol and the departure of would-be dictator Donald Trump, savage purveyor of lies and corruption, will enable the nation to have—also in Abraham Lincoln's phrase—"a new birth of freedom."

If we can find a way to face our many challenges and threats together, we cannot fail.

---

loc.gov/rr/program/bib/ourdocs/lincoln2nd.html.

EPILOGUE

WHERE LIES THE FUTURE for the Republican Party and for America? Does the party see Republicans as patriots and all others as traitors—the "traitors and patriots" of General Grant's 1861 letter to his father? Or can the party embrace Lincoln's unifying "with malice toward none" vision expressed in his second inaugural address?

After the January 6 violence at the Capitol, we witnessed a brief moment when at least some Republicans and Democrats spoke to each other as human beings, with hope that the nation could be repaired, but soon our leaders were recasting the relations between the parties as traitors versus patriots once again. Trump and other congressional Republicans quickly reinjected the hatred gene into discourse, and the Democrats moved toward impeachment for the second time during Trump's presidency. Trump—inexhaustible fountain of vituperation—continued to lie, threaten, and bad-mouth "opponents" as he had done extensively during his campaign and presidency. His purpose seemed to be to make sure he would not lose an election again; Americans would be too afraid of him. Then he would be president for the rest of his life.

Donald Trump doesn't understand very much about American public life. On June 15, 2018, when Sen. Kirsten Gillibrand (D-NY) was asked during an interview by a *Politico* reporter what she thought of President Trump, she replied, "His policies come from darkness and are evil in the biblical sense." In another part of the interview, she referred to the Trump administration as promoting "the devil's schemes."[1] Americans are not going to surrender their liberties to someone who carries out "the devil's schemes," or anyone else, for that matter.

In February of 2021, Michael Gerson penned a perceptive *Washington Post* column, "There's Only One Political Party Right Now," in which he assessed the state of party politics. He pointed to the strong disagreements in the Democratic Party between progressives and moderates, noting that for some people this seemed like dysfunction. For him, however, it was the "beating pulse of a healthy party." Post-Trump Republicans, by contrast, he believes, "have generally lost their standing to engage in these debates. Fiscal prudence? . . . Trump increased the national debt by some $7.8 trillion" without a whimper from anyone in the Republican Party. Executive overreach? Their president just led his party in an attempted coup with support from 90 percent of congressional Republicans—those who refused to impeach Trump in the aftermath. Gerson wrote:

> Elected Republicans who cheered Trump are not just hypocrites on these matters. They are jokes. From an ideological perspective, the Republican Party is a patient without a pulse. The only real question: are we ready to declare time of death? . . . That type of conservatism [that supports intraparty arguments] still exists, in offices at the American Enterprise Institute, among idealistic Capitol Hill staffers. . . . My advice? Given the entrenchment of the two-party system, the best option seems to be remaining in the GOP as long as conscience allows. Sometimes you struggle to win. Sometimes you struggle to keep something important alive. Both are noble callings.[2]

---

1   Edward-Isaac Dovere, "Trump's Policies 'Come from the Darkness.'"
2   Michael Gerson, "There's Only One Political Party Right Now," *Washington Post*,

The *Post* editorialized, "The country cannot forget that Mr. Trump betrayed his oath, that most Republican officeholders remain loyal to him nevertheless—and that it could be worse next time."[3]

After the coup attempt, Amy Sorkin reported in the *New Yorker* that Steny Hoyer, the Democratic House Majority Leader, had inquired of Capitol Police what the rules were for members carrying weapons in the Capitol. It is worrisome that representatives in the House were probing to find out just how far they might go were something like January 6 to occur again. Sorkin wrote:

> Last time, the violence of the Capitol elicited enough angry shock that some Fox News anchors and leading Republicans tweeted Meadows, asking for Trump to calm the mob. If there is a next time, the texts to whoever plays Meadows's role might have a different, and more dangerous, message.[4]

After all, Representative Boebert has openly stated that she brings her Glock onto the floor with her.

Trump has continued a nationwide effort to discredit Republicans who refused to go along with his coup plans, and he and others are continuing a campaign to change voting laws to make it more difficult for non-Whites to vote. Those twin efforts have been largely successful; many Republican election officials other than proven Trumpists have been removed from the national bureaucracies that implement the elections, and 19 states have passed new and highly restrictive

February 22, 2021, https://www.washingtonpost.com/opinions/theres-only-one-political-party-right-now/2021/02/22/5f8cc42e-7541-11eb-948d-19472e683521_story.html.

3   "A Trove of Preposterous Emails Raises the Question: How Can Republicans Still Be Loyal to This Man?," editorial, *Washington Post*, June 15, 2021, https://www.washingtonpost.com/opinions/the-nation-cannot-forget-donald-trumps-betrayal-of-his-oath/2021/06/15/c4a7790e-ce0a-11eb-8014-2f3926ca24d9_story.html.

4   Amy Davidson Sorkin, "Mark Meadows and the Republican Response to the January 6th Investigation," *New Yorker*, December 19, 2021, https://www.newyorker.com/magazine/2021/12/27/mark-meadows-and-the-republican-response-to-the-january-6th-investigation.

election laws. A half year previous to the 2020 election, Florida had expressed pride in its election vote, completed with the use of mail-in ballots and drop boxes, but because it turned out that too many Democrats used mail-in ballots, Florida Republicans passed legislation to make voting by mail much more difficult. For instance, the legislation virtually eliminated drop boxes.

The work of Trump and his followers goes well beyond reasonable political action. Trump and other Republicans, including many who participated in or supported the attack on the Capitol from Congress as well as from elsewhere around the country, began efforts to rerun elections where the vote was close, such as in Arizona, Georgia, Wisconsin, Michigan, and Pennsylvania. Though this effort has proved to be substantially unsuccessful—50 courts have thrown out their claims—a look at efforts in Arizona and a passing glance at those in Michigan during 2021 is instructive as to how these efforts have affected the nation.

Eleven days after the insurrection, Trump's election lies bloomed anew in Phoenix. Republicans in the Arizona State Senate subpoenaed Maricopa County, demanding that it turn over its nearly 2.1 million paper ballots, which had been packed up in cardboard boxes and stored in a facility known as the Vault. Trump had narrowly lost the state thanks to Biden's 45,000-vote margin in that county, home to Phoenix and to 60 percent of all Arizonans.[5] It mattered not to the Republican state senators that the accuracy of this count had been confirmed several times by federal and state judges.

> After a grueling year as chairman of the Maricopa County Board of Supervisors, the Republican [Clint Hickman] had eagerly handed off his gavel at a long-planned ceremony on

---

5   Amy Goodman and Rosalind S. Helderman, "The Attack (After): Contagion. The Jan. 6 Siege of the US Capitol Was Neither a Spontaneous Act Nor an Isolated Event," *Washington Post*, October 31, 2021, https://www.washingtonpost.com/politics/interactive/2021/warnings-jan-6-insurrection/.

the morning of January 6, only to arrive home to find two sheriff's deputies waiting in an unmarked car in his doorway.

Their tone was urgent. "You shouldn't be home tonight," one said.

"It's not that bad," Hickman responded. As chairman, he had faced threats and a large protest outside his home after he and the board had certified Joe Biden's win in the county in late November. The deputy asked whether he had been listening to the news. There are massive protests in Washington, the deputy said. They've broken into the Capitol.

Hickman had to see for himself. Following his wife into the house, he looked at the scenes on the television and blanched. If President Donald Trump's supporters were willing to attack the Capitol, who knows what they might do on a residential street in Phoenix. He and his wife rounded up their children and relocated to a relative's house, where he stayed up late, watching until Congress confirmed Biden's victory. Morning had come and Maricopa County was quiet. Hickman was unsure if the threat had passed. He called the family farm. He wouldn't be coming in to work today.

In Maricopa County, the venomous and profanity-laced attacks had poured in for months. The emails and calls attacked the county officials as traitors and called for their execution by firing squad or public hanging. Some were laced with anti-Semitic slurs.[6]

More trouble awaited Clint Hickman. Somewhat later his family egg farm, founded by his grandmother in 1944, caught fire. There had been fires there before. All afternoon firefighters fought the flames and finally subdued them, though the fire killed 165,000 hens. Then more trouble piled on. A headline on the right-wing website Gateway

---

6   Goodman and Helderman, "The Attack (After): Contagion."

Pundit announced, "After Finding Shredded Ballots in Dumpster Earlier Today—A Mysterious Fire Breaks Out at Maricopa County Official's Farm." As Amy Goodman and Rosalind Helderman would report in the *Washington Post*, "'There better be a good investigation into these fires,' the story concluded, questioning whether shredded ballots could have burned in the chicken coops."[7] Hostile calls and angry emails continued for months. Although officials quickly determined that the fire had not been started deliberately, online speculation accused Hickman of grinding up the ballots, putting them in the chicken feed, and then setting the farm on fire.

Karen Fann, president of the Arizona State Senate, was a former moderate Republican Arizona state representative who had evolved, in the eyes of one Democratic colleague, "from being a traditional Republican lawmaker to being a member of 'Trump's cult of personality.'"[8] Fann ordered a new audit of the vote in Maricopa County despite previous recounts and court reviews. With the financial support of the Heritage Foundation, the American Legislative Exchange Council, and a group tied to Leonard Leo, co-chairman of the Federalist Society—who helped to defray, along with others, the over $25 million cost—she hired Cyber Ninjas, a company with clients in the software security field but no experience in election audits. According to a *Washington Post* account, its head, Doug Logan, had been influenced by conspiracy theories about a fraudulent election.[9]

Fann's actions were well received by the Trump movement. Trump supporter and major financial backer Mike Lindell, CEO of MyPillow, proclaimed, "We need one state. They're all going to fall like dominoes."[10]

The recount began more than 100 days after President Biden had been sworn in. As the *Washington Post* reported:

7 Goodman and Helderman, "The Attack (After): Contagion."
8 Jane Mayer, "The Big Money Behind the Big Lie," *New Yorker*, August 9, 2021, https://www.newyorker.com/magazine/2021/08/09/the-big-money-behind-the-big-lie.
9 Mayer, "The Big Money Behind the Big Lie."
10 Goodman and Helderman, "The Attack (After): Contagion."

The whole process appears designed to introduce irregularities into the count, rather than discover ones the real experts failed to catch. The goal is to provide 'evidence' to justify Republicans' efforts to make voting harder, particularly for the poor and minority communities that tend to vote for Democrats. The danger is not only that they will succeed in passing more restrictive laws, but that every time the voters make decisions a partisan state legislature dislikes, lawmakers will seize the ballots from people who know what they are doing, conduct their own slanted count, and declare the will of the voters to be fraudulent. If it works in Arizona, expect Trump allies to push for similar efforts in Michigan, Pennsylvania, Wisconsin, and elsewhere. Republicans must stop. Democracy cannot work if one of the two major political parties is devoted to restricting the voters and rejecting their decisions.[11]

It turned out that the company hired to do what Karen Fann called a "forensic audit" performed it in a far more professional way than some had feared. Cyber Ninjas found no fraud. It confirmed the Maricopa County official machine count. It also said that there was no evidence of tampering with any of the ballots. Fann said, "This is the most encouraging finding of the audit [Cyber Ninjas' audit matching the Maricopa County official machine count]. This finding therefore addresses the sharpest concerns about the integrity of the certified results in the 2020 general election."[12] Contrary to Mike Lindell's prediction, no dominoes fell. Cyber Ninjas later declared bankruptcy, in part due to expenses related to the recount.[13]

11 "Democracy Can't Work," *Washington Post*.

12 Rosalind S. Helderman, "Arizona Ballot Report Commissioned by Republicans Reaffirms Biden's Victory," *Washington Post*, September 24, 2021, https://www.washingtonpost.com/politics/arizona-ballot-review-draft-report/2021/09/24/7c19ac08-1562-11ec-b976-f4a43b740aeb_story.html.

13 Erin Brady, "Cyber Ninjas to File for Bankruptcy, CEO Plans to Start New Firm with Same Employees," *Newsweek*, January 7, 2022, https://www.newsweek.com/

The *Washington Post* documented the following push for a recount in Michigan, in which Ed McBroom emerged as a pillar of patriotism. The story began, "Michigan State Sen. Ed McBroom, a conservative lawmaker with a deep religious faith, is known by his colleagues as 'the king of the Upper Peninsula.'" [14] This nickname suggests his personal popularity in a remote region of his state. A Lindell-produced film had falsely alleged that the vote in McBroom's county had been tampered with as part of a plot to throw the 2020 election to Biden. McBroom appeared on Zoom at a county commissioners meeting and said that all these charges were a fabrication. Some residents on the conference call insisted on a new audit of the results.

> Eight days later, McBroom's Senate Oversight Committee released a report, a withering 55-page dissection of the un-substantiated claims made by Trump and his allies. The conclusion: Citizens should be confident in the results of Michigan's election. [15]

The blowback was quick and devastating. Several local Republican committees passed resolutions censuring McBroom. He was denounced as "a servant of Satan." Trump attacked him personally, claiming that his report was a coverup, that he was "really a Democrat," and that Michigan voters would "not stand for Republican senators not to act on the crime of the century." [16]

> Disheartened, Mr. McBroom tried to take the long view. My reputation and image are in the hands of God, he told himself. Truth-tellers were no longer welcome in the GOP. Nor were those who saw the insurrectionists as anything other than patriots. . . . McBroom received scores of angry

---

cyber-ninjas-file-bankruptcy-ceo-plans-start-new-firm-same-employees-1667113.
14 Goodman and Helderman, "The Attack (After): Contagion."
15 Goodman and Helderman, "The Attack (After): Contagion."
16 Goodman and Helderman, "The Attack (After): Contagion."

calls, emails, or text messages, some calling for him to be "strung up" or "shot."[17]

How can Americans who do not hold elected positions related to elections work to support the continuance of democracy? This question was put to Liz Cheney:

> One summer evening [in 2021], she walked off the House floor and onto the Capitol steps, where she was greeted by one of her new and unlikely allies, Rep. Jamie Raskin (D-MD), a fellow member of the committee [the January 6 Commission]. A knot of students visiting from Miami University of Ohio were lingering nearby. A young woman approached Cheney. "I am not sure that I agree with you on many things," she told the Republican congresswoman, but added that she wanted to join her new cause: "How can I fight alongside you?" "Every single American has a responsibility," Cheney told her. "Our institutions are very fragile. Every single person has a duty."[18]

Michael Gerson opines that, given the entrenchment of the two-party system, it is best to stay with the Republicans as long as conscience permits and fight from within. But parties have been entrenched before and still become part of history. As Jelani Cobb points out in his *New Yorker* article "What is Happening to Republicans":

> The fraught discussions over the GOP's future are really debates about whether the current party is capable of adapting to modern circumstances again—or whether it will turn into a more malign version of itself, one even more dependent on White status anxieties.[19]

---

17 Goodman and Helderman, "The Attack (After): Contagion."
18 Goodman and Helderman, "The Attack (After): Contagion."
19 Jelani Cobb, "What Is Happening to the Republicans?" *New Yorker*, March 15, 2021, https://www.newyorker.com/magazine/2021/03/15/what-is-happening-to-the-

In a speech to the 1936 Republican convention, Herbert Hoover, just four years after he lost the White House, discussed what happens to parties that fail to navigate the difficult issues and circumstances of their time.

> "The Whig Party," Hoover said, "temporized, compromised upon the issue of slavery for the Black man. That party disappeared. It deserved to disappear." Hoover was speaking in the middle of the Great Depression, but his larger point was that parties are not necessarily permanent political fixtures. Considering that history, it's worth asking whether the party of Lincoln, now the party of Trump, is engaged in conflicts so intense that it will go the way of the Whigs.[20]

The few Republicans who can claim lineage from Lincoln fret about the future of the Republican Party.

> "The thing that's most concerning is that it [the Big Lie] has endured in the face of all evidence," said Rep. Adam Kinzinger, one of the vanishing few Republicans in Congress who remain committed to empirical reality and representative democracy. "And I've gotten to wonder if there is actually any evidence that would ever change certain people's minds." The answer, for now, appears to be no. Polling finds that the overwhelming majority of Republicans believe that President Biden was not legitimately elected and that about one-third of them approve of using violence to achieve political goals. Put those two numbers together, and you have a recipe for extreme danger.[21]

republicans.

20 Cobb, "What is Happening to the Republicans?"

21 "Every Day Is Jan. 6 Now," editorial, *New York Times*, January 1, 2022, https://www.nytimes.com/2022/01/01/opinion/january-6-attack-committee.html?searchResultPosition=1.

In her book *How Civil Wars Start*, Barbara Walter expresses the view that a serious risk of civil war in America will exist in the decade of the 2020s as a result of this situation. To summarize: The Constitution guarantees to all Americans a republican form of government. The essential features of such a government are the right of the people to choose their own officers and to have their votes counted equally in making that choice. Our chief national danger is the overthrow of majority control by the suppression or perversion of popular suffrage. If a state legislature were to succeed in substituting its own will for that of its voters, it is not too much to say that public peace might be seriously and widely endangered.

Writing for the *New Yorker* in January 2021, Adam Gopnik posited that it is faulty reasoning to look for the causes of America's decline into authoritarianism under Trump. We needn't focus our energies on why there is a crisis in democracy. Citing a character from Lewis Carroll in *Through the Looking-Glass*, Gopnik urged us to recognize about autocracy that "it always happens."[22] Democracy is not the normal state of humanity. "The default condition of humankind, traced across thousands of years of history, is some sort of autocracy."[23] Our Founders certainly believed this; that is why they put so many checks and balances in the Constitution. All of them feared domestic tyranny far more than foreign threats such as Great Britain.

The Republican Party refused to attend the House event marking the anniversary of the January 6 attack. According to Dana Milbank, about 50 Democrat members attended and, on the other side of the aisle, only one Republican, Liz Cheney, accompanied by her distinguished father, former House minority leader, secretary of defense, and vice president Dick Cheney.[24]

---

22 Adam Gopnik, "What We Get Wrong about America's Crisis of Democracy," *New Yorker*, January 4, 2021, https://www.newyorker.com/magazine/2021/01/04/what-we-get-wrong-about-americas-crisis-of-democracy.
23 Carter et al., "All 10 Living Former."
24 Dana Milbank, "On Jan. 6 Anniversary, Republicans Plumb New Depths,"

Speaking at a Federalist Society event in Florida on February 4, 2022, former vice president Pence said:

> This week, our former president said I had the right to overturn the election. President Trump is wrong. I had no such right. . . . John Quincy Adams reminds us: "Duty is ours. Results are God's." . . . Men and women, if we lose faith in the Constitution, we won't just lose elections, we'll lose our country.[25]

Pence also said, "The presidency belongs to the American people and the American people alone. Frankly, there is almost no idea more un-American than the notion that any one person could choose the American president."[26]

The Republican National Committee, on February 4, 2022, voted to censure Reps. Liz Cheney and Adam Kinzinger for doing their duty and serving on the January 6 Committee of the House. The RNC criticized Ms. Cheney and Mr. Kinzinger for interfering with citizens engaged in "legitimate political discourse"; by this criticism, the RNC legitimized the assault on the Capitol.[27] Sen. Mitt Romney said about this on the same day, "Shame falls on a party that would censure persons of conscience who seek truth in the face of vitriol. Honor attaches to Liz Cheney and Adam Kinzinger for seeking truth even when doing so comes at great personal cost."[28] The day before, Liz Cheney had said in

---

Washington Post, January 6, 2022, https://www.washingtonpost.com/opinions/2022/01/06/jan-6-anniversary-republicans-plumb-new-depths/.

25 S. V. Date, "Mike Pence Rebuts Trump's Claim that VP Can Overturn Election: 'President Trump Is Wrong,'" Yahoo News, February 4, 2022, https://www.yahoo.com/news/mike-pence-rebuts-trump-claim-204501632.html.

26 Brett Samuels, "Pence Breaks with Trump: 'I had no right to overturn the election,'" *The Hill*, February 4, 2022, https://thehill.com/homenews/administration/592878-pence-breaks-with-trump-i-had-no-right-to-overturn-the-election.

27 Jonathan Weisman and Reid J. Epstein, "GOP Declares Jan. 6 Attack 'Legitimate Political Discourse,'" *New York Times*, February 4, 2022, https://www.nytimes.com/2022/02/04/us/politics/republicans-jan-6-cheney-censure.html.

28 Weisman and Epstein, "GOP Declares."

Congress, "The leaders of the Republican Party have made themselves willing hostages to a man who admits he tried to overturn a presidential election and suggests he would pardon January 6 defendants, some of whom have been charged with seditious conspiracy."[29]

In his February 4 *Washington Post* column, Michael Gerson said:

> And the damning nature of his record heightens the case for durability of [Trump's] influence. A man who reintroduced raw racism and White grievance into our politics is approved of by more than 80 percent of Republicans. A man who gathered and incited an assault is approved of by more than 80 percent of Republicans. . . . A man who contemplated a military coup against the Constitution is approved of by more than 80 percent of Republicans. In so many ways, the infection is already deep in the bone. This is the hardest thing to swallow or ignore. One side of the American political rivalry is producing policy that some find mistaken and damaging, and which should be debated passionately within the bounds of the law. The other side endorses a strongman [Trump] who attempted to steal an election, employs political violence against opponents, is cultivating GOP governors and state officials to send fake presidential electors to Washington, and is revealing the frightening fragility of the American experiment.[30]

Donald Trump now appears to lead a cult more than a party.

We pass up the opportunity to stop Trump at our peril. As Liz Cheney warns, "Trump would do it again if given the chance, after

29 Liz Cheney, "Cheney: I Do Not Recognize Those in My Party Who Have Abandoned the Constitution to Embrace Donald Trump," Cheney for Wyoming, https://cheneyforwyoming.com/2022/02/cheney-i-do-not-recognize-those-in-my-party-who-have-abandoned-the-constitution-to-embrace-donald-trump/.

30 Michael Gerson, "Think Trump's Influence is Slipping? Think Again," *Washington Post*, February 4, 2022, https://www.washingtonpost.com/opinions/2022/02/03/suggestions-of-trump-influence-slipping-are-overstated/.

he dangled pardons for January 6 suspects and called for protests if prosecutors go after him."[31]

The *Washington Post* added an important element to the discussion with their February 5 editorial:

> The Republican Party on Friday took an official stand— against truth and democracy. At the Republican National Committee's winter meeting in Salt Lake City, party leaders censured Rep. Liz Cheney (R-WY) and moved to aid her primary opponent. . . . The Orwellian censure resolution accuses Ms. Cheney and fellow GOP dissident Rep. Adam Kinzinger (R-IL) of engaging in behavior "destructive to the institution of the US House of Representatives, the Republican Party, and our republic." Her transgressions? Co-leading the House committee investigating the Capitol invasion, an act of political violence Mr. Trump inspired when he was a sitting president charged with protecting the nation from enemies foreign and domestic. The investigation, the censure resolution claimed, is "a Democrat-led persecution of ordinary citizens engaged in legitimate political discourse."[32]

It may be that many Republicans consider violence, killing, treason, fascism, and hostile action toward the nation's principles and democracy "legitimate political discourse," but the majority of Americans do not. The editorial continues:

> Republicans assailing Ms. Cheney and siding with Mr. Trump and his lies about the 2020 election are the ones who imperil the republic. By asserting, as their censure resolution

---

31 Nikki Schwab, "Liz Cheney Says Trump Will 'Do It All Again If Given the Chance' After He Dangled Pardons for January 6 Suspects and Called for Protests if Prosecutors Go After Him," *Daily Mail*, January 31, 2022, https://www.daily-mail.co.uk/news/article-10460371/Liz-Cheney-says-Trump-given-chance.html.

32 "The Republican Party Formally Declares That Truth Is Fiction and Patriots Are Traitors," editorial, *Washington Post*, February 4, 2022, https://www.washington-post.com/opinions/2022/02/04/liz-cheney-republicans-censure-orwellian/.

did Friday, that truth is fiction and patriots are turncoats, they have exposed the dark festering core of what their party is becoming: an unruly revolt against fact and reason that betrays the principles leaders such as former president Ronald Reagan championed. . . . Republicans have started this election year by revealing what they really stand for. Voters must remember this moment in November.[33]

To this admonition Michael Gerson added in his February 7 *Washington Post* article:

> The ritual censure of the sane that came during the winter meeting of the Republican National Committee was another affirmation of Donald Trump's control over the GOP. As if we needed one. [The censure of Reps. Cheney and Kinzinger] seemed to imply that the violent shock troops of the anti-constitutional coup attempt carried a truer version of democratic ideals than the legislators investigating them. Support for seditious acts is now a normal and accepted element of Republican identity. . . . And yet one thing should comfort us: Even in a land of lies, truth is always an option—and it promises to set us free.[34]

Michael Gerson further urged that Americans not schedule more annual January 6 remembrance events at the Capitol—for the very reason that the attack on our constitutional order that was revealed on January 6, 2020, has not ended.[35] This date represents the commencement of a national movement to turn the Republican Party into

---

33 "The Republican Party Formally Declares," *Washington Post.*
34 Michael Gerson, "The Jan. 6 Committee Is an Organ of Truth. Of Course Trump Republicans Are Attacking It," *Washington Post*, February 7, 2022, https://www.washingtonpost.com/opinions/2022/02/07/trump-republicans-afraid-of-truth-attack-jan-6-committee/.
35 Michael Gerson, "Jan. 6 Wasn't the End of a Failed Plot. It Was a New Salvo in an Unfolding Uprising," *Washington Post*, January 6, 2020, https://www.washingtonpost.com/opinions/2022/01/06/jan-6-assault-on-democracy-unfolding/.

the carrier of pernicious legal theories that would prevent the peaceful transfer of presidential power, threaten the American project of self-government, and disqualify the Republican Party as an American political party.

The Republican Party has shown itself unwilling for some years to guarantee a republican form of government to all Americans as required by the Constitution. The Republican Party has apparently decided that it will no longer play by democratic rules. Therefore, having failed in its constitutional duties, unless drastic improvements are adopted in the near future, it is time for the Republican Party to go the way of the Whigs—to disappear—and to be replaced by the vibrant, principled conservative party we really need to help defend our Constitution. Truth, history, and our American principles are calling for this change.

On December 9, 2021, Liz Cheney said that the decision about how to deal with the legacy of January 6 is "the moral test of our generation." [36] Let it be so. And let us remain "one nation under God, indivisible, with liberty and justice for all."

---

36 Bart Jansen, "House Votes to Hold Mark Meadows in Contempt for Defying Jan. 6 Committee Subpoena," *USA Today*, December 13, 2021, https://www.usatoday.com/story/news/politics/2021/12/14/house-contempt-mark-meadows/6506569001/.

THE BEGINNINGS OF JUSTICE

ON JUNE 9, 2022, the Select Committee to Investigate the January 6th Attack on the United States Capitol, after more than a year of investigation—which included in-person and written responses to committee questions as well as exhaustive research and analysis by committee members and staff—held its first of a series of public hearings on the Trump coup attempt. The committee had amassed a mountain of incriminating evidence, some already public and some to be made public for the first time.

After an inspiring opening speech by the committee chair, Rep. Bennie Thompson, the vice chair, Rep. Liz Cheney, made a presentation characterized by Dana Milbank of the *Washington Post* as a "methodical indictment of Trump's role in planning and fomenting the violence, drawing occasional gasps and murmurs from the media, staff, and lawmakers in the room."[1] Perhaps most shocking

---

1 Dana Milbank, "Liz Cheney Got Her Chance to Rebut Her Dishonorable Peers. She Didn't Miss," *Washington Post*, June 9, 2022, https://www.washington post.com/opinions/2022/06/09/january-6th-committee-testimony-cheney-trump-dishonor/.

was Cheney's relating of Trump's response when it was mentioned that the mob might try to hang Mike Pence (for refusing to commit the illegal and unconstitutional act demanded of him by Trump): "Maybe our supporters have the right idea. [Mike Pence] deserves it."[2]

There was debate among some involved as to the point of maximum danger for the survival of American democracy. Liz Cheney made clear in the committee hearing that she thought that it was not Pence's heroic stand, as he was always determined, but rather that it was when Trump planned to replace the incumbent acting assistant attorney general and appoint a Justice Department official named Jeffrey Clark in his place. Clark had committed, if appointed, to sending a letter to officials in six of the states that Biden had won. The letter would have said that the DOJ had uncovered voting irregularities in their states and that the legislatures in those states might wish to reassign their electors. "The letter is a lie," Cheney said. This act by Trump was only narrowly averted by threats of mass resignations at DOJ.[3]

Cheney told stories of honor and duty in the White House. She also told tales of brutality and deceit by Trump loyalists. She detailed Trump's "sophisticated, seven-point plan to overturn the presidential election and prevent the transfer of presidential power."[4]

In addition to the evil of President Trump's continued assault on American democracy, we have witnessed the disgrace of many Republicans in the Congress who have enabled Trump and covered up his crimes. In a sort of coda for her speech, Cheney addressed these individuals: "I say this to my Republican colleagues who are defending the indefensible, there will come a day when Donald Trump is gone, but your dishonor will remain."[5] In his column the following day,

---

2   Milbank, "Liz Cheney Got Her Chance."

3   Amy Davidson Sorkin, "The GOP Heckles the January 6th Show," *New Yorker*, June 20, 2022, https://www.newyorker.com/magazine/2022/06/20/the-gop-heckles-the-january-6th-show.

4   Milbank, "Liz Cheney Got Her Chance."

5   Milbank, "Liz Cheney Got Her Chance."

Michael Gerson described Cheney's presentation as "calm, methodical, factual, and morally grounded" and noted that she was "fully aware of political risks that may come on the road of duty, and courageously prepared to accept them."[6]

American citizenship comes with obligations as well as benefits. The obligations include defending America, its Constitution, and its promised freedom with unrelenting moral resolve. In the select committee can be seen the strength of mind and courage needed for such a defense.

The warnings of our Founders are pertinent as we take the present toward the future:

"The Nation which can prefer disgrace to danger is prepared for a Master and deserves one." —Alexander Hamilton, 1797

"Liberty once lost is lost forever." —John Adams, in a letter to Abigail Adams, 1775

"The liberties of our country, the freedom of our civil constitution are worth defending at all hazards and it is our duty to defend them against all attacks." —Samuel Adams, 1777

---

6   Michael Gerson, "History Will Accept Only One Jan. 6 Narrative. This Committee Has It," *Washington Post*, June 10, 2022, https://www.washingtonpost.com/opinions/2022/06/10/house-january-sixth-committee-evidence/.

LOOKING TO THE FUTURE

ON JUNE 21, 2022, Speaker of the Arizona State House of Representatives and lifetime Republican Russell "Rusty" Bowers, along with two Georgia election officials, testified before the Select Committee about Bowers's refusal to help Donald Trump overturn the 2020 election. Bowers had been subpoenaed by the Select Committee to testify about post-election events in Arizona.

Bowers had voted and campaigned for Trump, but he had refused to violate the law for him. As a result, "his political future was jeopardized, his character was questioned and his family was harassed as his daughter lay dying."[1] Bowers's neighborhood in Mesa was occupied by Trump campaign caravans; he was screamed at through bullhorns and accused, in flyers distributed by pro-Trumpers, of corruption and even pedophilia. During his testimony before the Select Committee, his chin quivering with emotion, Bowers reported that his daughter

---

1   Yvonne Wingett Sanchez, "Alone in Washington, Rusty Bowers Tells World What Happened in Arizona," *Washington Post*, June 21, 2022, https://www.washington-post.com/national-security/2022/06/21/rusty-bowers-jan-6/.

had been upset by what was happening outside, although "my wife is a valiant person. Very, very strong. Quiet. Very strong woman . . . so, it was disturbing. It was disturbing."[2]

Bowers had rebuffed the call he'd received from an Arizona House attorney shortly before the hearing began—a call reporting "that Trump had put out a statement asserting that Bowers 'told me the election was rigged and that I won Arizona.'"[3] Bowers told the Select Committee that he'd had a conversation with the president, but "that certainly isn't it. Anywhere anyone, anytime, has said that I said the election was rigged—that would not be true."[4]

The first time Bowers met Trump—outside a church service in Phoenix—Rudy Giuliani was there as well. Trump asked Bowers to call the Arizona legislature into session to examine voter fraud in the election and to set in motion the creation of a new set of electors more favorable to him, to be chosen by the legislature. Bowers refused Trump and Giuliani: "'Look, you are asking me to do something that is counter to my oath'. . . . He told the men he would not break his oath and would uphold the Constitution."[5] Trump lied about that meeting when he issued his statement.

During the meeting, Bowers had asked Giuliani if he had proof of voter fraud, and Giuliani had said yes. Bowers had asked Giuliani to send the evidence to him, but none ever arrived. On December 1, Bowers saw Giuliani again. In the absence of proof from Giuliani, he had done nothing about a legislative session. He remembers Giuliani saying, "We've got lots of theories—we just don't have the evidence."[6] After relating this to the Select Committee, Bowers said, "The US Constitution does not say I can reverse the laws I work to

2 Sanchez, "Alone in Washington."
3 Sanchez, "Alone in Washington."
4 Sanchez, "Alone in Washington."
5 Sanchez, "Alone in Washington."
6 Sanchez, "Alone in Washington."

uphold which color this very issue."[7] Whatever the political or personal consequences, Bowers refused to break his oath to uphold the Constitution.

On the morning of January 6, shortly before the Capitol riot, the Trump campaign tried one more time to persuade Bowers. Andy Biggs (R-AZ)—Bowers's own US representative, former president of the Arizona State Senate, and part of the inner Trump group trying to overthrow the election and the country—"asked Bowers to support decertifying the electors. 'I said I would not,' Bowers recalled."[8]

In his campaign to overturn the 2020 election, Donald Trump and his supporters traveled the country in the weeks between November 3, 2020, and January 6, 2021. Such travel continued, to a degree, up to the date of the publication of this book. But the aforementioned period was particularly intense because Trump was still in office. During these months, Trump did not do any work for the American people as their president. He gave himself entirely over to his personal agenda of subverting the outcome of the election that he had lost, thereby further eroding the credibility of the office he then held. His actions taken to overthrow the election were accompanied by menace and violence, "afflicting everyone who resisted, from high-level elected officials to ordinary election workers."[9]

Also on the witness stand before the Select Committee were Georgia secretary of state Brad Raffensperger, who had recently won his Republican primary for reelection, and senior Georgia election official Gabriel Sterling, both 2020 election heroes whose stories were told earlier in this book. Each testified again to the demands of Trump and his supporters and to their own refusal to accede to those demands.

---

7 Sanchez, "Alone in Washington."
8 Sanchez, "Alone in Washington."
9 Rosalind S. Helderman and Jacqueline Alemany, "Trump's Pressure Drew Violence, Threats to Local Officials, Committee Shows," *Washington Post*, June 21, 2022, https://www.washingtonpost.com/national-security/2022/06/21/trumps-pressure-drew-violence-threats-local-officials-committee-shows/.

Following the three senior election officials, Shaye Moss, a former Georgia election worker, took the witness stand. She testified that Rudy Giuliani had publicly asserted "that she and her mother [Ruby Freeman], a fellow poll worker in Fulton County, Georgia, had rigged the outcome in her state."[10] Her supervisor had suggested that Moss check her social media accounts to see whether she had received threats as other Georgia election workers had. "She was stunned by what she saw. . . . Many of the messages were racist and 'hateful,' said Moss, who is black. 'It was just a lot of horrible things there. A lot of threats wishing death upon me, telling me I'll be in jail with my mother and saying things like 'Be glad it's 2020 and not 1920.'"[11]

Moss was speechless when her supervisors gave her access to a recording of Giuliani's statement about her and her mother—a statement made to a Georgia State Senate committee investigating the 2020 election. Giuliani accused Moss and Freeman of bringing in suitcases filled with fraudulent ballots, running them through the voting machines many times, and then adding the false data to a USB memory stick. Giuliani then described a surveillance video of the State Farm Arena—where votes were tabulated—in which Moss and Freeman, he said, "were exchanging USB memory sticks, presumably containing fraudulent vote counts. . . . [Giuliani said] 'I mean, it's obvious to anyone who's a criminal investigator or prosecutor that they are engaged in surreptitious, illegal activity. And they're still walking around Georgia. They should have been questioned already. Their homes should have been searched for evidence.'"[12]

When Select Committee member Representative Adam Schiff (D-CA) asked Moss, "None of that was true, was it?" Moss answered,

---

10 Amy Gardner, "Election Workers Describe 'Hateful' Threats After Trump's False Claims," *Washington Post*, June 21, 2022, https://www.washingtonpost.com/national-security/2022/06/21/ruby-freeman-shaye-moss-jan6-testimony/.

11 Gardner, "Election Workers Describe."

12 Gardner, "Election Workers Describe."

"None of it."[13] Schiff then asked about the alleged USB memory sticks. "What was your mom actually handing you on that video?" "A ginger mint," Moss said.[14]

Donald Trump also attacked Moss and Freeman directly, mentioning them in his phone call to Raffensperger. The president of the United States falsely accused Raffensperger's election workers. Mentioning Freeman 18 times, he described her at one point as "a professional vote scammer and hustler."[15] Additionally, Trump supporters found their way into Moss's grandmother's house in search of Moss and Freeman. Eventually both Moss and Freeman went into hiding, even cutting back trips to the grocery store to the extent they could. The FBI had in fact contacted Freeman the week of January 6, suggesting she leave her home for safety reasons. She stayed away two months but declared, "There is nowhere I feel safe."[16]

Georgia officials eventually concluded that there was no widespread fraud at State Farm Arena by election workers and that neither Moss nor Freeman engaged in any criminal activity.

These events are an illustration of the harm done in other incidents around the country by Trump in his effort to overturn the election. The damage was widespread and impacted thousands of people. The Select Committee is now shining light on such deeply reprehensible abuse in high places, showing it to be a widespread program of criminal abuse.

During Select Committee hearings, Liz Cheney outlined what she thought was perhaps the greatest risk to the republic in the entire Trump coup plan: the effort to appoint Jeffrey Clark as acting attorney general.

Before Attorney General Bill Barr resigned in late December 2020, he publicly stated more than once that the Justice Department, after

13 Gardner, "Election Workers Describe."
14 Gardner, "Election Workers Describe."
15 Gardner, "Election Workers Describe."
16 Gardner, "Election Workers Describe."

exhaustive investigation, had found no voter fraud anywhere in the country sufficient to change the result in the presidential election. After Barr's resignation, Trump immediately began to apply pressure to Barr's immediate successor, Acting Attorney General Jeff Rosen, and to some of Rosen's subordinates, particularly Acting Deputy Attorney General Richard Donoghue. In testimony before the Select Committee, the two officials described meetings with Trump in which "they rebutted his assertions about fraud, prompting Trump to make a remarkable demand: 'Just say that the election was corrupt + leave the rest to me and the R. Congressmen,' as Donoghue's contemporaneous notes put it."[17] Both Rosen and Donoghue refused to support any of Trump's plans for overturning the election. They kept the DOJ on the right side of this issue.

Trump then planned to fire Rosen and replace him with Jeffrey Clark. Clark had formally presented a plan of action to Trump on January 3, 2021, although informal discussions had been continuing for some time before that. Clark said that, if appointed, he would send letters to the relevant officials in six states that Biden won, falsely asserting that the Department of Justice was investigating irregularities in the 2020 presidential election, suggesting that some of these irregularities had occurred in those six states, and suggesting that the states might wish to reassign their electors.[18]

This, of course, would have created nationwide chaos right before the inauguration. Rosen and Donoghue fervently objected, saying that numerous high-ranking officials at the Justice Department would resign in protest. That threat ended the Clark plan.

---

17 Philip Bump, "Jan. 6 Committee Connects Two Strands of Trump's Effort to Retain Power," *Washington Post*, June 23, 2022, https://www.washingtonpost.com/politics/2022/06/23/jan-6-committee-connects-two-strands-trumps-effort-retain-power/.

18 Michael Kranish, "New Details Emerge of Oval Office Confrontation Three Days Before Jan. 6," *Washington Post*, June 14, 2022, https://www.washingtonpost.com/politics/2022/06/14/inside-explosive-oval-office-confrontation-three-days-before-jan-6/.

John Eastman—a Trump lawyer who was supposedly an expert on the Constitution—devised another plan to encourage various state legislatures to sign off on alternate, unofficial slates of electors that had been cobbled together on December 14. The idea was that the legislators in states won by Biden might pass resolutions setting aside electors who would vote for Biden and replacing them with electors who would support Trump.[19] That plan collapsed in the Senate only after the Capitol riot, when the properly submitted electors from each state were approved. But fake electoral certificates had been prepared and some handed to Pence during the electoral count, which attempt he immediately rebuffed.[20]

Shortly before the Select Committee took a brief recess on Tuesday, June 21, 2022, Committee Vice Chair Cheney revealed that Clark's letter plan and the Eastman elector plot were connected, part of the same Trump effort. Clark was working with a lawyer named Ken Klukowski to draft the letter, and at that time, Klukowski was already "one of the primary architects of President Trump's scheme to overturn the election."[21] Klukowski had been working with John Eastman at the Justice Department since December 15.

Perhaps scandals and government malfeasance are more likely to be uncovered and brought to public attention by young officials than by older, established public figures. John Dean was 31 when he made the Watergate crimes public. This time an even younger officer, 25-year-old Cassidy Hutchinson, who had served as an aide to White House Chief of Staff Mark Meadows, stepped forward to offer bombshell testimony before the Select Committee on June

---

19 Rosalind S. Helderman, "Trump Campaign Documents Show Advisers Knew Fake-Elector Plan Was Baseless," *Washington Post*, June 20, 2022, https://www.washingtonpost.com/politics/2022/06/20/trump-documents-fake-elector-plan/.

20 Nicholas Wu and Kyle Cheney, "Ron Johnson Tried to Hand Fake Elector Info to Mike Pence on Jan. 6, Panel Reveals," *Politico*, June 20, 2022, https://www.politico.com/news/2022/06/21/jan-6-panel-trump-overturn-2020-election-00040816.

21 Bump, "Jan. 6 Committee Connects Two Strands."

28.[22] Hutchinson's testimony to the Committee was broadcast live over CNN and other networks. The TV audience was estimated to be around 13 million.[23] There was considerable newspaper reportage as well.

The *Washington Post* reported:

> A former White House official revealed explosive new details Tuesday about President Donald Trump's actions on Jan. 6, 2021, telling Congress that [Trump] knew his supporters were carrying weapons, insisted on personally leading the armed mob to the Capitol, physically assailed the senior Secret Service agent who told him it was not possible, expressed support for the hanging of his own vice president, and mused about the pardoning of the rioters.
>
> The testimony of Cassidy Hutchinson . . . was the most chilling to date in the House Select Committee's Jan. 6 investigation. . . . She presented to the public a penetrating account of Trump's actions and mindset as the Capitol came under siege from his own supporters, who were determined to stop the electoral count and impede the certification of Biden's victory. . . .
>
> Informed that his supporters had come to the rally armed with weapons, Trump argued that security precautions at the rally be lifted, Hutchinson testified.
>
> "They're not here to hurt me," she recalled him saying. . . .
>
> She also recalled hearing discussion of violent far-right groups such as the Oath Keepers and the Proud Boys in

22 John Wagner, Eugene Scott, Amy B. Wang, and Mariana Alfaro, "Trump White House Aides Say Multiple Members of Congress Asked for Pardons," *Washington Post*, June 23, 2022, https://www.washingtonpost.com/national-security/2022/06/23/jan6-committee-hearings-live-updates-day-5/.

23 Gerry Smith, "Jan. 6 Surprise Witness Is Biggest TV Draw of Daytime Hearings," Bloomberg, June 30, 2022, https://www.bloomberg.com/news/articles/2022-06-30/surprise-witness-drew-most-viewers-to-daytime-jan-6-hearings#xj4y7vzkg.

Giuliani's presence in the run-up to the riot and confirmed serious discussion in Trump's cabinet of removing him from the presidency under the 25th Amendment.

[Hutchinson] was present when Tony Ornato, the deputy White House chief of staff for operations, shared reports with Meadows that marchers had been spotted with guns, knives, bear spray, body armor, and even spears. Meadows, she said, looked up and said, "Have you talked to the president?" And Tony said: "Yes sir, he's aware too." [Meadows] said, "All right, good."[24]

Hutchinson testified that Trump seemed not at all concerned about the possibility of people being hurt that day by the armed protesters. Instead, obsessed as usual with crowd size, he was upset that thousands had stayed outside the rally area for fear that the magnetometers would detect their weapons. Hutchinson overheard his angry response: "I don't f*ing care that they have weapons. They're not here to hurt me. Take the f*ing mags away. Let my people in." The magnetometers were removed—and the armed protesters, fired up by Trump's speech, were then allowed to march to the Capitol building unmolested.[25]

After his speech, Trump got back into his presidential vehicle. In the car were three Secret Service agents, including the chief of the presidential detail, Robert Engel. Hutchinson was not present, but she related to the Select Committee the story of what happened, saying she had heard it from Tony Ornato. According to Hutchinson's testimony, Trump said something about going to the Capitol to meet the protesters there. (Possibly he wanted to make another speech or even to enter the Senate chambers along with the mob.) Engel told Trump

---

24 Mike DeBonis and Jacqueline Alemany, "Trump Sought to Lead Armed Mob to Capitol on Jan 6, Aide Says," *Washington Post*, June 28, 2022, https://www.washingtonpost.com/national-security/2022/06/28/trump-sought-lead-armed-mob-capitol-jan-6-aide-says/.
25 DuBonis and Alemany, "Trump Sought to Lead."

he wasn't going to the Capitol, because it hadn't been secured that day for a presidential visit. Trump flew into a rage, shouting that he was "the f*ing president," and he reached over and grabbed at the steering wheel. Engel took Trump's arm away from the steering wheel, saying that Trump would have to return to the White House. Trump then lunged toward Engel and tried to grab him by the throat. Despite all this, the vehicle returned to the White House.

After Hutchinson's testimony, some of the agents involved disputed some of this account and offered to testify before the committee. Even if they describe some of the details differently, though, they have not disputed two major points: that Trump desperately wanted to join the mob at the Capitol and that he reacted with fury when he was told it was not possible.[26]

Hutchinson also testified that, apparently recognizing the seriousness of their actions after the election, a number of Republican representatives had asked for preemptive pardons for anything they might do in the lead-up to January 6 and on January 6 itself, thereby implying that they expected to be involved in illegal acts during that period. The representatives asking for the preemptive pardons were Matt Gaetz (R-FL), Mo Brooks (R-AL), Andy Biggs (R-AZ), Louie Gohmert (R-TX), Scott Perry (R-PA), and Marjorie Taylor Greene (R-GA). In response to questions asked publicly by Select Committee Vice Chair Liz Cheney in the hearing, Hutchinson subsequently added the names of Mark Meadows and Rudy Giuliani to the list of those who had requested pardons.[27]

After Cassidy Hutchinson completed her "smoking gun" testimony, Vice Chair Cheney said, "We are all in her debt. Our nation is

---

26 Isaac Arnsdorf, Josh Dawsey, and Carol D. Leonnig, "'Take Me to the Capitol Now': How Close Trump Came to Joining Rioters," *Washington Post*, July 1, 2022, https://www.washingtonpost.com/politics/2022/07/01/trump-capitol-riot-march/.

27 Harper Neidig, "Meadows, Giuliani Asked for Pardons Over Jan. 6," *The Hill*, June 28, 2022, https://thehill.com/homenews/house/3540140-meadows-giuliani-asked-for-pardons-over-jan-6/.

preserved by those who abide by their oath to our Constitution. Our nation is preserved by those who know the fundamental difference between right and wrong and I want all Americans to know that what Ms. Hutchinson has done today is not that easy." [28]

Only days after Hutchinson's testimony—and with the Select Committee's hearings continuing—the Supreme Court made several rulings that emphasized even further the willingness of the far right to hijack the American legal process for its own ends.

Many years ago, President George H. W. Bush appointed Justice Clarence Thomas to the Supreme Court, amidst much controversy, in a more-or-less-futile attempt to enhance his standing with the far right. When George W. Bush appointed Justice Samuel Alito and Chief Justice John Roberts, he too was worried about the far right. President Trump added three more conservatives, handpicked by far-right organizations, to the Court: Justices Neil Gorsuch, Brett Kavanaugh, and Amy Coney Barrett. These six Republicans currently join the three Democratic justices in deciding cases. In 2018, Chief Justice John Roberts said, "We do not have Obama judges or Trump judges, Bush judges or Clinton judges. What we have is an extraordinary group of dedicated judges doing their level best to do equal right to those appearing before them." [29] This nonpartisan view of the Court may have had its day, but since the case of *Bush v. Gore* in 2000, the Supreme Court has acted as a take-no-prisoners super-legislature.

It did so again during the week of June 20, 2022, during which it overturned several long-standing legal decisions, the most well known being *Roe v. Wade*. Five justices—some of whom had assured Congress and the American people that they would not do so—overturned *Roe*

---

28 DuBonis and Alemany, "Trump Sought to Lead."
29 Mark Sherman, "Roberts, Trump Spar in Extraordinary Scrap Over Judges," AP, November 21, 2018, https://apnews.com/article/north-america-donald-trump-us-news-ap-top-news-immigration-c4b34f9639e141069c08cf1e3deb6b84.

through their ruling in *Dobbs v. Jackson Women's Health Organization*. In doing so, the Court defied judicial tradition on precedents and took away what most Americans see as a constitutional right to bodily autonomy.

The damage done to the Court may be irreparable. Chief Justice Roberts recognized the risk in his concurring opinion in *Dobbs v. Jackson*. The *Washington Post* described Roberts's reasoning:

> Even if the justices did not find all of *Roe*'s reasoning compelling . . . the Court did not need to go as far as it did. The case before the Court involved Mississippi's ban on abortion after 15 weeks. . . . Such a holding would have modified, not obliterated, *Roe*'s longtime guarantee that pregnant people must be allowed to exercise some degree of free judgment on whether they will carry a child to term. "Surely we should adhere closely to principles of judicial restraint here, where the broader path the Court chooses entails repudiating a constitutional right we have not only previously recognized, but also expressly reaffirmed applying the doctrine of *stare decisis*." [30]

Roberts added that the majority's "dramatic and consequential ruling is unnecessary . . . a serious jolt to the legal system."

Justice Samuel Alito sarcastically replayed Roberts's argument in a second concurring opinion, "dismiss[ing] Roberts as unprincipled" and public opinion as an "extraneous" concern, according to the *Post*'s Dana Milbank:

> [Alito] likewise dismissed the pain the ruling would cause, writing that "this Court is ill-equipped to access 'generalized assertions about the national psyche.'" He washed his hands

---

30 "The Supreme Court's Radical Abortion Ruling Begins a Dangerous New Era," editorial, *Washington Post*, June 25, 2022, https://www.washingtonpost.com/opinions/2022/06/24/overturning-roe-dangerous-era/.

of answering the "empirical question" of "the effect of the abortion right . . . on the lives of women."[31]

A June 25 *Washington Post* editorial further described the impact of the Court's decision:

> In a stroke, a heedless majority has done more to undermine the Court's credibility than any other action it has taken in modern times. Fundamental to its place in American society is the notion that the justices are more than just politicians in robes—that they are committed to conscientiously interpreting the law, with regard to text, tradition, history, logic, judicial restraint and common practice, rather than imposing their political or ideological preferences as quickly and as far as they can. In much of this country, this image will now be shattered.[32]

The *Post* editorial further warns that "other legal guarantees, including same-sex marriage, access to contraceptives and even interracial marriage" might be threatened and that states might act to ban "other reproductive practices, such as in vitro fertilization or the use of intrauterine devices."[33] While these rights are not mentioned in the Constitution but rather derived from it, caution should be exercised in adjudicating such practices. In this regard, Justice Thomas's words in his concurring opinion in *Dobbs v. Jackson* are of note and must be taken seriously. They imply that the Supreme Court should reconsider the same-sex marriage and contraception issues as derived rights. Many around the country—both experts and laymen—believe it is only a matter of time before the Court moves on these other rights.

---

31 Dana Milbank, "The Supreme Court Radicals' New Precedent: Maximum Chaos," *Washington Post*, June 25, 2022, https://www.washingtonpost.com/opinions/2022/06/25/roe-guns-supreme-court-radicals-maximum-chaos/.
32 "The Supreme Court's Radical Abortion Ruling," *Washington Post*.
33 "The Supreme Court's Radical Abortion Ruling," *Washington Post*.

The *Dobbs* decision was not the only alarming ruling by the Court during this week. The Court also issued a ruling destroying a 109-year-old New York State regulation on carrying concealed weapons outside the home. Decrying the Court's decision in *New York State Rifle & Pistol Association, Inc., et al. v. Bruen,* which puts gun rights above human rights, the *New York Times* editorial of June 25 pointed out that "it was only in 2008, with its decision in *District of Columbia v. Heller,* that conservatives on the Court divined an individual right to bear arms hidden somewhere in the 27 words of the Second Amendment."[34] The ruling in the New York case, prominent experts said, would make any kind of regulation of firearms impossible.

Justice Thomas wrote the Court's opinion in this New York gun regulation case. His judicial reasoning is flawed because he fails to acknowledge that the Second Amendment makes no mention of an inherent right of individuals to carry weapons. The Second Amendment mentions only that state militias—a term that at that time referred to the militias of certain states, not to groups such as the modern Proud Boys—must retain the right to bear arms. Thus, the individual right to bear arms is derivative. When Joseph Ellis gives a historical account of the genesis of the Second Amendment, he reaches the same conclusion. Ellis demonstrates that when Madison drafted the words of the Second Amendment:

> [He] was responding to recommended amendments from five states, calling for the prohibition of a permanent standing army on the grounds that it had historically proven to be an enduring threat to republican values. It is clear that Madison's intention in drafting his proposed amendment was to assure those skeptical souls that the defense of the United

---

34 "The Supreme Court Puts Gun Rights Above the Human Life," editorial, *New York Times,* June 25, 2022, https://www.nytimes.com/2022/06/25/opinion/supreme-court-gun-control-bill.html.

States would depend on state militias rather than a professional, federal army. In Madison's formulation, the right to bear arms was not inherent but derivative, depending on service in the militia. The recent Supreme Court decision (*District of Columbia v. Heller*, 2008) that found the right to bear arms an inherent and nearly unlimited right is clearly at odds with Madison's original intentions.[35]

Like the *New York Times* editorial board, Ellis impugns the *Heller* decision for misconstruing the Founders' original intent. Acknowledging that the debate over the right to bear arms in our own time is deeply divisive, Ellis points out that

> for judicial devotees of the "original intent" doctrine, Madison's motives are clear beyond any reasonable doubt. To wit, the right to bear arms derived from the need to make state militias the core pillar of national defense. In order to avoid reaching that conclusion, the majority opinion in *Heller*, written by Justice Antonin Scalia, is an elegant example of legalistic legerdemain masquerading as erudition. Madison is rolling over in his grave."[36]

Thomas's opinion builds on the wobbly foundation of *Heller*, ignoring the actual original intent Court conservatives like to claim they value.

Alito also added a concurring opinion in the New York gun case, flaunting his callous indifference to the pain caused by gun violence. He writes, "It is hard to see what legitimate purpose can possibly be served by [Breyer's] mentions of mass shootings and growing firearm mayhem."[37] With breathtaking hard-heartedness, Alito dismisses the

---

35 Joseph J. Ellis, *The Quartet: Orchestrating the Second American Revolution, 1783–1789* (New York: Penguin Random House, 2015), 211–12.

36 Ellis, *Quartet*, 276.

37 Milbank, "Maximum Chaos."

ongoing plague of mass shootings in the United States as a legitimate consideration in gun regulation. Justice Breyer, in turn, scolded Justice Alito for writing an opinion on gun law that would unleash many more guns "without considering the state's compelling interest in preventing gun violence and protecting the safety of its citizens, and without considering the potential deadly consequences of its decision."[38]

It is notable that some of the conservative justices cited obscure, centuries-old writings in their opinions on both these cases, apparently reaching for anything that would bolster their shaky arguments. Defending the ruling in *Dobbs*, for instance, Justice Alito cited a treatise written around the year 1250 by the medieval cleric and jurist Henry de Bracton. Among other things, this treatise "referred to monsters, duels, burning at the stake—and to women as property, 'inferior' to men."[39] Henry de Bracton's complacent inhumanity is heartlessly included by Alito to justify an abortion ruling widely seen as regulating women as property. Perhaps the next justice should be an historian so that if the Court can't get the law and the politics right, at least it could begin to get the history right.

So there you have it. The Republican Supreme Court believes that women's rights should be placed firmly in the past—at least 50 years in the past—and it believes that the carrying of concealed handguns in public should only be subject to rather loose limits, so as to flood our cities with handguns causing, in Dana Milbank's apt phrase, "maximum chaos." For immediate destructive impact, such a double blow by the Court can perhaps only be rivaled by the Dred Scott decision of 1857, itself fashioned by that Court's six pro-slavery justices.

If we are uncertain of the way ahead, we might do well to carry around with us a little book for a few days. Written by Yale professor Timothy Snyder, *On Tyranny: Twenty Lessons from the Twentieth*

---

38 Milbank, "Maximum Chaos."
39 Milbank, "Maximum Chaos."

Century is 126 short pages. On the back of the book, Professor Snyder writes:

> The Founding Fathers tried to protect us from the threat they knew, the tyranny that overcame ancient democracy. Today, our political order faces new threats, not unlike the totalitarianism of the twentieth century. We are no wiser than the Europeans who saw democracy yield to fascism, Nazism or communism. Our one advantage is that we might learn from that experience.[40]

Benjamin Franklin's caution at our country's founding has never been more salient. At the close of the Constitutional Convention in Philadelphia in 1787, Franklin was approached by a woman outside Independence Hall. Eager for news of the convention's outcome, she queried, "Well, Doctor, what have we got—a republic or a monarchy?" "A republic," Franklin replied, "if you can keep it."[41]

---

40 Timothy Snyder, *On Tyranny: Twenty Lessons from the Twentieth Century* (New York: Crown, 2017).
41 "Papers of Dr. James McHenry on the Federal Convention of 1787," *American Historical Review* 11, no. 3 (April 1906): 618.

ACKNOWLEDGMENTS

MY PURPOSE IN WRITING this book has been to describe what the Republican Party, one of the two great parties of our nation, really has been and what it really is now. This assessment is based on the historical record as best as I can access it. I hope my assessment will be useful to voters as they contemplate the most important act that a citizen undertakes in a democracy: voting in an election.

I must recognize and thank my two supporting partners in this venture, Frances Eddy and Mary Eddy. Their efforts have been thoughtful, indefatigable, and insightful. They contributed greatly in aiding my efforts to complete this project, as did the prompt input of the original handwritten text and subsequent edits by Arlo Pignotti. I also want to express my gratitude to Sarah Jane Herbener for her outstanding editing at the end, which was important to the outcome. In addition, a number of friends, colleagues, and relatives, after I told them about this project, strongly encouraged me to pursue it, and quite a few of them asked me repeatedly about its progress. Their interest encouraged me to give to this project my very best efforts. I hope it will be a worthwhile contribution to political literature in America.

ABOUT THE AUTHOR

AMBASSADOR THOMAS GRAHAM JR. served as a senior US diplomat in every major international arms control and nonproliferation negotiation in which the United States took part from 1970 to 1997.

In 1995, he shared with Ambassador Jayantha Dhanapala of Sri Lanka, president of the 1995 NPT Review and Extension Conference, the Trainer Award for Distinction in the Conduct of Diplomacy from Georgetown University. Ambassador Graham has taught at a number of prestigious universities including the University of Virginia School of Law, Georgetown University, the Georgetown University Law Center, Stanford University, the University of Washington, Oregon State University, the University of Tennessee, and Dartmouth University.

Ambassador Graham has also written extensively, including some 12 books and nearly 100 articles. His books include *Disarmament Sketches: Three Decades of Arms Control and International Law*; *Unending Crisis: National Security Policy after 9/11*; *The Alternate Route: Nuclear-Weapon-Free Zones*; *America: The Founders' Vision*; and the novels *Sapphire: A Tale of the Cold War* and *On Tyranny and Crisis*, the story of an attempted coup in the US. Ambassador Graham's professional website is www.thomasgraham.info.